Advanced Bible History

for

LUTHERAN SCHOOLS

in the

WORDS OF HOLY SCRIPTURE

With Illustrations, Maps, and Notes

St. Louis, Mo.
CONCORDIA PUBLISHING HOUSE

Copyright, 1936
by
CONCORDIA PUBLISHING HOUSE
St. Louis, Mo.
Fifth Printing

PRINTED IN U. S. A.

PREFACE

The present volume is the *Comprehensive Bible History* in a new form. While the late text-book, used since 1918, was more comprehensive than our elementary books, some thought it insufficient in scope and for this and other reasons believed they should use the Bible. Others thought it too comprehensive. Various larger teachers' conferences as well as the conference of superintendents held that the content and its scope were satisfactory, but that various other improvements were necessary or at least desirable.

Changes Made. The textual content in this new book is practically the same as in the former book, and yet numerous changes were made.

1. Introductions and overviews as well as summary studies were supplied for the various historical units to emphasize the history aspect.

2. The very compact and formidable text of the old book has been broken up by a radical change in paragraphing, a revision and an increase of paragraph headings, and a larger type.

3. New illustrations were provided, eight of them full-page, and colored.

4. Wherever Bible-passages or the references to the Catechism and the hymn-book were missing, they have been supplied, and throughout the sources of the hymn stanzas were added.

5. Informative, explanatory, and interpretative notes were increased and arranged as footnotes.

6. Some additions and changes in the text of the stories were made, and in the New Testament the stories were arranged in better chronological order. Wherever it seemed advisable to retain the former combination of stories, footnotes were supplied to indicate the chronological order.

7. The self-pronouncing feature was dropped for the sake of economy and a *Pronouncing Vocabulary of Proper Names* printed in the rear of the book.

8. The *table of contents* is arranged in a more practical manner. Not only is it divided into periods, but also the Biblical sources of the stories are given and so arranged that at least in the Old Testament the pupil can see at a glance to what books of the Bible the stories belong. This should aid in Bible orientation.

9. The format is new. It is that of our readers. It makes for a shorter and slightly wider page and considerably enhances ease of reading and study.

10. The entire physical structure of the book is changed.

Introductions, Overviews, and Summary Studies. These features were embodied at the request of a teachers' conference. An earnest attempt has been made to meet the requirements. The newness of these features and the required brevity offered considerable difficulty. The summary-study questions at the end of historical periods are not meant to be followed verbatim, but rather to indicate the type of the exercise. Immediately following the study of a unit the teacher should be able to formulate the most appropriate summary-study directions himself.

Conclusion. Bible History should continue to occupy an important position in the educational curriculum of the Lutheran Church; it should be neither overemphasized nor underemphasized, but correctly evaluated and placed. It is hoped that this text-book in its new form will contribute toward the proper pursuit of the subject and, under God, bear rich fruit in the hearts and lives of Christian children. May the blessing of God rest upon all who teach and study His Word from the pages of this book, so that they may attain unto the wisdom of God's people for the salvation of their souls and the glory of God!

April, 1936   A. C. STELLHORN

CONTENTS

THE OLD TESTAMENT

	PAGE
Introduction	1

First Period: Primeval History (4000—2000 B.C.)

Overview		2
1. The Creation	Gen. 1. 2	3
2. Man and Paradise	Gen. 2	6
3. The Fall of Man	Gen. 3	8
4. Cain and Abel	Gen. 4. 5	11
4a. From Adam to Noah	Gen. 4. 5	13
5. The Flood	Gen. 6—9	17
6. The Curse of Canaan and the Tower of Babel	Gen. 9—11	20
Summary Study		23

Second Period: The Patriarchs (2000—1800 B.C.)

Overview		24
7. The Call of Abram	Gen. 12—14	24
8. Abraham's Faith	Gen. 15—18	27
9. Sodom and Gomorrah	Gen. 18. 19	30
10. The Offering of Isaac	Gen. 21—23	34
11. Isaac's Marriage	Gen. 24	37
12. Isaac Blesses His Children	Gen. 25—27	40
13. Jacob's Ladder	Gen. 27—29	44
14. Jacob and Laban	Gen. 29—32	47
15. Jacob's Return	Gen. 32—35	50
16. Joseph and His Brethren	Gen. 37	53
17. Joseph in Egypt	Gen. 39—41	57
18. Joseph before Pharaoh	Gen. 41	60
19. The First Journey of Joseph's Brethren	Gen. 42	65
20. The Second Journey of Joseph's Brethren	Gen. 43	68
21. Joseph Makes Himself Known	Gen. 44. 45	71
22. Jacob in Egypt	Gen. 45—50	75
23. Job	Book of Job	80
Summary Study		84

VIII   CONTENTS

Third Period: Moses and Joshua (1571—1426 B.C.)

		Page
Overview		85
24. Moses' Birth and Flight	Ex. 1. 2	85
25. The Call of Moses	Ex. 3. 4	88
26. Moses before Pharaoh. The Plagues	Ex. 5—10	92
27. The Last Plague and the Passover	Ex. 11. 12	95
28. The Exodus	Ex. 12—15	97
29. Israel in the Wilderness	Ex. 15—17	101
30. The Giving of the Law on Sinai	Ex. 19—24	105
31. The Golden Calf	Ex. 32—34	109
32. Public Worship and Discipline	Ex. 35—40	112
	Lev. 24. Num. 6 and 15	
33. Mutiny and Rebellion	Num. 13—16	117
34. The Water of Meribah and the Brazen Serpent	Num. 20. 21	121
35. Balaam	Num. 22—24	124
36. Moses' Last Days and Death	Deut. 1—34	127
	Num. 27	
37. Israel Enters Canaan	Josh. 1—5	129
38. The Fall of Jericho	Josh. 6. 7	132
39. Joshua's Victories and Last Days	Josh. 10—24	135
Summary Study		137

Fourth Period: The Judges (1427—1095 B.C.)

Overview		138
40. Gideon	Judges 2—7	138
41. Samson (Part I)	Judges 13—15	142
42. Samson (Part II)	Judges 16	145
43. Ruth	Book of Ruth	149
44. Samuel	1 Sam. 1—7	152
Summary Study		157

Fifth Period: The First Three Kings (1095—975 B.C.)

Overview		158
45. Saul, the First King of Israel	1 Sam. 8—15	158
46. David Anointed King	1 Sam. 16	163
47. David and Goliath	1 Sam. 17	166
48. David and Jonathan	1 Sam. 17—20	170
49. Persecution of David and Saul's Death	1 Sam. 21—31	174
	2 Sam. 1	

CONTENTS

			PAGE
50.	David Becomes King	2 Sam. 1—9	178
51.	David's Fall and Repentance	2 Sam. 11. 12	181
52.	Absalom's Rebellion	2 Sam. 14—19	183
53.	Solomon	1 Kings 1—11 1 Chron. 28. 29	186
54.	The Building of the Temple and Solomon's Death	1 Kings 5—8	189
	Summary Study		193

SIXTH PERIOD: FROM THE DIVISION OF THE KINGDOM TO THE CAPTIVITY AT BABYLON (975—588 B. C.)

	Overview		194
55.	The Division of the Kingdom	1 Kings 12—14	194
56.	The Prophet Elijah	1 Kings 16 2 Kings 2	198
57.	Elijah and the Prophets of Baal	1 Kings 18	201
58.	Elijah in the Wilderness	1 Kings 19	205
59.	Naboth's Vineyard	1 Kings 21. 22 2 Kings 9	207
60.	Elijah and Elisha	2 Kings 2—5	210
61.	Naaman and Elisha	2 Kings 5	213
62.	The Prophet Jonah	Jonah 1—4	216
63.	Overthrow of the Kingdom of Israel. Hezekiah.	2 Kings 17—20 2 Chron. 30	220
64.	The Babylonian Captivity	2 Kings 23—25 2 Chron. 36. Jer. 34—39	223
	Summary Study		226

SEVENTH PERIOD: FROM THE BABYLONIAN CAPTIVITY TO THE BIRTH OF CHRIST (588 B. C. TO CHRIST'S BIRTH)

	Overview		227
65.	The Prophet Daniel	Dan. 1, 2	227
66.	The Three Men in the Fiery Furnace	Dan. 3	233
67.	Belshazzar	Dan. 5	235
68.	Daniel in the Lions' Den	Dan. 6	237
69.	Esther	Book of Esther	241
70.	The Return from the Captivity	Ezra 1—6	245
	Appendix		249
	Summary Study		251

CONTENTS

THE NEW TESTAMENT

Biblical sources: Stories 1—57, the gospels. Stories 58—70, the Acts of the Apostles

PAGE

Introduction 253

First Period: The Childhood of Jesus

Overview 253
1. Zacharias 254
2. The Annunciation 256
3. The Birth of John the Baptist 259
4. The Birth of Jesus Christ 261
5. The Circumcision and the Presentation 264
6. The Wise Men from the East. The Flight to Egypt 267
7. The Child Jesus in the Temple 271
Summary Study 273

Second Period: The Public Ministry of Christ

Overview 274
8. John the Baptist 274
9. The Baptism of Jesus and His Temptation 278
10. The First Disciples 280
11. The Marriage in Cana (12)* 283
12. Nicodemus (14) 285
13. Jesus and the Samaritans 287
14. Bethesda. The Withered Hand (19) 290
15. Peter's Draught of Fishes. The Twelve Apostles 293
16. The Stilling of the Tempest. The Gergesenes. The Man Sick of the Palsy (17. 24 b) 296
17. The Daughter of Jairus. The Young Man of Nain (18) 300
18. The Sower (20) 303
19. The Tares among the Wheat. The Draw-Net (21) 304
20. The Sermon on the Mount (11) 307
21. The Leper. The Centurion of Capernaum (16) 310
22. Death of John the Baptist 312
23. Feeding of the Five Thousand 314
24. Jesus Walks on the Sea 317

---

* Former number

CONTENTS

		PAGE
25.	The Woman of Canaan. The Deaf-and-Dumb. The Ten Lepers	319
26.	Peter's Confession. Christ's Transfiguration	322
27.	The Unmerciful Servant (30)	324
28.	The Good Samaritan (27)	326
29.	Mary and Martha. Jesus and the Child. Jesus Blessing Little Children (28)	328
30.	The Rich Young Ruler. The Foolish Rich Man (31)	332
31.	The Great Supper. The Lost Sheep (29)	334
32.	The Prodigal Son	336
33.	The Rich Man and Poor Lazarus	339
34.	The Pharisee and the Publican	341
35.	The Raising of Lazarus (36)	342
36.	The Blind Man. Zacchaeus (35)	345
37.	Jesus Enters Jerusalem	348
38.	Jesus' Last Discourses	351
39.	The Ten Virgins	353
40.	The Signs of Christ's Coming	355
41.	The Day of Judgment	356
42.	The Lord's Supper	358
	Summary Study	361

THIRD PERIOD: THE PASSION OF OUR LORD JESUS CHRIST

	Overview	362
43.	Jesus in Gethsemane	362
44.	Jesus Taken Captive	365
45.	Jesus before the High Priest	367
46.	Peter's Denial and the Death of Judas	369
47.	Christ before Pilate	372
48.	The Savior Condemned	375
49.	The Crucifixion (Part I)	379
50.	The Crucifixion (Part II)	382
51.	The Burial of Jesus	385
	Summary Study	387

FOURTH PERIOD: THE GLORIFIED LORD

	Overview	388
52.	The Resurrection	388
53.	The First Appearances of the Risen Lord	391

CONTENTS

	PAGE
54. Jesus Appears on the Way to Emmaus	393
55. Christ Appears to the Disciples	396
56. Christ's Appearance in Galilee	398
57. The Ascension	401
Summary Study	403

FIFTH PERIOD: THE FOUNDING AND GROWTH OF THE CHRISTIAN CHURCH

Overview	404
58. Pentecost	404
59. The Healing of the Lame Man	407
60. Ananias and Sapphira	409
61. Stephen	411
62. The Eunuch of Ethiopia	414
63. The Conversion of Saul	417
64. Cornelius	420
65. Peter's Deliverance	423
66. Paul's First Missionary Journey	426
67. Paul's Second Missionary Journey	430
68. Paul's Third Missionary Journey	433
69. Paul the Prisoner	435
70. Paul is Taken to Rome	438
Summary Study	442
Books of the Bible	443
Pronouncing Vocabulary of Proper Names	445
Maps	

THE CREATION

THE OLD TESTAMENT

INTRODUCTION

When Jesus said to the Jews, John 5, 39: "Search the Scriptures; for in them ye think ye have eternal life, and they are they which testify of Me," He referred to the Old Testament, for the New Testament was not yet written. Even in the Old Testament, then, we have the testimony concerning Christ and eternal life.

Again, the Old Testament was referred to when St. Paul wrote to Timothy, 2 Tim. 3, 15—17: "And that from a child thou hast known the Holy Scriptures, which are able to make thee wise unto salvation through faith which is in Christ Jesus. All Scripture is given by inspiration of God and is profitable for doctrine, for reproof, for correction, for instruction in righteousness, that the man of God may be perfect, throughly furnished unto all good works." So also the Old Testament was given to make us wise unto salvation through faith in Christ Jesus and is profitable for all those things just mentioned.

For many centuries the Old Testament was the only part of Scripture that God's people on earth had and in which they could find eternal life through faith in the promised Savior and from which they could obtain all the instruction and guidance necessary for a true child of God.

This part of Holy Scripture is an account of the revelations, works, miracles, guidance, mercies, promises, prophecies, and general dealings of God with mankind during the period of waiting and longing for the Savior's coming into the flesh, which found its climax, ending, and fulfilment in the New Testament.

With this conception, then, approach the study of the Old Testament. Do not think of it alone as something meant for people of the long ago, but as the holy Word of God to you for your instruction unto eternal life.

The seventy Bible accounts of our ADVANCED BIBLE HISTORY, taken from the Old Testament, are divided into seven periods, or epochs: —

First Period: Primeval History (ca. 4000—2000 B. C.), from the Creation to the Tower of Babel; 6 stories.

Second Period: The Patriarchs (ca. 2000—1500 B. C.), from Abraham to Joseph and Job; 17 stories.

Third Period: Moses and Joshua (ca. 1571—1426 B. C.), from the birth of Moses to the death of Joshua; 16 stories.

Fourth Period: The Time of the Judges (ca. 1426—1095 B. C.), from Gideon to Samuel; 5 stories.

Fifth Period: The First Three Kings (ca. 1095—975 B. C.), from Saul to Solomon; 10 stories.

Sixth Period: From the Division of the Kingdom to the Captivity at Babylon (ca. 975—588 B. C.); 10 stories.

Seventh Period: From the Babylonian Captivity to the Birth of Christ (606 B. C. to the birth of Christ); 6 stories.

FIRST PERIOD
PRIMEVAL HISTORY
(Ca. 4000—2000 B. C.*)

"Primeval" means "of the first age." Primeval history treats of the first age of the world. Here God reveals to us the beginning of things: the beginning of heaven and earth in all their greatness, beauty, and perfection; the beginning of time, of nature, of animals and plants; the first human beings in their blissful knowledge of God, perfect righteousness and holiness; the beginning of marriage and of government; the fall of man and its terrible results; the first promise of a Savior and the history of godly people from Adam to Noah, who accepted this Savior by faith; the beginning of man's temporal activity; the great length of life of persons during this early period of the world (even Noah, at the end of this period, living 950 years, 600 years before the Flood and 350 years after the Flood); the beginning of the Church of God and public worship; the beginning of various languages through the confusion of tongues at Babel.

Only six stories in this book (from the Creation to the Tower of Babel) and only eleven chapters of the Bible (Gen. 1—11) are devoted to this first age of the world; yet in point of time this period covers about one half of the Old Testament record. It is by far the longest of the twelve periods into which our BIBLE HISTORY has been divided. You should therefore think of a tremendous span of time as you study this section, a time about as long as from Abraham to the birth of Christ.

---

* Dates in this book according to the chronology of Bishop Ussher.

1. The Creation
Gen. 1. 2

Heaven and Earth; Light; Night and Day. In the beginning God created [1] the heaven and the earth. And the earth was without form and void; [2] and darkness was upon the

"In the beginning"

face of the deep. And the Spirit of God moved upon the face of the waters.

And God [3] said, "Let there be light." And there was light. And God saw the light that it was good.

And God divided the light from the darkness. And God called the light Day, and the darkness He called Night.

And the evening and the morning were the *first* day.[4]

---

[1] Called forth out of nothing by His word.   [2] Empty, bare.
[3] The Son of God. (John 1.)   [4] Twenty-four hours.

The Firmament. And God said, "Let there be a firmament [5] in the midst of the waters." And God divided the waters which were under the firmament from the waters which were above the firmament; and it was so. And God called the firmament Heaven.

And the evening and the morning were the *second* day.

Land and Seas; Plants. And God said, "Let the waters under the heaven be gathered together unto one place, and let the dry land appear." And it was so. And God called the dry land Earth; and the gathering together of the waters called He Seas. And God saw that it was good.

And God said, "Let the earth bring forth grass, the herb yielding seed and the fruit-tree yielding fruit after his kind, whose seed is in itself upon the earth." And it was so.

And the evening and the morning were the *third* day.

Sun, Moon, and Stars. And God said, "Let there be lights in the firmament of the heaven to divide the day from the night; and let them be for signs, and for seasons, and for days, and years, and to give light upon the earth." And it was so.

And God made two great lights; the greater light to rule the day and the lesser light to rule the night; He made the stars also. And God saw that it was good.

And the evening and the morning were the *fourth* day.

Birds and Water Animals. And God said, "Let the waters bring forth abundantly the moving creature that hath life and fowl that may fly above the earth in the open firmament of heaven."

And God created great whales [6] and every living creature

---

5) The sky.   6) Sea-monsters.

that moveth, which the waters brought forth abundantly after their kind, and every winged fowl after his kind. And God saw that it was good. And God blessed them, saying, "Be fruitful and multiply."

And the evening and the morning were the *fifth* day.

Land Animals and Man. And God said, "Let the earth bring forth the living creature after his kind, cattle, and creeping thing, and beast of the earth after his kind." And it was so. And God saw that it was good."

And God said, *"Let Us[7] make man in Our image, after Our likeness:*[8] and let them have dominion over the fish of the sea, and over the fowl of the air, and over the cattle, and over all the earth, and over every creeping thing that creepeth upon the earth."

So God created man in His own image, in the image of God created He him; male and female created He them. And God blessed them and said, "Be fruitful, and multiply, and replenish the earth, and subdue it; and have dominion over the fish of the sea, and over the fowl of the air, and over every living thing that moveth upon the earth."

And God saw everything that He had made, and, behold, it was very good.

And the evening and the morning were the *sixth* day.

The Sabbath. Thus the heavens and the earth were finished, and all the host of them. And God rested on the *seventh* day from all His work. And He blessed the seventh day and sanctified it,[9] because that in it He had rested from all His work.

---

7) The Triune God.

8) Different from other visible creatures; resembling God: rational, knowing God, righteous, holy.

9) Set it apart.

First Article.

Ps. 104, 24. O Lord, how manifold are Thy works! In wisdom hast Thou made them all; the earth is full of Thy riches.

> Holy, holy, holy, Lord God Almighty!
> All Thy works shall praise Thy name
>   in earth and sky and sea.
> Holy, holy, holy, merciful and mighty!
> God in Three Persons, blessed Trinity! (246, 4.)

---

2. Man and Paradise *
Gen. 2

Creation of the Man. And the LORD God formed man of the dust of the ground and breathed into his nostrils the breath of life;[1] and man became a living soul.[2]

Paradise. And the LORD God planted a garden eastward in Eden. And out of the ground made the LORD God to grow every tree that is pleasant to the sight and good for food; the tree of life[3] also in the midst of the garden and the tree of knowledge of good and evil.[4]

And the LORD God took the man and put him into the garden of Eden to dress[5] it and to keep it.

The Divine Commandment. And the LORD God commanded the man, saying, "Of every tree of the garden thou mayest freely eat; but of the tree of the knowledge of good and evil, thou shalt not eat of it; for in the day that thou eatest thereof, thou shalt surely die."

Creation of the Woman. Institution of Marriage. And

---

* The incidents of this story occurred on the sixth day of Creation.
1) Gave him life.   2) A rational, *immortal* being.
3) Its fruit gave "life forever" (Gen. 3, 22).
4) A tree to test man's obedience.   5) Cultivate.

the Lord God said, "It is not good that the man should be alone; I will make him an help meet [6] for him."

For when the Lord God had formed every beast of the field and every fowl of the air, He brought them unto Adam to see what he would call them. And Adam gave names to all cattle and to the fowl of the air and to every beast of

Man in Paradise

the field; but for Adam there was not found an help meet for him.

And the Lord God caused a deep sleep to fall upon Adam, and he slept; and He took one of his ribs and closed up the flesh. And the rib made He a woman and brought her unto the man.

And Adam said, "This is, now, bone of my bones and

---

[6] "Meet" = suited. A helping companion.

flesh of my flesh. She shall be called Woman because she was taken out of Man. Therefore shall a man leave his father and his mother and shall cleave unto his wife: and they shall be one flesh."

And they were both naked, the man and his wife, and were not ashamed.[7]

First Article.

Ps. 139, 14. I will praise Thee; for I am fearfully and wonderfully made. Marvelous are Thy works, and that my soul knoweth right well.

Praise to the Lord, who hath fearfully, wondrously, made thee;
Health hath vouchsafed and, when heedlessly falling, hath stayed thee.
What need or grief
Ever hath failed of relief? —
Wings of His mercy did shade thee. (39, 3.)

3. The Fall of Man

Gen. 3

The Temptation. Now, the serpent was more subtile[1] than any beast of the field. And he said unto the woman: "Yea, hath God said, Ye shall not eat of every tree of the garden?"

And the woman said unto the serpent, "We may eat of the fruit of the trees of the garden; but of the fruit of the tree which is in the midst of the garden, God hath said, 'Ye shall not eat of it, neither shall ye touch it, lest ye die.'"

And the serpent said unto the woman, "Ye shall not surely die; for God doth know that in the day ye eat thereof, then your eyes shall be opened, and ye shall be as gods, knowing good and evil."

---

[7] Proof of their holiness and purity.

[1] More cunning, wily, crafty. It was the devil who spoke through the serpent.

The Fall. And when the woman saw that the tree was good for food and that it was pleasant to the eyes and a tree to be desired to make one wise, she took of the fruit thereof and did eat and gave also unto her husband, and he did eat.

Immediate Effects. And the eyes of them both were opened, and they knew that they were naked; and they sewed fig-leaves together and made themselves aprons.

And they heard the voice of the LORD God walking in the garden in the cool of the day; and Adam and his wife hid themselves from the presence of the LORD God amongst the trees of the garden. And the LORD God called unto Adam and said unto him, "Where art thou?"

And he said, "I heard Thy voice in the garden, and I was afraid because I was naked; and I hid myself."

And He said, "Who told thee that thou wast naked? Hast thou eaten of the tree whereof I commanded thee that thou shouldest not eat?"

And the man said, "The woman whom Thou gavest to be with me, she gave me of the tree, and I did eat."

And the LORD God said unto the woman, "What is this that thou hast done?"

And the woman said, "The serpent beguiled me, and I did eat."

The Sentence and Promise. And the LORD God said unto the serpent, "Because thou hast done this, thou art cursed above all cattle and above every beast of the field; upon thy belly shalt thou go, and dust shalt thou eat all the days of thy life. *And I will put enmity between thee and the woman and between thy seed and her Seed; It shall bruise thy head, and thou shalt bruise His heel.*"

Unto the woman He said, "In sorrow thou shalt bring forth children; and thy desire shall be to thy husband, and he shall rule over thee."

And unto Adam He said, "Because thou hast hearkened unto the voice of thy wife, cursed is the ground for thy sake; in sorrow shalt thou eat of it all the days of thy life; thorns and thistles shall it bring forth to thee; and thou shalt eat the herb of the field. In the sweat of thy face shalt thou eat

"And He drove out the man"

bread till thou return unto the ground; for out of it wast thou taken; for dust thou art, and unto dust shalt thou return."

Paradise Closed. And Adam called his wife's name Eve, because she was the mother of all living. Unto Adam also and to his wife did the LORD God make coats of skins and clothed them.

And lest man put forth his hand, and take also of the

tree of life, and eat, and live forever, the LORD God sent him forth from the garden of Eden to till the ground from whence he was taken.

And He placed at the east of the garden of Eden cherubim and a flaming sword, which turned every way, to keep the way of the tree of life.

Conclusion of the Commandments.

Rom. 5, 12. By one man, sin entered into the world and death by sin; and so death passed upon all men for that all have sinned.

> He saw me ruined in the Fall,
> Yet loved me notwithstanding all.
> He saved me from my lost estate, —
> His loving-kindness, oh, how great! (340, 2.)

---

4. Cain and Abel
Gen. 4. 5

The Two Brothers. Adam [1] called his wife Eve; and she bare Cain [2] and said, "I have gotten a man from the Lord." [3] And she again bare his brother Abel. [4] And Abel was a keeper of sheep, but Cain was a tiller of the ground.

Cain's Envy. And it came to pass that Cain brought of the fruit of the ground an offering unto the LORD. And Abel also brought of the firstlings of his flock. And the LORD had respect unto Abel and to his offering; but unto Cain and his offering He had not respect. And Cain was very wroth, and his countenance fell.

And the LORD said unto Cain, "Why art thou wroth, and why is thy countenance fallen? If thou doest well, shalt thou not be accepted? and if thou doest not well, sin lieth

---

[1] Adam means Man. [2] Cain means Possession, or Gain.
[3] Or: "I have the Man, the Lord" (the "Woman's Seed," the Savior). [4] Abel means A Breath; Vanity.

at the door.[5] And unto thee shall be his desire,[6] and thou shalt rule over him."

The Murder. And Cain talked with Abel, his brother; and it came to pass, when they were in the field, that Cain rose up against his brother and slew him.

"And Cain was very wroth"

The Punishment. And the Lord said unto Cain, "Where is Abel, thy brother?"

And he said, "I know not; am I my brother's keeper?"

But the Lord said, "What hast thou done? The voice of thy brother's blood crieth unto Me from the ground.[7]

"And now art thou cursed from the earth, which hath opened her mouth to receive thy brother's blood from thy

---

5) Like a fierce animal, ready to attack.
6) Sin desires to overcome you; but you should **rule over it.**
7) Calls to heaven for justice and vengeance.

hand. When thou tillest the ground, it shall not henceforth yield unto thee her strength; a fugitive and a vagabond [8] shalt thou be in the earth."

Cain's Despair. And Cain said unto the LORD, "My punishment is greater than I can bear. Behold, Thou hast driven me out this day from the land; and from Thy face shall I be hid; and I shall be a fugitive and a vagabond in the earth; and it shall come to pass that every one that findeth me shall slay me."

And the LORD said unto him, "Whosoever slayeth Cain, vengeance shall be taken on him sevenfold." And the LORD set a mark upon Cain that no one should kill him.

Fifth Commandment.

Heb. 11, 4. By faith Abel offered unto God a more excellent sacrifice than Cain.

Gen. 9, 6. Whoso sheddeth man's blood, by man shall his blood be shed; for in the image of God made He man.

> Abel's blood for vengeance
> Pleaded to the skies;
> But the blood of Jesus
> For our pardon cries. (158, 4.)

4a. From Adam to Noah
Gen. 4. 5

NOTE. — The world knows little or nothing of the first two thousand years of human history. Yet in school histories and other books unbelieving scientists boldly assert that man began as a savage. It is therefore necessary to pay particular attention to this period of history as revealed by God. The truth is, man began as a perfect being, perfect in body and soul, in knowledge and wisdom, in ability and skill. Even after the Fall, Adam and Eve were the highest type of human beings, and so were their immediate descendants.

You will observe that the following brief account covers a very long historical period, namely, about 1500 years, or about as long as from the birth of Moses to the birth of Christ.

---

[8] Exiled, restless roamer, tramp.

The Generations of Adam.* And Adam lived an hundred and thirty years and begat a son in his own likeness,[1] in his image, and called his name Seth.[2] "For God," said his wife, "hath appointed me another seed instead of Abel, whom Cain slew."

And the days of Adam, after he had begotten Seth, were

"Then began men to call upon the name of the Lord"

eight hundred years; and he begat sons and daughters. And all the days that Adam lived were nine hundred and thirty years; and he died.[3]

---

* The chain of family heads in the Church of God, or the patriarchs, who were the preachers of God in that long era. There were no doubt millions of people as time went on.

1) Sinful; not in the likeness of God.
2) Seth means Substitute.   3) As God had said before the **Fall.**

And *Seth* lived an hundred and five years and begat Enos. Then began men to call upon the name of the LORD.[4)]

And Seth lived, after he begat Enos, eight hundred and seven years, and begat sons and daughters. And all the days of Seth were nine hundred and twelve years; and he died.[5)]

Enos begat Cainan and other sons and daughters and lived nine hundred and five years.

Cainan begat Mahalaleel and other sons and daughters and lived nine hundred and ten years.

Mahalaleel begat Jared and other sons and daughters and lived eight hundred and ninety-five years.

Jared begat Enoch and other sons and daughters and lived nine hundred and sixty-two years.

Enoch begat Methuselah and other sons and daughters and lived three hundred and sixty-five years. And Enoch walked with God, and he was not, for God took him.[6)]

Methuselah begat Lamech and other sons and daughters and lived nine hundred and sixty-nine years.

Lamech begat Noah, saying, "This same shall comfort us concerning our work and toil of our hands because of the ground which the LORD hath cursed." [7)] And Lamech begat other sons and daughters and lived seven hundred and seventy-seven years.

Noah begat Shem, Ham, and Japheth. And Noah was six hundred years old when the flood of waters was upon the earth, and he lived nine hundred and fifty years. (Gen. 7, 6; 9, 29.)

---

4) Began public worship and preaching.

5) Like Adam. And so it became the rule with all flesh.

6) Enoch did not die, but was in some unrevealed manner taken by God into heaven. Note the faith and godly life of these patriarchs.

7) Lamech speaks of the curse of sin. Like Eve, he believes his son to be the expected Savior.

The Descendants of Cain. And Cain went out from the presence of the LORD [8] and dwelt in the land of Nod,[9] on the east of Eden. And he built a city and called the name of the city, after the name of his son, Enoch.[10]

And unto Enoch was born Irad; and Irad begat Mehujael; and Mehujael begat Methusael; and Methusael begat Lamech. And the sons of Lamech were Jabal, Jubal, and Tubal-cain.

Jabal was the father of such as dwell in tents and of such as have cattle.

Jubal was the father of all such as handle the harp and organ.

Tubal-cain was an instructor of every artificer [11] in brass and iron.

First and Fourth Commandments. (Promise.)

Ps. 90, 12. Teach us to number our days that we may apply our hearts unto wisdom.

Heb. 11, 5. By faith Enoch was translated that he should not see death.

> What the fathers most desired,
> What the prophets' heart inspired,
> What they longed for many a year,
> Stands fulfilled in glory here. (91, 2.)

NOTE.—When Adam died at the age of 930 years, Noah's father was 56 years old. Shem, the son of Noah, was about 97 years old when the Flood came, and lived until Abraham was 149 years and Isaac 49 years old. So it was possible to transmit the correct history of Creation and the human race as well as the promise of the Savior by word of mouth from Adam to the patriarchs of Israel. God later caused Moses to write the account.

---

8) Left the Church of God and became the father of "children of men," unbelievers, who in time grew far more numerous than the "children of God" and provoked God to bring about the great destruction in the Flood.

9) The land of wandering, or exile.

10) The builder of a city could not have been a savage.

11) A skilled or artistic worker.

5. The Flood

Gen. 6—9

Cause of the Flood. And men began to multiply on the face of the earth. Then the sons of God [1] saw the daughters of men [2] that they were fair; and they took them wives of all which they chose. And God saw that the wickedness of man was great in the earth and that every imagination of the thoughts of his heart was only evil continually. And He said, "My Spirit shall not always strive with man; I will destroy man from the earth; yet his days shall be one hundred and twenty years."

The Ark. But Noah found grace in the eyes of the LORD, for he was a just man and walked with God. And God said unto Noah, "The end of all flesh is come before Me; for the earth is filled with violence. Make thee an ark of gopherwood,[3] three hundred cubits in length, fifty cubits in breadth, and thirty cubits in height. Make rooms therein and pitch it within and without with pitch. A window and a door shalt thou make to the ark; with lower, second, and third stories shalt thou make it.

"And, behold, I do bring a flood of waters upon the earth to destroy all flesh. But with thee will I establish My covenant [4] and thou shalt come into the ark, thou, and thy sons, and thy wife, and thy sons' wives with thee.

"And of every living thing of all flesh, two of every sort, shalt thou bring into the ark to keep them alive with thee; they shall be male and female.

"And take thou unto thee of all food that is eaten, and it shall be for food for thee and for them." And Noah did all that the LORD commanded him.

---

[1] Believers.
[2] Unbelievers.
[3] Perhaps a species of cypress.
[4] Solemn agreement.

THE FLOOD

The Flood. And the Lord said unto Noah, "Come thou and all thy house into the ark; for thee have I seen righteous before Me in this generation.

"Of every clean beast thou shalt take to thee by sevens, the male and his female; and of beasts that are not clean by two, the male and his female. Of fowls also of the air by sevens, the male and the female, to keep seed alive upon the face of all the earth."

"And all flesh died"

And Noah was six hundred years old when the flood of waters was upon the earth.

And he went into the ark with his three sons, Shem, Ham, and Japheth, his wife, and the three wives of his sons; and of beasts and fowls and everything that creepeth upon the earth there went in two and two unto Noah into the ark, as God had commanded Noah. And the Lord shut him in.

In the six-hundredth year of Noah's life, on the seventeenth day of the second month, the same day were all the fountains of the great deep broken up, and the windows of heaven were opened. And it rained upon the earth forty days and forty nights.

And the waters increased greatly upon the earth and bare up the ark; and all the high hills and mountains that were under the whole heaven were covered fifteen cubits. And all flesh died, both of fowl, and of cattle, and of beast, and creeping thing, and every man. And the waters prevailed upon the earth an hundred and fifty days.

End of the Flood. And God remembered Noah. And God made a wind to pass over the earth, and the waters assuaged.[5] And the ark rested on the seventeenth day of the seventh month upon the mountains of Ararat. On the first day of the tenth month were the tops of the mountains seen.

At the end of forty days Noah opened the window of the ark and sent forth a raven, which went forth to and fro until the waters were dried up from the earth. Also he sent forth a dove from him. But the dove found no rest for the sole of her foot and returned unto him into the ark.

And after seven days he again sent forth the dove. And the dove came to him in the evening, and, lo, in her mouth was an olive-leaf. Noah stayed yet other seven days and sent forth the dove, which returned not again.

The Covenant. And Noah removed the covering of the ark. And on the seven-and-twentieth day of the second month was the earth dried. And God spake unto Noah, saying, "Go out of the ark, thou and thy wife, thy sons and thy sons' wives, and every living thing that is with thee." And Noah builded an altar unto the LORD and offered burnt offerings.[6]

And the LORD said, "I will not again curse the ground any more for man's sake; for *the imagination of man's heart is evil from his youth. While the earth remaineth, seed-time*

---

5) Grew less.
6) The whole animal was consumed by fire in the burnt sacrifices. It was to signify the yielding up of oneself to God with body and soul.

and harvest, cold and heat, summer and winter, day and night, shall not cease."

And God blessed Noah and his sons and said, "Be fruitful and multiply and replenish the earth. And, behold, I establish My covenant with you; neither shall there any more be a flood to destroy the earth. I do set My bow in the cloud, and it shall be for a token of a covenant between Me and the earth."

Conclusion of the Commandments.

1 John 2, 15—17. Love not the world, neither the things that are in the world. If any man love the world, the love of the Father is not in him. For all that is in the world, the lust of the flesh and the lust of the eyes and the pride of life, is not of the Father, but is of the world. And the world passeth away and the lust thereof; but he that doeth the will of God abideth forever.

> Before Jehovah's awe-full throne,
> Ye nations, bow with sacred joy.
> Know that the Lord is God alone;
> He can create and He destroy. (13, 1.)

NOTE. — On the mountains of many countries are found fishes, and seashells turned to stone, indicating the great Flood.

---

6. The Curse of Canaan and the Tower of Babel

Gen. 9—11

Ham's Sin. And Noah began to be a husbandman, and he planted a vineyard. And he drank of the wine and was drunken; and he was uncovered within his tent. And Ham, the father of Canaan, saw the nakedness of his father and told his two brethren without.

And Shem and Japheth took a garment, and laid it upon both their shoulders, and went backward, and covered the nakedness of their father; and their faces were backward, and they saw not their father's nakedness.

The Curse and the Blessing. And Noah awoke from his

THE CURSE OF CANAAN AND THE TOWER OF BABEL

wine and knew what his younger son [1] had done unto him. And he said, "Cursed be Canaan; [2] a servant of servants shall he be unto his brethren."

And he said, "Blessed be the LORD God of Shem; [3] and Canaan shall be his servant. God shall enlarge Japheth, [4]

"So the Lord scattered them abroad"

and he shall dwell in the tents of Shem; [5] and Canaan shall be his servant."

---

1) Ham was the youngest son of Noah.

2) Canaan, following in the footsteps of Ham, bears the sin of his father. (Close of Ten Commandments.)

3) From Shem were later to come Abraham, Isaac, Jacob, and the house of Judah, or the Jews. And the Savior was to come out of Judah. "Salvation is of the Jews," said Jesus, John 4, 22.

4) His descendants, especially Europeans, "have had the destinies of the world in their hands, under God."

5) Share in the spiritual blessings of Shem.

The Building of the Tower.* From Noah's sons, Shem, Ham, and Japheth, were the people divided in the earth after the Flood. And the whole earth was of one language. And as they journeyed from the East, they found a plain in the land of Shinar; and they dwelt there.

And they said one to another, "Go to, let us make brick and burn them thoroughly; and let us build us a city and a tower whose top may reach unto heaven; and let us make us a name lest we be scattered abroad upon the face of the whole earth."

The Confusion of Tongues. And the LORD said, "Behold, the people is one, and they have all one language; and now nothing will be restrained from them which they have imagined to do. Go to, let Us confound their language that they may not understand one another's speech."

So the LORD scattered them abroad from thence upon the face of all the earth; and they left off to build the city. Therefore is the name of it called Babel, because the Lord did there confound the language of all the earth.

First Commandment.

1 Pet. 5, 5. God resisteth the proud.

> The world seeks to be praised
> And honored by the mighty,
> Yet never once reflects
> That they are frail and flighty,
> But what I truly prize
> Above all things is **He,**
> My Jesus, He alone, —
> What is the world to me! (430, 3.)

NOTE. — From Mount Ararat the descendants of Noah began to spread out in all directions. The Shemites (Semites) gradually peopled Anterior Asia and Asia Minor; the Japhetic nations, Northern Asia and Europe; the Hamites, Africa and Southern Asia.

---

* 115 years after the Flood.

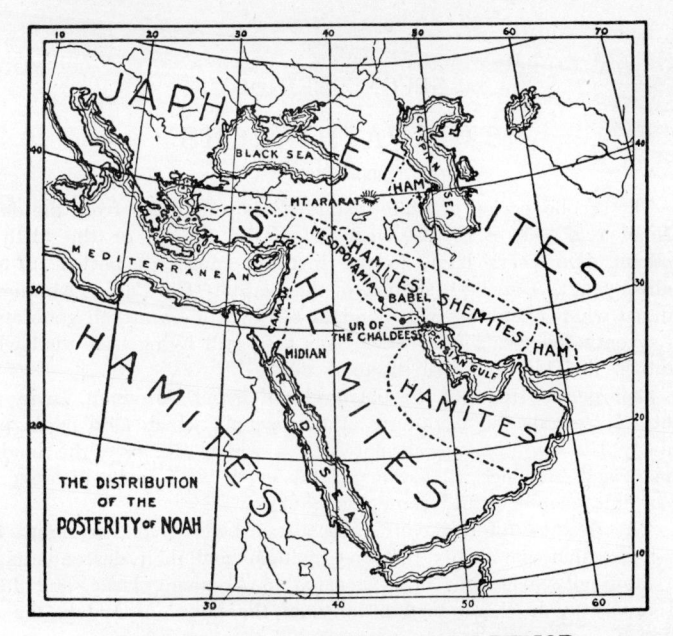

SUMMARY STUDY OF THE FIRST PERIOD

Read again the overview of this period on page 2.

Formulate a brief statement, oral or written, in which you name the length, the main incidents, and the general purpose of this period.

Beginning with the holy estate of Adam and Eve, describe the life of mankind on earth during this period, that of the godly as well as that of the ungodly.

Give several proofs that men from Adam to Noah believed **and** understood the promise concerning the Woman's Seed.

Explain why it was possible for the men of God to teach and preach about the works and the will of God and concerning the Savior even without our present Bible.

Name and discuss in class a number of the lessons which a Christian should derive from this period for his own personal faith and life.

BEHOLD WHAT GOD HATH WROUGHT IN HIS WISDOM, POWER, MERCY, AND RIGHTEOUSNESS!

SECOND PERIOD

THE PATRIARCHS

(Ca. 2000—1600 B. C.)

The second period of Bible history dates practically from the death of Noah (ca. 2000 B. C., 350 years after the Flood) or the birth of Abraham, two years later, to the birth of Moses, a period of four hundred years. But the first story of this period, "The Call of Abraham," occurred when Abraham, a descendant of Shem in the tenth generation, was seventy-five years old. Shem was then still living. He died when Abraham was 149 and Isaac 49 years old.

This period treats of the patriarchs of Israel, Abraham, Isaac, and Jacob. It reveals the beginning of that people which God made particularly His own among all nations, to which He gave the land of Canaan, and in which all nations of the earth were to be blessed; for out of this people should come the Savior.

The promise of a Savior, which had been given to Adam and Eve and which was firmly believed by them and their descendants for two thousand years, was now repeated to Abraham, Isaac, and Jacob and finally made the special promise of the house of Judah, the son of Jacob.

7. The Call of Abram

Gen. 12—14

His Father's House. Terah, a descendant of Shem, with his sons Abram, Nahor, and Haran, lived at Ur of the Chaldees, where Haran also died. And Terah took his family and removed to Haran in Mesopota'-mia [1] and dwelt there. But Terah served other gods.

God's Call. And the LORD said unto Abram, "Get thee out of thy country and from thy kindred and from thy father's house unto a land that I will show thee.

"And I will make of thee a great nation, and I will bless

---

1) A country between the Euphrates and the Tigris rivers.

thee and make thy name great; and *in thee shall all families of the earth be blessed.*"

Removal to Canaan. So Abram, seventy and five years old, departed with Sarai, his wife, and Lot, his brother Haran's son. And when they came into the land of Canaan, to Sichem, unto the Plain of Moreh, the LORD appeared unto Abram and said, "Unto thy seed will I give this land."

"Separate thyself from me"

And there builded he an altar unto the LORD who appeared unto him.

Separation of Abram and Lot. Abram was very rich in cattle, in silver, and in gold. And Lot also had flocks and herds. And the land was not able to bear them that they might dwell together; therefore there was always strife between their herdmen.

An Abram said unto Lot, "Let there be no strife, I pray

thee, between me and thee and between my herdmen and thy herdmen; for we be brethren. Is not the whole land before thee? Separate thyself, I pray thee, from me. If thou wilt take the left hand, then I will go to the right; or if thou depart to the right hand, then I will go to the left."

And Lot beheld all the Plain of Jordan that it was well watered everywhere, even as the garden of the LORD. Then Lot chose him all the Plain of Jordan and pitched his tent toward Sodom. But the men of Sodom were wicked and sinners before the LORD exceedingly.

Abram Reassured. And the LORD said unto Abram, after Lot was separated from him, "Lift up now thine eyes and look; for all the land which thou seest, to thee will I give it and to thy seed forever."

And Abram came and dwelt in the Plain of Mamre, which is in Hebron, and built there an altar unto the LORD.

Lot Captured and Rescued. And it came to pass that four kings made war upon the king of Sodom, and put him to flight, and took all the goods of Sodom and Gomorrah and all their victuals, and Lot also, and went their way.

When Abram heard this, he armed his three hundred and eighteen trained servants, pursued and smote the enemy, and brought back all the goods and people, and also Lot.

First Commandment. — Seventh Commandment.

Ps. 37, 5. Commit thy way unto the Lord; trust also in Him; and He shall bring it to pass.

> And let me with all men,
>   As far as in me lieth,
> In peace and friendship live.
>   And if Thy gift supplieth
> Great wealth and honor fair,
>   Then this refuse me not,
> That naught be mingled there
>   Of goods unjustly got. (395, 5.)

8. Abraham's Faith
Gen. 15—18

God's Renewed Promise. Abram dwelt in the Plain of Mamre, which is in Hebron. And the word of the Lord came unto Abram, saying, "Fear not, Abram; I am thy Shield and thy exceeding great Reward."

"So shall thy seed be"

And Abram said, "Lord God, what wilt Thou give me, seeing I go childless?"

And He brought him forth abroad and said, "Look now toward heaven and tell the stars, if thou be able to number them." And He said unto him, "So shall thy seed be."

And Abram believed in the Lord; *and He counted it to him for righteousness.*

The Covenant. And when Abram was ninety-nine years old, the Lord appeared unto him and said, *"I am the almighty*

God; walk before Me and be thou perfect. And I will make My covenant between Me and thee and will multiply thee exceedingly."

And Abram fell on his face. And God talked with him, saying, "My covenant is with thee, and thou shalt be a father of many nations. Neither shall thy name any more be called Abram, but thy name shall be Abraham.[1]

"This is My covenant which ye shall keep: Every man child among you that is eight days old shall be circumcised. And the man child whose flesh is not circumcised, that soul shall be cut off from his people; he hath broken My covenant.

"As for Sarai, thy wife, thou shalt not call her name Sarai, but Sarah [2] shall her name be. And I will bless her, and give thee a son of her; and she shall be a mother of nations; kings of people shall be of her.

Announcement of Isaac's Birth. And the LORD again appeared unto Abraham in the Plains of Mamre as he sat in the tent door in the heat of the day. And he lifted up his eyes and looked, and, lo, three men [3] stood by him.

And when he saw them, he ran to meet them from the tent door and bowed himself toward the ground and said, "My Lord, if, now, I have found favor in Thy sight, pass not away, I pray Thee, from Thy servant. Let a little water be fetched, and wash your feet and rest yourselves under the tree. And I will fetch a morsel of bread, and comfort ye your hearts; after that ye shall pass on."

And they said, "So do as thou hast said."

And Abraham hastened into the tent unto Sarah and

---

[1] Father of a multitude, of nations.

[2] Princess, mother of nations, of kings, of the heavenly King Jesus Christ.

[3] The Son of God and two angels.

said, "Make ready quickly three measures of fine meal, knead it, and make cakes."

And he ran unto the herd and fetched a calf, tender and good, and gave it unto a young man; and he hasted to dress it. And he took butter and milk and the calf which

"I will fetch a morsel of bread"

he had dressed and set it before them; and he stood by them under the tree, and they did eat.

And they said, "Where is Sarah, thy wife?"

And he said, "Behold, in the tent."

And He said, "I will certainly return unto thee a year hence; and, lo, Sarah, thy wife, shall have a son."

And Sarah heard it in the tent door, which was behind him, and laughed within herself.

And the Lord said unto Abraham, "Wherefore did Sarah laugh? Is anything too hard for the Lord?"

Then Sarah denied, saying, "I laughed not"; for she was afraid.

And He said, "Nay, but thou didst laugh."

Third Article: Justification. — *First Article:* Good Angels.

Heb. 11, 1. Now, faith is the substance of things hoped for, the evidence of things not seen.

> Lo, what the Word in times of old
> Of future days and deeds foretold
> Is all fulfilled while ages roll,
> As traced on the prophetic scroll. (290, 3.)

9. Sodom and Gomorrah
Gen. 18. 19

The Lord's Revelation to Abraham. And the three men arose and looked toward Sodom. And Abraham went with them to bring them on their way.

And the Lord said, "Shall I hide from Abraham the thing which I do, seeing that Abraham shall surely become a great and mighty nation and all the nations of the earth shall be blessed in him?

"For I know him that he will command his children and his household after him, and they shall keep the way of the Lord to do justice and judgment [1] that the Lord may bring upon Abraham that which He hath spoken of him."

And the Lord said, "Because the cry of Sodom and Gomorrah is great, and because their sin is very grievous, I will go down now and see."

---

1) The descendants of Abraham would live in true piety and strive to do right in the sight of God.

Abraham's Intercession. And the men went toward Sodom; but Abraham stood yet before the Lord and said, "Wilt Thou also destroy the righteous with the wicked? Perhaps there are fifty righteous in the city; wilt Thou not spare the place for the fifty righteous that are therein?" And the Lord said, "If I find in Sodom fifty righteous, then I will spare all the place for their sakes."

Abraham answered and said, "Behold now, I have taken upon me to speak unto the Lord, which am but dust and ashes; perhaps there shall lack five; wilt Thou destroy all the city for the lack of five?" And He said, "If I find there forty-five, I will not destroy it."

And he spake unto Him again and said, "Perhaps there shall be forty found there." And He said, "I will not do it for forty's sake."

Abraham said, "Oh, let not the Lord be angry, and I will speak: Perhaps there shall be thirty found there." He said, "I will not do it if I find thirty there."

And he said, "Behold now, I have taken upon me to speak unto the Lord, Perhaps there shall be twenty found there." And He said, "I will not destroy it for twenty's sake."

And Abraham said, "Oh, let not the Lord be angry, and I will speak yet but this once: Perhaps ten shall be found there." And He said, "I will not destroy it for ten's sake."

And the Lord went His way as soon as He had left communing with Abraham; and Abraham returned unto his place.

The Angels at Sodom. The two angels came to Sodom in the evening. Lot sat in the gate,[2] and seeing them, he rose up to meet them, bowed down, and said, "Turn in, I pray you, into your servant's house and tarry all night."

---

[2] Gate of the city; an arched entrance with seats on either side. Here men would assemble not only for social talk, but also to transact business, and here judges would also hold court trials.

And they said, "Nay; but we will abide in the street."

And he pressed them greatly; and they entered into his house; and he made them a feast and did bake bread; and they did eat.

The Wickedness of the People. But before they lay down, the men of Sodom surrounded the house, both old and young, and said, "Where are the men which came in to thee this night? Bring them out unto us." [3]

Lot went out and shut the door after him and said, "I pray you, brethren, do not so wickedly."

But they said, "This one fellow came in to sojourn, and he will needs be a judge!" [4] And they pressed sore upon Lot and came near to break the door.

But the men put forth their hand and pulled Lot into the house and shut to the door. And they smote the men that were at the door with blindness, so that they wearied themselves to find the door.

The Saving of Lot. And the men said unto Lot, "Hast thou here any besides, son-in-law, sons, and daughters? Bring them out of this place, for the LORD hath sent us to destroy it."

And Lot went out and spake unto his sons-in-law and said, "Up, get you out of this place; for the LORD will destroy this city." But he seemed unto them as one that mocked.

And when the morning came, the angels hastened Lot. And while he lingered, they laid hold upon his hand, and upon the hand of his wife and his two daughters, and brought them forth without the city, and said, "Escape for thy life; look not behind thee; escape to the mountain lest thou be consumed."

And Lot said, "Oh, not so, my Lord. I cannot escape to

---

3) Into the shameful life of the city.

4) They meant to say: Lot is a newcomer, an alien, and he wants to teach us.

the mountain lest some evil take me and I die. This city is near; let me escape thither."

And he said, "Haste thee, escape thither." Therefore the name of the city was called Zoar, that is, *Little*.

Destruction of Sodom and Gomorrah. Then the LORD rained upon Sodom and Gomorrah brimstone and fire and

"But Lot's wife looked back"

overthrew those cities and all the plain. But Lot's wife looked back, and she became a pillar of salt.

And Abraham got up early in the morning to the place where he stood before the LORD. And he looked toward Sodom and Gomorrah and toward all the land of the plain, and, lo, the smoke of the country went up as the smoke of a furnace.

Conclusion of the Commandments. — Seventh Petition.

2 Pet. 2, 6. 7. He turned the cities of Sodom and Gomorrah into ashes, condemned them with an overthrow, making them an ensample

unto those that after should live ungodly; and delivered just Lot, vexed with the filthy conversation of the wicked.

> He knows, and He approves,
> The way the righteous go;
> But sinners and their works shall meet
> A dreadful overthrow. (414, 6.)

NOTE. — Sodom and Gomorrah stood at a place that now forms the southern part of the Dead Sea. The Dead Sea is forty-six miles long, ten miles wide, up to thirteen hundred feet deep, and thirteen hundred feet below sea-level. The water is bitter and more salty than ocean water (the Dead Sea, 25 per cent.; the ocean, 4.6 per cent.). No creature can live in it. Excavators have found clear traces of the former cities, even the pillar of salt mingled with clay and brimstone.

10. The Offering of Isaac
Gen. 21—23

Birth of Isaac. When Abraham was an hundred years old, his wife Sarah bare him a son at the set time of which the LORD had spoken to him. And Abraham called the name of his son Isaac [1] and circumcised him being eight days old, as God had commanded him.

God's Command. After these things God did tempt Abraham and said unto him, "Abraham!" And he said, "Here I am." And He said, "Take now thine only son Isaac, whom thou lovest, and get thee into the land of Moriah; [2] and offer him there for a burnt offering upon one of the mountains which I will tell thee of."

Abraham's Obedience. And Abraham rose up early in the morning, and saddled his ass, and took two of his young men with him, and Isaac, his son, and clave the wood for the burnt offering, and rose up, and went unto the place of which God had told him.

---

1) Isaac means *Laughter*.
2) Moriah is the mountain on which the Temple in Jerusalem was afterward built.

Then on the third day Abraham lifted up his eyes and saw the place afar off. And he said unto his young men, "Abide ye here with the ass; and I and the lad will go yonder and worship and come again to you."

And Abraham took the wood of the burnt offering and

"Now I know that thou fearest God"

laid it upon Isaac, his son; and he took the fire in his hand and a knife; and they went both of them together.

And Isaac said, "My father." And Abraham said, "Here am I, my son." And he said, "Behold the fire and the wood; but where is the lamb for a burnt offering?"

And Abraham said, "My son, God will provide Himself a lamb for a burnt offering."

And they came to the place which God had told him of; and Abraham built an altar there, and laid the wood in order, and bound Isaac, his son, and laid him on the altar upon the wood. And he stretched forth his hand and took the knife to slay his son.

The Purpose of the Trial Revealed. And the Angel of the LORD called unto him out of heaven and said, "Abraham, Abraham!" And he said, "Here am I." And He said, "Lay not thine hand upon the lad, neither do thou anything unto him; for now I know that thou fearest God, seeing thou hast not withheld thine only son from Me."

And Abraham lifted up his eyes and saw behind him a ram caught in a thicket by his horns; and he went and took the ram and offered him up for a burnt offering instead of his son.

The Promise Renewed. And the Angel of the LORD called unto Abraham out of heaven the second time and said, "By Myself have I sworn, saith the Lord, because thou hast done this thing and hast not withheld thine only son that I will bless thee and will multiply thy seed as the stars of heaven and as the sand upon the seashore; and thy seed shall possess the gate of his enemies. *And in thy Seed shall all the nations of the earth be blessed* because thou hast obeyed My voice."

So Abraham returned unto his young men, and they rose up and went together to Beersheba and dwelt there.

Sarah's Death. When Sarah was an hundred and twenty and seven years old, she died, and Abraham buried Sarah, his wife, in the cave of the field of Machpelah before Hebron.

First Commandment.

Matt. 10, 37. He that loveth father or mother more than Me is not worthy of Me; and he that loveth son or daughter more than Me is not worthy of Me.

> Though Thou hast called me to resign
> What most I prized, it ne'er was mine;
> I have but yielded what was Thine —
>   "Thy will be done!"   (418, 4.)

11. Isaac's Marriage
Gen. 24

Abraham Sends Eliezer. And Abraham was old and well stricken in age, and the LORD had blessed him in all things.

And Abraham said to his eldest servant, "I will make thee swear by the LORD, the God of heaven and of the earth, that thou shalt not take a wife unto my son of the daughters of the Canaanites among whom I dwell; but thou shalt go unto my country and to my kindred and take a wife unto my son Isaac. And if the woman will not be willing to follow thee into this land, then thou shalt be clear from this my oath." And the servant sware to him.

And he took ten camels and departed and went to Mesopotamia, unto the city of Nahor. And he made his camels to kneel down without the city by a well of water, at the time of the evening that women go out to draw water.

The Servant's Prayer. And he said, "O LORD God, show kindness unto my master Abraham. Behold, I stand here by the well of water; and the daughters of the men of the city come out to draw water. And let it come to pass that the damsel to whom I shall say, 'Let down thy pitcher, I pray thee, that I may drink,' and she shall say, 'Drink, and I will give thy camels drink also,' let the same be she that Thou hast appointed for Thy servant Isaac."

The Prayer Heard. And before he had done speaking, behold, Rebekah, the daughter of Bethuel, the son of Nahor, came out with her pitcher upon her shoulder. And she went down to the well and filled her pitcher and came up.

And the servant ran to meet her and said, "Let me, I pray thee, drink a little water of thy pitcher."

And she said, "Drink, my lord"; and she hasted, and let down her pitcher upon her hand, and gave him drink, and said, "I will draw water for thy camels also until they have done drinking." And she hasted, and emptied her pitcher into the trough, and ran again unto the well, and drew for all his camels.

Eliezer's Gratitude. And when the camels had done drinking, the man gave her a golden earring and two golden bracelets and said, "Whose daughter art thou? Is there room in thy father's house for us to lodge in?"

"Let me, I pray thee, drink a little water"

And she said unto him, "I am the daughter of Bethuel. We have both straw and provender enough and room to lodge in."

And the man bowed down his head and worshiped the LORD and said, "Blessed be the LORD God, who hath led me to the house of my master's brethren."

And the damsel ran and told them of her mother's house these things.

Eliezer Sues for Rebekah. And when Laban, Rebekah's

brother, saw the earring and bracelets and heard the words of Rebekah, he ran to the servant and said, "Come in, thou blessed of the Lord; wherefore standest thou without? For I have prepared the house and room for the camels."

And the man came into the house. And Laban ungirded his camels and gave straw and provender for the camels and water to wash his feet and set meat before him to eat.

But he said, "I will not eat until I have told mine errand." And he said, "Speak on." And the servant told them all that had taken place and said, "Now, if ye will deal kindly and truly with my master, tell me."

Then Laban and Bethuel answered, "The thing proceedeth from the Lord. Behold, Rebekah is before thee; take her and go and let her be thy master's son's wife."

The Marriage. And in the morning he rose up and said, "Send me away unto my master."

And they called Rebekah and said unto her, "Wilt thou go with this man?" And she said, "I will go." And they blessed Rebekah and sent her away.

And Isaac went out to meditate in the field at eventide. And Eliezer came and told Isaac all things that he had done. And Isaac brought Rebekah into his mother Sarah's tent, and she became his wife; and he loved her.

The Death of Abraham. And Abraham gave all that he had unto Isaac and died an hundred threescore and fifteen years old. And his sons Isaac and Ishmael buried him in the cave of Machpelah at Hebron.

Second Commandment: Swearing.— *Fourth Petition:* Pious Spouse. *Sixth Commandment.*

Deut. 6, 13. Thou shalt fear the Lord, thy God, and serve Him and shalt swear by His name.

> Be present, loving Father,
>   To give away this bride
> As Thou gav'st Eve to Adam,
>   A helpmeet at his side. ((622, 2.)

12. Isaac Blesses His Children
Gen. 25—27

Esau Despises His Birthright. Isaac had two sons, Esau and Jacob. The first was red, all over like a hairy garment. And the boys grew, and Esau was a cunning hunter, a man of the field; and Jacob was a plain man, dwelling in tents. And Isaac loved Esau, but Rebekah loved Jacob.

And Jacob sod pottage; and Esau came from the field and he was faint and said to Jacob, "Feed me, I pray thee, with that same red pottage, for I am faint."

And Jacob said, "Sell me this day thy birthright." And Esau said, "Behold, I am at the point to die; and what profit shall this birthright do to me?"

And Jacob said, "Swear to me this day." And he sware unto him; and he sold his birthright unto Jacob.

Then Jacob gave Esau bread and pottage of lentils; and he did eat and drink, and rose up and went his way. Thus Esau despised his birthright.

And when Esau was forty years old, he took two wives of the Hittites, which were a grief of mind unto Isaac and to Rebekah.

Isaac and Rebekah Differ. And when Isaac was old and his eyes were dim so that he could not see, he called Esau and said unto him, "Behold, now I am old; I know not the day of my death. Now, therefore, take thy quiver and thy bow and go out to the field and take me some venison; and make me savory meat, such as I love, that my soul may bless thee before I die." [1]

And Rebekah heard these words and said unto Jacob,

---

[1] A mistake on the part of Isaac. God had told Rebekah, "The elder shall serve the younger," Gen. 25, 23. Also, Esau had despised the blessing and sold his birthright.

"Go now to the flock and fetch me from thence two good kids of the goats; and I will make them savory meat for thy father, such as he loveth. And thou shalt bring it to thy father that he may eat and that he may bless thee before his death." [2]

And Jacob said to Rebekah, his mother, "Behold, Esau, my brother, is a hairy man, and I am a smooth man. My father perhaps will feel me, and I shall seem to him as a deceiver; and I shall bring a curse upon me and not a blessing."

And his mother said, "Upon me be thy curse, my son; only obey my voice." [3] And he went, and fetched, and brought them to his mother.

The Blessing Given to Jacob. And his mother made savory meat and took goodly raiment of her eldest son, Esau, which were with her in the house, and put them upon Jacob. And she put the skins of the kids of the goats upon his hands and upon the smooth of his neck.

And Jacob came unto his father and said, "My father"; and he said, "Who art thou, my son?"

And Jacob said, "I am Esau, thy first-born; I have done according as thou badest me. Arise, sit, and eat of my venison that thy soul may bless me."

And Isaac said, "How is it that thou hast found it so quickly, my son?" And he said, "Because the LORD, thy God, brought it to me."

And Isaac said, "Come near that I may feel thee, my son, whether thou be my very son Esau or not." And he felt

---

[2] Rebekah recognized Isaac's mistake and aimed to prevent it. This was right. But her method was wrong and showed lack of confidence in God. Even Jacob considered it wrong.

[3] Rebekah was ready to take the consequences of frustrating Isaac's plans.

him and said, "The voice is Jacob's voice, but the hands are the hands of Esau."

And he said, "Art thou my very son Esau?" And he said, "I am." And Isaac did eat and drink.

And Isaac said, "Come near now and kiss me, my son." And he came near and kissed him. And he smelled the smell

"Isaac blessed him"

of his raiment and blessed him and said, "God give thee of the dew of heaven and the fatness of the earth and plenty of corn and wine. Let people serve thee and nations bow down to thee. Be lord over thy brethren, and let thy mother's sons bow down to thee. Cursed be every one that curseth thee, and blessed be he that blesseth thee."

Esau's Return. And as soon as Isaac had made an end of blessing Jacob and Jacob was yet scarce gone out, Esau, his brother, came in from his hunting. And he also made savory meat and brought it unto his father and said, "Let my father arise and eat of his son's venison that thy soul may bless me."

And Isaac, his father, said unto him, "Who art thou?"

And he said, "I am thy son, thy first-born, Esau."

And Isaac trembled very exceedingly and said, "Who? Where is he that hath taken venison and brought it me, and I have eaten of all before thou camest and have blessed him? Yea, and he shall be blessed.[4] Thy brother came with subtilty and hath taken away thy blessing."

And when Esau heard these words, he cried with a great and exceeding bitter cry and said unto his father, "Hast thou but *one* blessing, my father?" And he lifted up his voice and wept.

And Isaac answered, "Behold, thy dwelling shall be the fatness of the earth and of the dew of heaven from above; and by thy sword shalt thou live and shalt serve thy brother.[5] And it shall come to pass when thou shalt have the dominion that thou shalt break his yoke from off thy neck."

Third Petition.

Heb. 11, 20. By faith Isaac blessed Jacob and Esau concerning things to come.

> Thy ways, O Lord, with wise design
> Are framed upon Thy throne above,
> And every dark and bending line
> Meets in the center of Thy love. (530, 1.)

NOTE. — *Esau* means *Hairy.* — *Jacob* means *Supplanter.*

---

[4] Isaac realized the mistake of his plan to bless Esau.
[5] As the Lord had said.

13. Jacob's Ladder
Gen. 27—29

Esau's Hatred. And Esau hated Jacob because of the blessing and said, "The days of mourning for my father are at hand; then will I slay my brother."

And these words of Esau were told to Rebekah. And she sent and called Jacob and said unto him, "Arise, flee thou to Laban, my brother, to Haran; and tarry with him a few days [1] until thy brother's fury turn away; then I will send and fetch thee from thence."

Plans for Jacob's Marriage. And Rebekah said to Isaac, "I am weary of my life because of the daughters of Heth; if Jacob take a wife of the daughters of Heth, what good shall my life do me?"

And Isaac called Jacob and blessed him and said, "Thou shalt not take a wife of the daughters of Canaan. Arise, take thee a wife of the daughters of Laban."

And Isaac blessed him and said, "God Almighty bless thee and make thee fruitful and multiply thee that thou mayest be a multitude of people; and give thee the blessing of Abraham that thou mayest inherit the land wherein thou art a stranger, which God gave unto Abraham." [2]

Thus Isaac sent away Jacob to Mesopotamia unto Laban.

Jacob's Dream and Blessing. And Jacob went out from Beersheba and went toward Haran. And he lighted upon a certain place and tarried there all night; and he took of the stones and put them for his pillows and lay down in that place to sleep.

And he dreamed; and, behold, a ladder set up on the

---

[1] A short time.
[2] Isaac was now fully convinced that the blessing of Abraham was to go to Jacob and not to Esau.

earth, and the top of it reached to heaven; and, behold, the angels of God ascending and descending on it.[3)]

And the LORD stood above it and said, "I am the LORD God of Abraham, thy father, and the God of Isaac: the land whereon thou liest, to thee will I give it and to thy seed; and thy seed shall be as the dust of the earth; *and in thee and in*

"The angels of God ascending and descending"

thy seed shall all the families of the earth be blessed.[4)] And, behold, I am with thee and will keep thee whither thou goest and will bring thee again into this land."

Jacob's Vow. Jacob awaked out of his sleep, and he

---

3) Picturing the union between God and man, to be established by Jesus.

4) God Himself here again reveals that the Savior was to come from Jacob and not from Esau. This is the reason why Rebekah acted promptly, though unwisely, to secure the best blessing for Jacob.

said, "Surely the LORD is in this place, and I knew it not. How dreadful [5]) is this place! This is none other but the house of God, and this is the gate of heaven."

And Jacob rose up early in the morning, and took the stone that he had put for his pillows, and set it up for a pillar,

"Then Jacob rolled the stone from the well's mouth"

and poured oil upon it. And he called the name of that place Bethel.

And Jacob vowed a vow, saying, "If God will be with me and will keep me in this way that I go and will give me bread to eat and raiment to put on, so that I come again to my father's house in peace, then shall the LORD be my God; and this stone shall be God's house."

Arrival at Laban's Home. Now, when Jacob went on into

---

5) Awe-inspiring.

the land of the East, he came to a well in the field. And he said to the shepherds who were waiting there to water their flocks, "My brethren, whence be ye?"

And they said, "Of Haran are we."

And he said unto them, "Know ye Laban, the son of Nahor?"

And they said, "We know him, and, behold, Rachel, his daughter, cometh with the sheep."

Then Jacob went near, and rolled the stone from the well's mouth, and watered the flock of Laban, and kissed Rachel, and lifted up his voice and wept, and told her that he was Rebekah's son.

And she ran and told her father. And Laban ran to meet him, and embraced him, and kissed him, and brought him to his house.

Evening Prayer: "Let Thy holy angel be with me that the wicked Foe may have no power over me." — *Good Angels.*

John 1, 51. Verily, verily, I say unto you, Hereafter ye shall see heaven open and the angels of God ascending and descending upon the Son of Man.

> Abram's promised great Reward,
> Zion's Helper, Jacob's Lord, —
> Him of twofold race behold, —
> Truly came, as long foretold. (91, 3.)

NOTE. — Jacob probably never saw his mother again.

---

14. Jacob and Laban
Gen. 29—32

Service with Laban. Now, when Jacob had been with Laban a month, Laban said, "Because thou art my brother, shouldest thou therefore serve me for naught? Tell me, what shall thy wages be?"

And Laban had two daughters; the name of the elder

was Leah, and the name of the younger was Rachel. Leah was tender-eyed;[1)] but Rachel was beautiful and well-favored. And Jacob loved Rachel and said, "I will serve thee seven years for Rachel."

And Jacob served seven years for Rachel; and they seemed unto him but a few days for the love he had to her.

Jacob's Marriage. And Laban made a feast and took Leah and brought her to him and gave her Zilpah for an handmaid.

And Jacob said to Laban, "What is this thou hast done unto me? Did not I serve thee for Rachel?"

And Laban said, "It must not be so done in our country to give the younger before the first-born.[2)] Fulfil her week,[3)] and we will give thee this also for the service which thou shalt serve with me yet seven other years."

And Jacob did so and fulfilled her week,[4)] and he gave him Rachel, his daughter, to wife also. And Laban gave to Rachel his handmaid Bilhah to be her maid.

And the LORD gave Jacob twelve sons: Reuben, Simeon, Levi, Judah, Dan, Naphtali, Gad, Asher, Issachar, Zebulun, Joseph, and Benjamin. Joseph and Benjamin were sons of Rachel.

God Enriches Jacob. — And Jacob said to Laban, "Let me go to my country; give me my wives and my children and let me go."

And Laban said unto him, "I pray thee, if I have found favor in thine eyes, tarry; for I experience that the LORD hath blessed me for thy sake. Appoint me thy wages, and I will give it." Jacob demanded as hire all the sheep and goats

---

1) Pale-eyed; lacking in beauty.
2) Laban should have said this in the beginning.
3) The week's wedding celebration.
4) Acknowledged Leah as his wife.

that were spotted and speckled and all the brown among the sheep.

Thus Jacob served Laban six other years for wages of cattle. And although Laban changed his wages ten times, he became exceedingly rich in maid-servants and men-servants, sheep, camels, and asses. But Laban and his sons were jealous of Jacob on account of his wealth.

And the LORD said unto Jacob, "Return unto the land of thy fathers; and I will be with thee."

Jacob Departs Secretly. And Jacob sent and called Rachel and Leah to the field and said unto them, "I see your father's countenance that it is not toward me as before; and ye know that with all my power I have served your father. And your father hath deceived me and changed my wages ten times; but God suffered him not to hurt me."

And Rachel and Leah answered, "Whatsoever God hath said unto thee do."

Then Jacob rose up and set his sons and his wives upon camels; and he carried away all his cattle and all his goods for to go to Isaac, his father, in the land of Canaan.

And it was told Laban on the third day that Jacob was fled. And he pursued after him and overtook him in Mount Gilead. And God told Laban in a dream, "Take heed that thou speak not to Jacob either good or bad." [5]

And Laban overtook Jacob and said, "Wherefore didst thou flee away secretly and didst not tell me? It is in my power to do you hurt; but the God of your father spake unto me yesternight, 'Take heed that thou speak not to Jacob either good or bad.'" And Jacob and Laban made a covenant with each other.

---

[5] Luther's translation: Take heed that you do not speak otherwise than friendly to Jacob.

And Jacob went on his way, and the angels of God met him. And when he saw them, he said, "This is God's host." And he called the name of that place Mahanaim.

Fourth Commandment.

1 Pet. 2, 18. Servants, be subject to your masters with all fear; not only to the good and gentle, but also to the froward.

>All depends on our possessing
>God's abundant grace and blessing,
>>Though all earthly wealth depart.
>
>He who trusts with faith unshaken
>In his God is not forsaken
>>And e'er keeps a dauntless heart. (425, 1.)

---

15. Jacob's Return
Gen. 32—35

Jacob's Message to Esau. And Jacob sent messengers before him to Esau, his brother, saying, "Thy servant Jacob saith thus, 'I have sent that I may find grace in thy sight.'"

And the messengers returned to Jacob, saying, "We came to thy brother Esau, and also he cometh to meet thee and four hundred men with him."

Then Jacob was greatly afraid, and he divided the people that was with him and the herds into two bands and said, "If Esau come to the one company and smite it, then the other company which is left shall escape."

Jacob's Prayer. And Jacob said, "O God of my father Abraham and God of my father Isaac, the LORD which saidst unto me, 'Return unto thy country,' *I am not worthy of the least of all the mercies and of all the truth which Thou hast showed unto Thy servant;* for with my staff I passed over this Jordan, and now I am become two bands. Deliver me, I pray Thee, from the hand of my brother Esau."

Then he prepared presents for Esau, and that night he took his wives and children and all that he had and sent them over the ford Jabbok. And Jacob was left alone.

Jacob's Faith. And there wrestled a Man [1] with him until the breaking of the day. And when He saw that He prevailed not against him,[2] He touched the hollow of his

"I will not let Thee go except Thou bless me"

thigh; and the hollow of Jacob's thigh was out of joint as he wrestled with Him.

And He said, "Let me go, for the day breaketh."

And Jacob said, "I will not let Thee go except Thou bless me."

---

[1] The Son of God.
[2] He did not use His divine power; He had come only to test Jacob's faith and spiritual strength and willingly permitted Jacob to obtain the victory through faith.

And He said unto him, "What is thy name?" And he said, "Jacob." And He said, "Thy name shall be called no more Jacob, but Israel;[3] for as a prince hast thou power with God and with men and hast prevailed." And He blessed him there.

And Jacob called the name of the place Peniel.[4] "For," said he, "I have seen God face to face, and my life is preserved." And as he passed over Peniel, the sun rose upon him.

Jacob and Esau Meet. And Jacob lifted up his eyes, and saw his brother Esau coming with four hundred men. And he bowed himself to the ground seven times until he came to his brother. And Esau ran to meet him and fell on his neck and kissed him; and they wept.

And Jacob said, "If, now, I have found grace in thy sight, then receive my present at my hand."

And Esau said, "I have enough; keep that thou hast." And Jacob urged him, and he took it.

Jacob Settles in Canaan. And Jacob came to Shalem, a city of Shechem, and bought a parcel of a field where he spread his tent, and he erected there an altar.

And God said unto Jacob, "Arise, go up to Bethel, and make there an altar unto God that appeared unto thee when thou fleddest from the face of Esau, thy brother." And Jacob did so.

Isaac's Death. And Jacob came unto Isaac, his father, unto Mamre, which is Hebron. And the days of Isaac were an hundred and fourscore years, and he died. And his sons Esau and Jacob buried him.

---

3) Israel means "He who prevails with God," "A prince who has power with God and men."
4) Face of God.

First Article. Fourth and Seventh Petitions.

Ps. 91, 10. There shall no evil befall thee, neither shall any plague come nigh thy dwelling.

> If God Himself be for me,
> I may a host defy;
> For when I pray, before me
> My foes, confounded, fly.
> If Christ, my Head and Master,
> Befriend me from above,
> What foe or what disaster
> Can drive me from His love? (528, 1.)

NOTE. — Isaac was probably one hundred and fifty-seven years old when Jacob returned and lived twenty-three years after that.

16. Joseph and His Brethren
Gen. 37

Israel's Preference for Joseph. Joseph, being seventeen years old, was feeding the flock with his brethren and brought unto his father their evil report.

Now, Israel loved Joseph more than all his children because he was the son of his old age; and he made him a coat of many colors.[1)] And when his brethren saw that their father loved him more than all his brethren, they hated him, and could not speak peaceably unto him.

Joseph's Dreams. And Joseph dreamed a dream, and he told it his brethren, saying, "Hear, I pray you, this dream which I have dreamed: We were binding sheaves in the field, and, lo, my sheaf arose and also stood upright; and your sheaves stood round about and made obeisance [2)] to my sheaf."

---

1) A coat of distinction, probably made of rich materials and worn by prominent persons. Shepherds or herdsmen wore plain, one-colored garments, reaching only to the knees. The coat of many colors reached to the feet.   2) Bowed down.

And his brethren said to him, "Shalt thou indeed reign over us?" And they hated him yet the more.

And he dreamed yet another dream and told it his brethren and said, "Behold, I have dreamed a dream more; and, behold, the sun and the moon and the eleven stars made

"And Joseph dreamed a dream"

obeisance to me." And he told it to his father and to his brethren.

And his father rebuked him and said unto him, "What is this dream that thou hast dreamed? Shall I and thy mother and thy brethren indeed come to bow down ourselves to thee to the earth?" And his brethren envied him; but his father observed the saying.

The Plot against Joseph's Life. And his brethren went to feed their father's flock in Shechem. And Jacob said unto Joseph, "Go, see whether it be well with thy brethren and with the flocks."

And when his brethren saw him afar off, they said, "Behold, this dreamer cometh. Let us slay him and say,

"And they sold Joseph"

'Some evil beast hath devoured him'; and we shall see what will become of his dreams."

And Reuben [3] heard it; and he delivered him out of their hands and said, "Shed no blood, but cast him into this pit that is in the wilderness and lay no hand upon him"; that he might rid him out of their hands, to deliver him to his father again.

And when Joseph was come unto his brethren, they

---

[3] As the eldest son he had the greatest responsibility.

stripped him out of his coat of many colors and cast him into a pit; and the pit was empty, there was no water in it. And they sat down to eat bread.

Joseph Sold. And, behold, a company of Ishmaelites came with their camels bearing spicery and balm and myrrh, going to carry it down to Egypt.

And Judah said, "What profit is it if we slay our brother? Come, let us sell him to the Ishmaelites, and let not our hand be upon him; for he is our brother."

And his brethren were content.[4] Then they drew Joseph out of the pit and sold him for twenty pieces of silver.

And Reuben returned unto the pit; and, behold, Joseph was not in the pit; and he rent his clothes.[5] And he returned unto his brethren and said, "The child is not; and I, whither shall I go?"

And they killed a kid of the goats, and dipped Joseph's coat in the blood, and sent it to their father, and said, "This have we found; know now whether it be thy son's coat or no."

Jacob's Sorrow. And he knew it and said, "It is my son's coat; an evil beast hath devoured him; Joseph is without doubt rent in pieces."

And Jacob rent his clothes and put sackcloth upon his loins and mourned his son many days. And all his sons and all his daughters rose up to comfort him; but he refused to be comforted; and he said, "I will go down into the grave unto my son mourning."

Fifth Commandment.

1 John 3, 15. Whosoever hateth his brother is a murderer; and ye know that no murderer hath eternal life abiding in him.

Are we weak and heavy laden, Cumbered with a load of care?
Precious Savior, still our Refuge, — Take it to the Lord in prayer.
Do thy friends despise, forsake thee? Take it to the Lord in prayer;
In His arms He'll take and shield thee, Thou wilt find a solace there.

(457, 3.)

---

4) They were satisfied.   5) A sign of shock or grief.

17. Joseph in Egypt
Gen. 39 and 40

In Potiphar's House. And Joseph was brought down to Egypt; and Potiphar, an officer of Pharaoh, captain of the guard, bought him of the Ishmaelites, which had brought him down thither.

And the LORD was with Joseph and made all that he did to prosper in his hand. And Potiphar made him overseer over his house, and all that he had he put into his hand.

Joseph's Purity. And Joseph was a goodly person and well favored. And it came to pass that his master's wife cast her eyes upon Joseph, and she said, "Lie with me."

But he refused and said unto her, "Behold, my master hath committed all that he hath to my hand; neither hath he kept back anything from me but thee, because thou art his wife. How, then, can I do this great wickedness and sin against God?" [1]

And as she spake to Joseph day by day, he hearkened not unto her to be with her.

And it came to pass about this time that Joseph went into the house to do his business; and there was none of the men of the house there within. And she caught him by his garment, saying, "Lie with me." And he left his garment in her hand and fled and got him out.

And she called the men of her house and said, "See, he hath brought in a Hebrew [2] unto us to mock us; [3] and when he heard that I cried with a loud voice, he fled and got him out."

---

1) It is the fear of God that saved Joseph in his temptation. He confessed his fear of God frankly before this heathen woman.

2) The word *Hebrew* is derived from Eber, one of the ancestors of Abraham, Gen. 10, 24; 11, 13.

3) To bring shame or scandal upon us.

And she laid up his garment by her until his lord came home. And she spake unto him, saying, "The Hebrew servant which thou hast brought unto us came in unto me to mock me. And it came to pass, as I lifted up my voice and cried, that he left his garment with me and fled out."

Joseph in Prison. And his master's wrath was kindled, and he put him into the prison where the king's prisoners were.

But the LORD was with Joseph and showed him mercy and gave him favor in the sight of the keeper of the prison, so that he committed to his hands all the prisoners. The keeper of the prison looked not to anything because the LORD was with Joseph, and that which he did, the LORD made it to prosper.

The Butler's Dream. And it came to pass after these things that the butler of the king of Egypt and his baker had offended their lord, the king of Egypt. And Pharaoh put them into prison.

And they dreamed a dream, both of them, in one night. And when Joseph, in the morning, saw that they were sad, he asked them, saying, "Wherefore look ye so sadly to-day?"

They said, "We have dreamed a dream, and there is no interpreter of it."

And Joseph said, "Do not interpretations belong to God? Tell me them, I pray you."

And the chief butler told his dream and said, "In my dream a vine was before me; and in the vine were three branches; and it budded, and her blossoms shot forth and brought forth ripe grapes. And Pharaoh's cup was in my hand; and I took the grapes and pressed them into the cup, and I gave the cup into Pharaoh's hand."

And Joseph said unto him, "This is the interpretation of it: The three branches are three days. Yet within three days shall Pharaoh lift up thine head and restore thee unto thy place. But think on me when it shall be well with thee, and show kindness, I pray thee, unto me, and make mention of me unto Pharaoh, and bring me out of this house; for

"This is the interpretation"

I have done nothing that they should put me into the dungeon."

The Baker's Dream. When the chief baker saw that the interpretation was good, he said, "I, in my dream, had three white baskets on my head; and in the uppermost basket there was of all manner of bakemeats for Pharaoh; and the birds did eat them out of the basket."

And Joseph answered, "This is the interpretation thereof: The three baskets are three days. Yet within three days shall Pharaoh lift up thy head and shall hang thee on a tree; and the birds shall eat thy flesh from off thee."

And it came to pass the third day, which was Pharaoh's birthday, that he restored the chief butler unto his butlership again; but he hanged the chief baker, as Joseph had interpreted to them. Yet did not the chief butler remember Joseph, but forgot him.

Sixth Commandment. — Sixth Petition.

Ps. 119, 9. Wherewithal shall a young man cleanse his way? By taking heed thereto according to Thy Word.

> How shall the young secure their hearts
> And guard their lives from sin?
> Thy Word the choicest rules imparts
> To keep the conscience clean. (286, 1.)

NOTE. — Pharaoh is not a name, but was the title of the kings of Egypt in the Old Testament.

18. Joseph before Pharaoh
Gen. 41

Pharaoh's Dreams. At the end of two full years, Pharaoh dreamed; and, behold, he stood by the river. And there came up out of the river seven well-favored and fat-fleshed kine,[1] and they fed in a meadow. And seven other kine came up after them out of the river, ill favored and lean-fleshed; and they did eat up the seven well favored and fat kine. So Pharaoh awoke.

And he slept and dreamed the second time; and, behold,

---

1) Cows.

seven ears of corn [2] came up upon one stalk, rank [3] and good. And, behold, seven thin ears, and blasted [4] with the east wind, sprung up after them. And the seven thin ears devoured the seven rank and full ears. And Pharaoh awoke.

And it came to pass in the morning that his spirit was troubled; and he sent and called for all the magicians [5] of Egypt and all the wise men [6] thereof; but there was none that could interpret the dream unto Pharaoh.

Then spake the chief butler unto Pharaoh, saying, "I do remember my faults this day. Pharaoh was wroth with his servants and put me in ward in the captain of the guard's house, both me and the chief baker. And we dreamed a dream in one night. And there was there with us a young man, a Hebrew, and he interpreted to us our dreams. And it came to pass, as he interpreted to us, so it was; me he restored unto mine office, and him he hanged."

Joseph's Interpretation and Advice. Then Pharaoh sent and called Joseph; and they brought him hastily out of the dungeon. And he shaved himself and changed his raiment and came in unto Pharaoh.

And Pharaoh said unto him, "I have dreamed a dream, and there is none that can interpret it; and I have heard say of thee that thou canst understand a dream to interpret it."

And Joseph answered, "It is not in me; God shall give Pharaoh an answer of peace." [7]

---

[2] Here meaning grain; evidently wheat.
[3] Very large; of unusual size.
[4] Withered and burned by hot winds.
[5] Persons performing supernatural deeds by the aid of the devil or deceiving people by trickery.
[6] Magicians and wise men were a priestly caste in Egypt; leaders in both religion and science.
[7] Note how Joseph here and in the following confesses God before this heathen king. He shows the hand of the true God in world affairs, also in heathen countries.

And Pharaoh told him his dreams. And Joseph said, "The dream of Pharaoh is one: God hath showed Pharaoh what He is about to do.

"The seven good kine are seven years; and the seven good ears are seven years; the dream is one. And the seven

"The dream of Pharaoh is one"

thin and ill-favored kine that came up after them and the seven empty and blasted ears shall be seven years of famine.

"Behold, there come seven years of great plenty throughout all the land of Egypt. And there shall arise after them seven years of famine; and all the plenty shall be forgotten in the land by reason of that famine following; for it shall be very grievous.

"And for that the dream was doubled unto Pharaoh twice, it is because the thing is established by God, and God will shortly bring it to pass.

"Now, therefore, let Pharaoh look out a man discreet and wise and set him over the land of Egypt. And let him take up the fifth part of the land of Egypt in the seven plenteous years. And let them gather all the food of those good years that come, and let them keep food in the cities. And that food shall be for store to the land against the seven years of famine that the land perish not through the famine."

Joseph Exalted. And the thing was good in the eyes of Pharaoh and in the eyes of all his servants. And Pharaoh said, "Can we find such a one as this is, a man in whom the Spirit of God is?"

And he said unto Joseph, "Forasmuch as God hath showed thee all this, there is none so discreet and wise as thou art.[8] Thou shalt be over my house, and according unto thy word shall all my people be ruled; only in the throne will I be greater than thou."

And Pharaoh took off his ring from his hand, and put it upon Joseph's hand, and arrayed him in vestures of fine linen, and put a gold chain about his neck; and he made him to ride in the second chariot which he had; and they cried before him, "Bow the knee!"

And he made him ruler over all the land of Egypt. And he gave him to wife Asenath, the daughter of Potipherah, priest of On.

And Joseph was thirty years old when he stood before Pharaoh. And Joseph went out throughout all the land of

---

[8] Note what respect for the true God Joseph has created in the heart of Pharaoh.

Egypt. And he gathered up all the food of the seven plenteous years and laid up the food. And he gathered corn as the sand of the sea very much, until he left numbering; for it was without number.

And unto Joseph were born two sons before the years

"And they cried before him, 'Bow the knee'"

of famine came. And Joseph called the first-born Manasseh and the second Ephraim.

And the seven years of plenteousness were ended. And the seven years of dearth began to come; and the dearth was in all lands. And when all the people cried to Pharaoh for bread, Pharaoh said, "Go unto Joseph; what he saith to you do."

And Joseph opened all the storehouses and sold unto the Egyptians. And all countries came into Egypt to Joseph for to buy corn.

First Article: Preservation; God's Rule.

1 Pet. 5, 5. 6. God resisteth the proud and giveth grace to the humble. Humble yourselves therefore under the mighty hand of God that He may exalt you in due time.

> Sing, pray, and keep His ways unswerving,
>   Perform thy duties faithfully,
> And trust His Word, though undeserving,
>   Thou yet shalt find it true for thee.
> God never yet forsook in need
> The soul that trusted Him indeed. (518, 7.)

---

19. The First Journey of Joseph's Brethren
Gen. 42

Famine Brings the Sons of Jacob to Egypt. Now, when Jacob saw that there was corn in Egypt, he said unto his sons, "Get you down and buy for us that we may live and not die."

And Joseph's ten brethren went down to buy corn in Egypt. But Benjamin, Joseph's brother, Jacob sent not with them; for he said, "Lest, peradventure, mischief befall him."

On Trial before Joseph. And Joseph was the governor over the land. And they bowed down themselves before him with their faces to the earth.

And Joseph saw his brethren, and he knew them, but made himself strange unto them and spake roughly unto them and said, "Whence come ye?" And they said, "From the land of Canaan to buy food."

And Joseph knew his brethren, but they knew not him. And he remembered the dreams which he dreamed of them and said unto them, "Ye are spies; to see the nakedness of the land ye are come."

And they said, "Nay, my lord, but to buy food are thy servants come. We are all one man's sons; we are true men;

thy servants are no spies. We are twelve brethren, the sons of one man in the land of Canaan; and the youngest is with our father, and one is not."

And Joseph said unto them, "That is it that I spake

"Ye are spies"

unto you, saying, 'Ye are spies'; hereby ye shall be proved: ye shall not go forth hence except your youngest brother come hither. Send one of you and let him fetch your brother, and ye shall be kept in prison, that your words may be proved whether there be any truth in you.". And he put them all together into ward three days.

Simeon Held as Hostage. And Joseph said unto them the third day, "This do and live; for I fear God.[1] If ye be true men, let one of your brethren be bound in your prison. Go ye, carry corn for the famine of your houses, but bring your youngest brother unto me; so shall your words be verified, and ye shall not die."

And they said one to another, "We are verily guilty concerning our brother in that we saw the anguish of his soul when he besought us, and we would not hear; therefore is this distress come upon us."

And they knew not that Joseph understood them; for he spake unto them by an interpreter.[2] And he turned himself about from them and wept[3] and returned to them again, and took from them Simeon, and bound him before their eyes.

The Return Home. Then Joseph commanded to fill their sacks with corn and to restore every man's money into his sack and to give them provision for the way. And they departed thence.

And as one of them opened his sack to give his ass provender in the inn, he espied his money; for, behold, it was in his sack's mouth. And their heart failed them, and they were afraid, saying one to another, "What is this that God hath done unto us?"

And when they came unto Jacob, their father, they told

---

[1] I shall not treat you unjustly. This confession evidently made the brethren wonder all the more and inspired confidence. Who would expect such a thing in Egypt!

[2] A man who spoke both Egyptian and Hebrew.

[3] Joseph had a deep, burning love for his brethren. His real object was to make sure that they would return with Benjamin, not to take revenge.

him all that befell unto them. And it came to pass, as they emptied their sacks, that, behold, every man's bundle of money was in his sack; and they and their father were afraid.

And Jacob said unto them, "Me have ye bereaved of my children: Joseph is not, and Simeon is not, and ye will take Benjamin away; all these things are against me."

And Reuben spake unto his father, saying, "Slay my two sons if I bring him not to thee."

And Jacob said, "My son shall not go down with you; for his brother is dead, and he is left alone; if mischief befall him by the way, then shall ye bring down my gray hairs with sorrow to the grave."

Confession.

Ps. 51, 17. The sacrifices of God are a broken spirit; a broken and a contrite heart, O God, Thou wilt not despise.

Before Thee, God, who knowest all, With grief and shame I prostrate fall. I see my sins against Thee, Lord, The sins of thought, of deed, and word. They press me sore; I cry to Thee: O God, be merciful to me! (318, 1.)

---

20. The Second Journey of Joseph's Brethren
Gen. 43

Benjamin Goes with the Brethren. And the famine was sore in the land. And it came to pass, when they had eaten up the corn, their father said unto them, "Go again, buy us a little food."

And Judah said, "The man did solemnly protest unto us, saying, 'Ye shall not see my face except your brother be with you.' If thou wilt send our brother with us, we will go down and buy thee food; but if thou wilt not send him, we will not go down."

And Israel said, "Wherefore dealt ye so ill with me as to tell the man whether ye had yet a brother?"

And they said, "The man asked us straitly of our kindred. Could we certainly know that he would say, 'Bring your brother down'?"

And Judah said unto his father, "Send the lad with me; I will be surety for him. If I bring him not unto thee, then let me bear the blame forever."

And their father said unto them, "If it must be so now, do this; take of the best fruits in the land and carry the man a present, a little balm, and a little honey, spices and myrrh, nuts and almonds. And take double money in your hand and the money that was brought again in the mouth of your sacks; peradventure it was an oversight. Take also your brother and go.

"And God Almighty give you mercy before the man that he may send away your other brother and Benjamin. If I be bereaved of my children, I am bereaved."

A Kind Reception. And they rose up and went to Egypt and stood before Joseph. And when Joseph saw Benjamin with them, he said to the ruler of his house, "Bring these men home and slay and make ready; for these men shall dine with me at noon."

And they were afraid because they were brought into Joseph's house; and they said, "Because of the money that was returned in our sacks are we brought in that he may fall upon us and take us for bondmen."

And they came near to the steward of Joseph's house and communed with him and wanted to give him the money again. And he said, "Peace be to you, fear not; your God and the God of your father hath given you treasure in your sacks. I had your money." And he brought Simeon out unto them.

And when Joseph came home, they brought him the present and bowed themselves to him to the earth. And he asked them of their welfare and said, "Is your father well, the old man of whom ye spake? Is he yet alive?"

And they answered, "Thy servant, our father, is in good

"Is this your younger brother?"

health." And they bowed down their heads and made obeisance.

Joseph and Benjamin. And Joseph saw his brother Benjamin and said, "Is this your younger brother, of whom ye spake unto me?" And he said, "God be gracious unto thee, my son."

And Joseph made haste; for his bowels [1] did yearn upon his brother; and he entered into his chamber and wept there.

---

1) His innermost being. We would say "his heart."

And he washed his face, and went out, and refrained himself, and said, "Set on bread." And they set on for him by himself and for the Egyptians which did eat with him, because the Egyptians might not eat bread with the Hebrews; for that is an abomination unto the Egyptians.

And they sat before him, the first-born according to his birthright and the youngest according to his youth; and the men marveled one at another. And he sent messes unto them from before him; but Benjamin's mess was five times so much as any of theirs.

Sum of Second Table. Fifth Petition.

Rom. 12, 10. Be kindly affectioned one to another with brotherly love.

> Thou sacred Love, grace on us bestow,
> Set our hearts with heavenly fire aglow,
> That with hearts united we love each other,
> Of one mind, in peace with every brother.
> Lord, have mercy! (231, 3.)

NOTE.— Joseph was about thirty-nine years old and Benjamin about twenty-four.

21. Joseph Makes Himself Known
Gen. 44. 45

A Final Test. And Joseph commanded the steward of his house, saying, "Fill the men's sacks with food, as much as they can carry, and put every man's money in his sack's mouth. And put my silver cup in the sack's mouth of the youngest and his corn-money." And he did so.

As soon as the morning was light, the men were sent away. And when they were gone out of the city, Joseph said unto his steward, "Up, follow after the men; and when thou dost overtake them, say unto them, 'Wherefore have ye rewarded evil for good? Is not this it in which my lord drinketh? Ye have done evil in so doing.'"

And he overtook them, and he spake unto them these same words.

And they said unto him, "Wherefore saith my lord these words? God forbid that thy servants should do according to this thing. Behold, the money which we found in our sack's mouth we brought again unto thee; how, then, should we steal out of thy lord's house silver or gold? With whomsoever it be found, both let him die, and we also will be my lord's bondmen."

And he said, "Now also let it be according unto your words: he with whom it be found shall be my servant, and ye shall be blameless."

Then they took down every man his sack to the ground and opened every man his sack. And he searched and began at the eldest and left at the youngest; and the cup was found in Benjamin's sack. Then they rent their clothes and returned to the city.

Judah's Pleading. And Judah and his brethren came to Joseph's house, and they fell before him on the ground.

And Joseph said unto them, "What deed is this that ye have done?"

And Judah said, "What shall we say unto my lord? God hath found out the iniquity of thy servants; behold, we are my lord's servants."

And he said, "God forbid that I should do so; but the man in whose hand the cup is found, he shall be my servant; and as for you, get you up in peace unto your father."

Then Judah came near unto him and said, "O my lord, let thy servant, I pray thee, speak a word in my lord's ears. Our father's life is bound up in this lad's life.[1] Now, therefore, when I come home and the lad be not with us, it shall

---

1) Since Joseph was gone, Benjamin was especially dear to him.

come to pass when he seeth that the lad is not with us, that he will die; thus we would bring down the gray hairs of our father with sorrow to the grave. For thy servant became surety for the lad unto my father. Therefore let me abide instead of the lad a bondman to my lord, and let the lad go up with his brethren. For how shall I go up to my father

"I am Joseph"

and the lad be not with me? lest, peradventure, I see the evil that shall come on my father." [2]

Joseph Reveals Himself. Then Joseph could not refrain himself any longer; and he cried, "Cause every man to go out from me."

And he wept aloud and said unto his brethren, "I am Joseph! Doth my father yet live?"

2) Judah a type of Christ. — "I do not doubt that Joseph trembled in his whole body while Judah uttered his plea. . . . Every word must have pierced his heart." (*Luther.*)

And his brethren could not answer him; for they were troubled at his presence.

And Joseph said unto his brethren, "Come near to me, I pray you. I am Joseph, your brother, whom ye sold into Egypt. Now, therefore, be not grieved nor angry with yourselves that ye sold me hither; for God did send me before you to preserve life. So now it was not you that sent me hither, but God; and He hath made me a ruler throughout all the land of Egypt.

"Haste ye and go up to my father and say unto him, 'Thus saith thy son Joseph, "God hath made me lord of all Egypt; come down unto me, tarry not, and I will nourish thee; for yet there are five years of famine."'

"And ye shall tell my father of all my glory in Egypt; and ye shall haste and bring down my father hither."

And he fell upon his brother Benjamin's neck and wept. Moreover, he kissed all his brethren and wept upon them; and after that his brethren talked with him.

Pharaoh's Kindness. And when Pharaoh heard that Joseph's brethren were come, it pleased him well. And he said unto Joseph, "Say unto thy brethren, 'Go unto the land of Canaan and take your father and your households and come unto me. Take you wagons out of the land of Egypt for your little ones and for your wives and bring your father and come. Also regard not your stuff;[3] I will give you the good of the land of Egypt, and ye shall eat of the fat of the land.'"

And Joseph gave them wagons according to the commandment of Pharaoh and many good things of Egypt for his father and sent them away. And he said unto them, "See that ye fall not out by the way."[4]

---

[3] Do not trouble about bringing your personal property.
[4] Do not quarrel.

Fifth Petition. First Article: God's Care.

Matt. 5, 44. But I say unto you, Love your enemies, bless them that curse you, do good to them that hate you, and pray for them which despitefully use you and persecute you.

> I, a sinner, come to Thee
> With a penitent confession;
> Savior, mercy show to me,
> Grant for all my sins remission. (324, 5.)

22. Jacob in Egypt
Gen. 45—50

Israel's Departure from Canaan. And Joseph's brethren came into the land of Canaan unto Jacob, their father, and told him, saying, "Joseph is yet alive, and he is governor over all the land of Egypt."

And Jacob's heart fainted, for he believed them not.

And they told him all the words of Joseph which he had said unto them. And when he saw the wagons which Joseph had sent to carry him, the spirit of Jacob revived. And Israel said, "It is enough; Joseph, my son, is yet alive. I will go and see him before I die."

And Israel took his journey with all that he had and came to Beersheba and offered sacrifices unto the God of his father Isaac.

And God spake unto him in the visions of the night and said, "I am God, the God of thy father. Fear not to go down into Egypt; for I will make of thee a great nation. I will go down with thee into Egypt; and I will also surely bring thee up again; and Joseph shall put his hand upon thine eyes." [1]

And all the souls of the house of Jacob which came into Egypt were threescore and ten, besides his sons' wives and the servants.

---

[1] He shall be present at your death.

Reunion of Father and Son. And Jacob sent Judah before him unto Joseph. And Joseph made ready his chariot and went up to meet Israel, his father, to Goshen and presented himself unto him; and he fell on his neck and wept on his neck a good while.

And Israel said unto Joseph, "Now let me die since I have seen thy face, because thou art yet alive."

"And Jacob blessed Pharaoh"

Jacob before Pharaoh. Then Joseph came and told Pharaoh. And Pharaoh spake unto Joseph, saying, "Thy father and thy brethren are come unto thee; the land of Egypt is before thee; in the best of the land make thy father and brethren to dwell; in the land of Goshen let them dwell."

And Joseph brought in Jacob, his father, and set him before Pharaoh. And Pharaoh asked him, "How old art thou?"

And Jacob said, "The days of my pilgrimage are one

hundred and thirty years; few and evil have the years of my life been and have not attained unto the years of the life of my fathers in their pilgrimage." And Jacob blessed Pharaoh.

And Joseph nourished his father and his brethren and all his father's household with bread in the best of the land, as Pharaoh had commanded. And Jacob lived in Egypt seventeen years.

Jacob Blesses the Sons of Joseph. And when the time drew nigh that Israel must die, he called Joseph and said, "Deal kindly and truly with me; bury me not in Egypt, but in my father's burying-place."

And Joseph said, "I will do as thou hast said." And he said, "Swear unto me." And he sware unto him.

And it came to pass after these things that one told Joseph, "Behold, thy father is sick."

And he took with him his two sons Manasseh and Ephraim.

And Israel strengthened himself and sat upon the bed and said to Joseph, "Who are these?"

And Joseph said, "They are my sons whom God hath given me."

And Israel stretched out his hands upon them and said, "God, before whom my fathers Abraham and Isaac did walk, bless the lads and let them grow into a multitude in the midst of the earth."

And Israel said unto Joseph, "Behold, I die; but God shall be with you and bring you again unto the land of your fathers."

Jacob Blesses His Own Sons. And Jacob called his sons, and blessed them.

And when he blessed Judah, he said, "Judah, thou art he whom thy brethren shall praise; thy father's children shall bow down before thee. Judah is a lion's whelp;[2] from the prey, my son, thou art gone up.[3] *The scepter shall not depart from Judah nor a lawgiver from between his feet until Shiloh come; and unto Him shall the gathering of the people be.* I have waited for Thy salvation, O Lord."

"God bless the lads"

Jacob's Death. And when Jacob had made an end, he yielded up the ghost and was gathered unto his people.

And Joseph fell upon his father's face and wept upon him and kissed him.

And Joseph commanded his servants, the physicians, to embalm his father.

And the Egyptians mourned for him threescore and ten days.

---

2) A young lion, a cub.
3) You shall become important through many victories.

Then Joseph and his brethren went up into the land of Canaan and buried Jacob in the cave of Machpelah which Abraham had bought.

Joseph's Renewed Assurance of Forgiveness. And when Joseph's brethren saw that their father was dead, they said, "Joseph will peradventure hate us and will certainly requite us all the evil which we did unto him."

And they sent unto Joseph, saying, "Thy father did command before he died, saying, 'So shall ye say unto Joseph, "Forgive, I pray thee now, the trespass of thy brethren and their sin; for they did unto thee evil."'"

And Joseph wept and said unto them, "Fear not; for am I in the place of God? *Ye thought evil against me; but God meant it unto good, to bring to pass as it is this day, to save much people alive.*"

And he comforted them and spake kindly unto them.

And Joseph said, "When God shall bring you unto the land which He sware to Abraham, to Isaac, and to Jacob, ye shall carry up my bones from hence."

And Joseph died, being one hundred and ten years old. And they embalmed him, and he was put in a coffin in Egypt.

Fourth Commandment.

1 Tim. 5, 4. Let them learn to requite their parents; for that is good and acceptable before God.

> What God ordains is always good;
> His will abideth holy.
> As He directs my life for me,
> I follow meek and lowly. (521, 1.)

NOTE. — Goshen lay in Northern Egypt, on the eastern side of the Nile. Jacob is not reported to have crossed the river; nor does it appear that the Israelites did so in their flight out of Egypt. — The Egyptians observed the custom of embalming their dead. The preserved dead bodies are called mummies. — Abraham died, aged one hundred and seventy-five, Isaac one hundred and eighty, Jacob one hundred and forty-seven, and Joseph one hundred and ten years.

23. Job
Book of Job

Job's Character and Wealth. There was a man in the land of Uz whose name was Job;[1)] and that man was perfect and upright and one that feared God and eschewed [2)] evil.

And there were born unto him seven sons and three daughters; his substance [3)] also was seven thousand sheep, three thousand camels, five hundred yoke of oxen, and five hundred asses, and a very great household.

And his sons feasted in their houses, every one his day, and sent for their three sisters to eat and drink with them. And when the days of their feastings were gone about, Job sent and sanctified them and offered burnt offerings according to the number of them all; for Job said, "It may be that my sons have sinned."

Satan's Accusation. Now, when the sons of God came to present themselves before the LORD, Satan came also among them.

And the LORD said unto Satan, "Whence comest thou?" Then Satan answered, "From going to and fro in the earth."

And the LORD said, "Hast thou considered My servant Job that there is none like him in the earth?"

Then Satan answered, "Doth Job fear the LORD for naught? Thou hast blessed the work of his hands. Put now forth Thine hand, touch all that he hath, and he will curse Thee to Thy face."

And the LORD said, "Behold, all that he hath is in thy power; only upon himself put not forth thine hand." So Satan went forth from the presence of the LORD.

---

1) Near the northern end, and east, of the Red Sea was the land of Uz. Job appears to have lived during the time of Isaac or Jacob.
2) Avoided; shunned.
3) Property.

Job's Losses. And there was a day when his sons and his daughters were eating and drinking wine.

And there came a messenger unto Job and said, "The oxen were plowing and the asses feeding beside them; and the Sabeans fell upon them and took them away and slew the servants with the edge of the sword; and I only am escaped alone to tell thee."

While he was yet speaking, there came another and said, "The fire of God is fallen from heaven and hath burned up the sheep and the servants; and I only am escaped alone to tell thee."

While he was yet speaking, there came also another and said, "The Chaldeans took the camels and slew the servants with the edge of the sword; and I only am escaped alone to tell thee."

While he was yet speaking, there came also another and said, "Thy sons and thy daughters were eating and drinking; and, behold, there came a great wind and smote the house, and it fell upon the young men, and they are dead."

Then Job arose, and rent his mantle, and shaved his head, and fell down upon the ground, and worshiped, and said, "The LORD gave, and the LORD hath taken away; blessed be the name of the LORD."

Satan's Second Accusation. Again the sons of God came to present themselves before the LORD, and Satan came among them.

And the LORD said, "Hast thou considered Job? Still he holdeth fast his integrity." [4]

And Satan answered, "All that a man hath will he give for his life. But put forth Thine hand and touch his bone and his flesh, and he will curse Thee to Thy face."

And the LORD said, "He is in thy hand, but spare his life."

---

4) Piety.

Job's Bodily Affliction. Then went Satan forth from the presence of the LORD and smote Job with sore boils from the sole of his foot unto his crown. And he took a potsherd [5] to scrape himself with and sat down among the ashes.

Then said his wife unto him, "Dost thou still retain thine integrity? Curse God and die."

Job's Suffering

But he said, "What? shall we receive good at the hand of God, and shall we not receive evil?"

In all this did not Job sin.

Job's Friends. Then came Job's three friends, Eliphaz, Bildad, and Zophar, to comfort him. And they knew him not, and they wept.

So they sat down with him upon the ground seven days

---

[5] A piece of a broken pot.

and seven nights, and none spake a word unto him; for they saw that his grief was very great.

After this opened Job his mouth and cursed his day.[6]

Then Eliphaz said, "Who ever perished being innocent? Happy is the man whom God correcteth; therefore despise not thou the chastening of the Almighty."

And Job answered and said, "The arrows of the Almighty are within me. My brethren have dealt deceitfully as a brook. Is there iniquity in my tongue? Cannot my taste discern perverse things?"

Then Bildad answered, "How long wilt thou speak those things? Doth the Almighty pervert justice?"

Then Job answered, "I know it is so. How should a man be just with God? If he will contend with Him, he cannot answer Him one of a thousand. My soul is weary of life. I will say unto God, 'Show me wherefore Thou contendest with me.'"

Then answered Zophar, "If iniquity be in thine hand, put it far away; for then shalt thou lift up thy face without spot and shalt not fear."

Then Job answered, "Miserable comforters are ye all. Oh, that my words were now written! For *I know that my Redeemer liveth and that He shall stand at the Latter Day upon the earth; and though after my skin worms destroy this body, yet in my flesh shall I see God; whom I shall see for myself and mine eyes shall behold and not another.*"

Job Comforted. Then the Lord answered Job out of the whirlwind and said, "Where wast thou when I laid the foundations of the earth, when the morning stars sang together and all the sons of God shouted for joy?"

And Job answered, "Behold, I am vile. I have uttered what I understood not, things too wonderful for me, which

---

6) The day of his birth.

I knew not. Wherefore I abhor myself and repent in dust and ashes."

And the Lord said to Eliphaz and his two friends, "Ye have not spoken of Me the thing that is right as My servant Job hath."

Then the Lord accepted Job and turned the captivity of Job; He blessed him and gave him twice as much as he had before. He had also seven sons and three daughters. And Job saw his sons and his sons' sons, even four generations. So Job died, being old and full of days.

Sixth and Seventh Petitions.

Heb. 12, 6. Whom the Lord loveth He chasteneth.

> I know that my Redeemer lives!
> What comfort this sweet sentence gives!
> He lives, He lives, who once was dead,
> He lives, my ever-living Head. (200, 1.)

SUMMARY STUDY OF THE SECOND PERIOD

Show the connection between the house of Noah and the people of Israel.

Tell the entire story of this period in a few sentences, keeping in mind God's purpose in calling Abraham and preparing for Himself a people.

Recount the occasions on which God appeared, or manifested Himself, to the patriarchs of Israel; on which either God or one of the patriarchs speaks of the coming Savior.

What evidences of the sinful nature of men are found in this period? What evidences of faith and the fear of God?

Name the trials to which God subjected the believers and tell how in each case He delivered them. What is God's object in sending such trials?

List for yourself, or discuss in class, a number of the practical lessons which a Christian should draw from this period for his own better knowledge of God, knowledge of self, his faith and life.

"I WILL MAKE OF THEE A GREAT NATION, . . . AND IN THEE SHALL ALL THE FAMILIES OF THE EARTH BE BLESSED." Gen. 12, 2. 3.

THIRD PERIOD
MOSES AND JOSHUA
(Ca. 1571—1426 B. C.)

We have here a period of one hundred forty-five years, extending from the birth of Moses to the death of Joshua. It is the period in which God delivered the children of Israel, now a populous nation, from the bondage and tyranny of Egypt, gave them His Law, established formal worship in the Tabernacle, kept them wandering in the desert for forty years, and finally established them in the Promised Land, the land of Canaan. It is a period in which the Lord made Himself known to His people in many different ways that they might recognize Him and believe in Him as the only true God; a period in which He tested and tried His people and schooled them in true obedience to Him alone.

24. Moses' Birth and Flight
Ex. 1. 2

Israel in Bondage. Now, when Joseph had died and all his brethren, the children of Israel increased abundantly.

And there rose up a new king over Egypt which knew not Joseph. And he said unto his people, "Behold, the people of the children of Israel are mightier than we. Come on, let us deal wisely [1] with them lest they multiply and it come to pass that, when there falleth out any war, they join also unto our enemies and fight against us."

Therefore they did set over them taskmasters [2] to afflict them with burdens. And they built for Pharaoh treasure-cities, Pithom and Raamses.

But the more they afflicted them, the more they multiplied and grew. And Pharaoh charged all his people, saying, "Every son that is born ye shall cast into the river, and every daughter ye shall save alive."

---

1) By a scheme to keep down their number.
2) Cruel overseers.

Moses Hidden. And there went a man of the house of Levi, named Amram, and took to wife a daughter of Levi, Jochebed by name. And the woman bare a son; and when she saw that he was a goodly child, she hid him three months.

And when she could not longer hide him, she took an ark of bulrushes, and daubed it with slime and with pitch, and put the child therein, and laid it in the flags by the

"And, behold, the babe wept"

river's brink. And his sister Miriam stood afar off to see what would be done to him.

Adopted by a Princess. And the daughter of Pharaoh came down to wash herself at the river; and her maidens walked along by the river's side; and when she saw the ark among the flags, she sent her maid to fetch it.

And when she had opened it, she saw the child; and, behold, the babe wept. And she had compassion on him and said, "This is one of the Hebrews' children."

Then said his sister to Pharaoh's daughter, "Shall I go and call to thee a nurse of the Hebrew women that she may nurse the child for thee?" And Pharaoh's daughter said to her, "Go."

And the maid went and called the child's mother. And Pharaoh's daughter said unto her, "Take this child away and nurse it for me, and I will give thee thy wages." And the woman took the child and nursed it.

And the child grew; and she brought him unto Pharaoh's daughter, and he became her son. And she called his name Moses; and she said, "Because I drew him out of the water."

Attempt to Help His People. When Moses was grown, he went out unto his brethren and looked on their burdens. And he spied an Egyptian smiting an Hebrew, one of his brethren. And he slew the Egyptian,[3] and hid him in the sand.

And when he went out the second day, behold, two men of the Hebrews strove together; and he said to him that did the wrong, "Wherefore smitest thou thy fellow?"

And he said, "Who made thee a prince and a judge over us? Intendest thou to kill me as thou killedst the Egyptian?"

And Moses feared and said, "Surely this thing is known."

Moses Flees to Midian. Now, when Pharaoh heard this thing, he sought to slay Moses. But Moses fled from the face of Pharaoh to the land of Midian,[4] and he sat down by a well.

Now, the priest of Midian had seven daughters; and they came and drew water and filled the troughs to water their

---

[3] "He supposed his brethren would have understood how that God by his hand would deliver them." Acts 7, 25. However, it was a premature zeal; God's hour had not yet come.

[4] The land of Midian lies in Arabia, around the northeastern arm of the Red Sea.

father's flock. And the shepherds came and drove them away; but Moses stood up and helped them and watered their flock.

And when they came to Reuel, their father, he said, "How is it that ye are come so soon to-day?"

And they said, "An Egyptian delivered us out of the hand of the shepherds and also drew water enough for us and watered the flock."

And he said unto his daughters, "And where is he? Why is it that ye have left the man? Call him that he may eat bread."

And Moses was content to dwell with the man; and he gave Moses Zipporah, his daughter.

First Article: Preservation. *Table of Duties:* Masters, Servants.

Ps. 91, 10. There shall no evil befall thee, neither shall any plague come nigh thy dwelling.

> If God had not been on our side
> And had not come to aid us,
> The foes with all their pow'r and pride
> Would surely have dismayed us;
> For we, His flock, would have to fear
> The threat of men both far and near
> Who rise in might against us. (267, 1.)

25. The Call of Moses
Ex. 3. 4

Moses to Deliver Israel from Egypt. Now, Moses kept the flock of Jethro, his father-in-law, the priest of Midian, and came to the mountain of God, even to Horeb.

And the Angel of the LORD [1] appeared unto him in a flame of fire out of the midst of a bush; and, behold, the bush burned with fire, and the bush was not consumed. And when the LORD saw that he turned aside to see, God called

---

[1] In the following He is called "the Lord" and "God of Abraham." By Angel of the Lord is meant "the Word," the Son of God, the same who appeared to Abraham with two angels.

unto him out of the bush and said, "Moses, Moses!" And he said, "Here am I." And He said, "Put off thy shoes from off thy feet; for the place whereon thou standest is holy ground. I am the God of Abraham, the God of Isaac, and the God of Jacob."

And Moses hid his face; for he was afraid to look upon God.

And the LORD said, "I have surely seen the affliction of

"The bush burned with fire"

My people which are in Egypt. And I am come down to deliver them out of the hand of the Egyptians and to bring them up out of that land unto a land flowing with milk and honey. Come, now, and I will send thee unto Pharaoh that thou mayest bring forth My people out of Egypt."

Moses Hesitates. And Moses said, "Who am I that I should go unto Pharaoh and bring forth the children of Israel out of Egypt?" And He said, "Certainly I will be with thee."

And Moses said unto God, "Behold, when I come unto the children of Israel and shall say unto them, 'The God of your fathers hath sent me unto you,' and they shall say to me, 'What is His name?' what shall I say unto them?"

And God said unto Moses, "I AM THAT I AM; thus shalt thou say unto the children of Israel, I AM hath sent me unto you."

And God said moreover unto Moses, "Thus shalt thou say unto the children of Israel, 'The LORD God of your fathers, the God of Abraham, the God of Isaac, and the God of Jacob, hath sent me unto you.' This is My name forever, and this is My memorial unto all generations."

God's Reassurance to Moses. And Moses answered and said, "But, behold, they will not believe me; for they will say, 'The LORD hath not appeared unto thee.'"

And the LORD said unto him, "What is that in thine hand?" And he said, "A rod." And He said, "Cast it on the ground." And he cast it on the ground, and it became a serpent; and Moses fled from before it.

And the LORD said, "Put forth thine hand and take it by the tail." And he put forth his hand and caught it; and it became a rod in his hand.

And the LORD said furthermore unto him, "Put now thine hand into thy bosom." And when he took it out, behold, his hand was leprous as snow.

And He said, "Put it into thy bosom again"; and, behold, is was turned again as his other flesh.

And the LORD said, "If they will not believe these two signs, thou shalt take of the water of the river and pour it upon the dry land, and it shall become blood."

Moses Declines. And Moses said unto the LORD, "O my Lord, I am not eloquent, but I am slow of speech and of a slow tongue."

And the Lord said unto him, "Who hath made man's mouth, or who maketh the dumb, or deaf, or the seeing, or the blind? Have not I, the Lord? Now therefore go, and I will teach thee what thou shalt say."

And he said, "O my Lord, send, I pray Thee, whom Thou wilt send."

And the anger of the Lord was kindled against Moses, and He said, "I know that Aaron, thy brother, can speak well. He shall be thy spokesman unto the people. And thou shalt take this rod in thine hand, wherewith thou shalt do signs."

Moses Obeys. And Moses went to Jethro, and took his wife and his sons, and set them upon an ass, and returned to the land of Egypt.

And the Lord said to Aaron, "Go into the wilderness to meet Moses." And he went and met him in the mount of God and kissed him.

And Moses told Aaron all the words of the Lord who had sent him and all the signs which He had commanded him.

And they went and gathered together all the elders of the children of Israel. And Aaron spake all the words which the Lord had spoken unto Moses and did the signs in the sight of the people. And the people believed; and when they heard that the Lord had looked upon their affliction, then they bowed their heads and worshiped.

Third Petition. Office of the Keys.

2 Cor. 12, 9. My grace is sufficient for thee; for My strength is made perfect in weakness.

> Thy way, not mine, O Lord,
>   However dark it be!
> Lead me by Thine own hand,
>   Choose Thou the path for me. (532, 1 a.)

Note. — At the age of forty, Moses was ready in his ambition to deliver his people. Now, at the age of eighty, after forty years of exile and plain shepherd life, he is thoroughly humble and realizes the gravity of that task as well as his own inability, even to the extent of hesitating and declining when the call of God comes to him. In such weakness the strength of God was made perfect in order that to Him and not to Moses might be all glory.

26. Moses before Pharaoh. The Plagues
Ex. 5—10

Pharaoh's Refusal. And afterward Moses and Aaron went in and told Pharaoh, "Thus saith the Lord God of Israel, 'Let My people go that they may hold a feast unto Me in the wilderness.'"

And Pharaoh said, "Who is the Lord that I should obey His voice? I know not the Lord, neither will I let Israel go."

Increased Tyranny. And Pharaoh commanded the same day the taskmasters of the people and their officers, saying, "Let there more work be laid upon the men that they may labor therein; and let them not regard vain words."

And the taskmasters of the people went out, and their officers, and they spake to the people, saying, "Thus saith Pharaoh, 'I will not give you straw; go ye and get ye straw where ye can find it; yet not aught of your work shall be diminished.'"

So the people were scattered abroad to gather stubble instead of straw.

Complaint of Hebrew Officers. Then the officers of the children of Israel came and cried unto Pharaoh, saying, "Wherefore dealest thou thus with thy servants?"

But he said, "Ye are idle, ye are idle; therefore ye say, 'Let us go and do sacrifice to the Lord.' Go therefore now and work."

Moses Appeals to the Lord. And Moses returned unto the Lord and said, "Lord, wherefore hast Thou so entreated this people? Why is it that Thou hast sent me? For since I came to Pharaoh, he hath done evil to this people; neither hast Thou delivered Thy people at all."

Then the Lord said unto Moses, "Now shalt thou see what I will do to Pharaoh; for with a strong hand shall he let them go. And the Egyptians shall know that I am the Lord."

Pharaoh Not Moved by Miracles. And Moses and Aaron went in unto Pharaoh, and Aaron cast down his rod before Pharaoh, and it became a serpent.

Then Pharaoh called the wise men and the sorcerers. They also did in like manner with their enchantments. But Aaron's rod swallowed up their rods.

"Thus saith the Lord, 'Let My people go'"

And the Lord hardened Pharaoh's heart that he hearkened not unto them.

The Plagues. And Aaron lifted up the rod and smote the waters, and all the waters were turned to *blood*. And the fish in the river died; and the river stank, and the Egyptians could not drink of the water; and there was blood throughout all the land of Egypt. And the magicians of Egypt did so with their enchantments; and Pharaoh's heart was hardened.

And Aaron stretched out his hand over the waters of

Egypt; and *frogs* came up and covered the land of Egypt. And the frogs came into the houses, the bedchambers, the beds, the ovens, and into the kneading-troughs. Then Pharaoh called for Moses and Aaron and said, "Entreat the Lord that He may take away the frogs from us; and I will let the people go." And Moses cried unto the Lord, and the frogs died; and they gathered them together upon heaps; and the land stank. But when Pharaoh saw that there was respite, he hardened his heart and hearkened not unto them.

And Aaron stretched out his rod and smote the dust of the earth, and it became *lice* in man and in beast; all the dust became lice throughout all the land of Egypt. And the magicians could not do this, but said, "This is the finger of God." But Pharaoh's heart was hardened; and he hearkened not unto them.

And the Lord sent swarms of *flies* upon Pharaoh and his people; *murrain*,[1] that all the cattle died; *boils and blains*[2] on man and beast (and the magicians could no longer stand before Moses because of the boils); *hail,* thunder, and fire mingled with the hail in all the land, that smote all that was in the field, man and beast, every herb and every tree; *locusts,* which ate up all that the hail had left; *darkness* in all the land of Egypt three days, thick darkness that could be felt; they saw not one another, neither rose any from his place for three days. But all the children of Israel had light in their dwellings. And the Lord hardened Pharaoh's heart, and he would not let them go.

Conclusion of the Lord's Prayer.

Ps. 50, 15. Call upon Me in the day of trouble; I will deliver thee, and thou shalt glorify Me.

> "Fear not, I am with thee, oh, be not dismayed;
> For I am thy God and will still give thee aid;
> I'll strengthen thee, help thee, and cause thee to stand,
> Upheld by My righteous, omnipotent hand." (427, 3.)

---

1) A contagious fever.   2) Skin disease, like smallpox.

27. The Last Plague and the Passover
Ex. 11. 12

The First-Born to Die. And the LORD said unto Moses, "Yet will I bring one plague more upon Pharaoh, afterwards he will let you go hence.

"About midnight will I go out into the midst of Egypt; and all the *first-born* in the land of Egypt shall die, from the first-born of Pharaoh even unto the first-born of the maid-servant, and all the first-born of beasts.

"But against any of the children of Israel shall not a dog move his tongue, that ye may know how that the LORD doth put a difference between the Egyptians and Israel."

The Passover. And the LORD spake unto Moses and Aaron, saying, "Speak ye unto all the congregation of Israel, saying, 'In the tenth day of this month they shall take to them every man a lamb without blemish,[1] a male of the first year. And ye shall keep it until the fourteenth day of the month and shall kill it in the evening.

"'And ye shall take the blood and strike it on the two side-posts and on the upper door-post of the houses wherein ye shall eat it.

"'And ye shall eat the flesh in that night and unleavened bread. And ye shall let nothing of it remain until the morning.

"'With your loins girded, your shoes on your feet, and your staff in your hand, ye shall eat it in haste: it is the LORD's Passover.

"'For I will pass through the land of Egypt this night and will smite all the first-born, both man and beast. And the blood shall be to you for a token upon the houses where ye are. And when I see the blood, I will pass over you, and

---

[1] A type of Christ, who was without sin.

the plague shall not be upon you to destroy you when I smite the land of Egypt.

"'And this day shall be unto you a feast to the Lord throughout your generations.

"'And when ye be come to the land which the Lord will give you, and your children say unto you, "What mean ye by this service?" ye shall say, "It is the Lord's Passover,

The Passover

who passed over the houses of the children of Israel when He smote the Egyptians and delivered our houses."'"

And the people bowed the head and worshiped. And the children of Israel went away and did as the Lord had commanded Moses and Aaron.

The First-Born Slain. And it came to pass that at midnight the Lord smote all the first-born in the land of Egypt; from the first-born of Pharaoh that sat on his throne unto the first-born of the captive that was in the dungeon, and all the first-born of the cattle.

And Pharaoh rose up in the night, he and all his servants, and all the Egyptians; and there was a great cry in Egypt; for there was not a house where there was not one dead.

Sacrament of the Altar.

John 1, 29. Behold the Lamb of God, which taketh away the sin of the world.

1 John 1, 7. The blood of Jesus Christ, His Son, cleanseth us from all sin.

> Here the true Paschal Lamb we see,
>   Whom God so freely gave us;
> He died on the accursed tree —
>   So strong His love! — to save us.
> See, His blood doth mark our door,
> Faith points to it, Death passes o'er,
>   And Satan cannot harm us.
>   Hallelujah!   (195, 3.)

28. The Exodus
Ex. 12—15

Israel Urged to Leave. Pharaoh called for Moses and Aaron by night and said, "Rise up and get you forth from among my people; take also your flocks and your herds."

And the Egyptians were urgent upon the people that they might send them out of the land in haste; for they said, "We be all dead men."

And the people took their dough before it was leavened, their kneading-troughs bound up in their clothes upon their shoulders. And they baked unleavened cakes of the dough,[1] because they could not tarry, neither had they prepared for themselves any victual.

---

[1] Hence the Passover was also known as the Feast of Unleavened Bread.

Advanced Bible History.

And the children of Israel borrowed [2] of the Egyptians jewels of silver, and jewels of gold, and raiment, as the Lord had commanded them. And the Lord gave the people favor in the sight of the Egyptians, so that they lent [3] unto them such things; and they spoiled the Egyptians.[4]

The Departure. And the children of Israel journeyed, about six hundred thousand on foot that were men, beside children. And a mixed multitude also went up with them; [5] and flocks and herds, even very much cattle.

And Moses took the bones of Joseph with him.

And the Lord led the people through the way of the wilderness of the Red Sea and went before them by day in a pillar of cloud and by night in a pillar of fire.

Now, the sojourning of the children of Israel in Egypt was four hundred and thirty years. And at the end of the four hundred and thirty years, even the selfsame day, all the hosts of the Lord went out of Egypt.

Pharaoh's Pursuit. And when it was told the king of Egypt that the people fled, he said, "Why have we let Israel go from serving us?"

And he made ready his chariot and took his people with him; and he took six hundred chosen chariots and all the chariots of Egypt and pursued after the children of Israel and overtook them encamping by the sea.

And the children of Israel lifted up their eyes, and, behold, the Egyptians marched after them. And they were sore afraid and cried out unto the Lord.

---

[2] Asked.   [3] Gave as they were asked.

[4] The Egyptians gave of their wealth to the children of Israel. This was a small payment for their years of service.

[5] The six hundred thousand were men able to fight. Including women, children, and all other people, Israel numbered about two million souls; a procession about twelve miles long.

"A Very Present Help in Trouble." And Moses said unto the people, "Fear ye not; stand still and see the salvation of the LORD which He will show to you; the LORD shall fight for you, and ye shall hold your peace."

And the LORD said unto Moses, "Wherefore criest thou unto Me? Speak unto the children of Israel that they go forward. But lift thou up thy rod and stretch out thine hand

"And the waters returned"

over the sea and divide it. And the children of Israel shall go on the dry ground through the midst of the sea."

Israel Delivered. The Angel of God, which went before the camp of Israel, removed and went behind them; and the pillar of the cloud went between the camp of the Egyptians and the camp of Israel; and it was a cloud of darkness to them, but it gave light by night to these, so that the one came not near the other all the night.

And Moses stretched out his hand over the sea; and the LORD caused the sea to go back by a strong east wind all that night and made the sea dry land, and the waters were divided. And the children of Israel went into the midst of the sea upon the dry ground; and the waters were a wall unto them on their right hand and on their left.

And the Egyptians pursued and went in after them to the midst of the sea. And the LORD said unto Moses, "Stretch out thine hand over the sea that the waters may come again upon the Egyptians, upon their chariots, and upon their horsemen."

And Moses stretched forth his hand over the sea, and the sea returned, and the LORD overthrew the Egyptians in the midst of the sea. And the waters returned and covered the chariots and the horsemen and all the host of Pharaoh; there remained not so much as one of them.

Thus the LORD saved Israel that day out of the hand of the Egyptians; and Israel saw the Egyptians dead upon the seashore.

Israel's Thanksgiving. And Israel saw that great work which the LORD did. Then sang Moses and the children of Israel this song unto the LORD, and spake: —

> "I will sing unto the LORD,
> For He hath triumphed gloriously:
> The horse and his rider
> Hath He thrown into the sea."

And Miriam, the prophetess, the sister of Aaron, and the women answered them: —

> "Sing ye to the LORD,
> For He hath triumphed gloriously:
> The horse and his rider
> Hath He thrown into the sea."

Seventh Petition.

Ps. 34, 7. The angel of the Lord encampeth round about them that fear Him and delivereth them.

A mighty Fortress is our God,	Now means deadly woe;
A trusty Shield and Weapon;	Deep guile and great might
He helps us free from every need	Are his dread arms in fight;
That hath us now o'ertaken.	On earth is not his equal.
The old evil Foe	(262, 1.)

---

29. Israel in the Wilderness
Ex. 15—17

The Sweetened Waters of Marah. So Moses brought Israel from the Red Sea into the Wilderness of Shur; and they went three days in the wilderness and found no water. And when they came to Marah, they could not drink of the waters, for they were bitter.

And the people murmured against Moses, saying, "What shall we drink?"

And he cried unto the LORD; and the LORD showed him a tree, which when he had cast into the waters, the waters were made sweet. And the LORD said, "I am the LORD that healeth thee." [1]

And they came to Elim, where were twelve wells of water and threescore and ten palm-trees. And from Elim they came unto the wilderness of Sin.

Yearning after the Flesh-Pots and Bread of Egypt. And the whole congregation of the children of Israel murmured against Moses and Aaron and said unto them, "Would to God we had died in the land of Egypt, when we sat by the flesh-pots and did eat bread to the full! For ye have brought us into this wilderness to kill us with hunger."

---

[1] The Lord means to say: As I have sweetened this water, so will I also heal you spiritually.

And Moses said, "What are we? Your murmurings are not against us, but against the LORD."

And the LORD said unto Moses, "I have heard the murmurings of the children of Israel. Say unto them, 'At even ye shall eat flesh, and in the morning ye shall be filled with bread; and ye shall know that I am the LORD, your God.'"

God Sends Meat and Bread. And in the evening quails came up and covered the camp.[2]

"It is manna"

And in the morning, when the dew was gone, behold, upon the face of the wilderness there lay a small round thing, as small as the hoar frost on the ground. And when the children of Israel saw it, they said one to another, "It is manna."[3]

And Moses said unto them, "This is the bread which the

---

2) At the season when the Israelites gathered them, quails still migrate from Africa northward in immense numbers.

3) Manna means, What is this? Israel needed about two million pounds daily of this heavenly bread, which God supplied in a miraculous manner.

Lord hath given you to eat. Gather of it every man according to his eating."

And the children of Israel gathered, some more, some less. And when they did measure it, he that gathered much had nothing over, and he that gathered little had no lack; they gathered every man according to his eating.

Regulations Concerning the Manna. And Moses said, "Let no man leave of it till the morning."

Notwithstanding they hearkened not unto Moses; but some of them left of it until the morning; and it bred worms and stank.

And they gathered it every morning; and when the sun waxed hot, it melted.

And Moses said, "To-morrow is the holy Sabbath unto the Lord; that which remaineth over lay up for you to be kept until the morning. Six days ye shall gather it; but on the seventh day, which is the Sabbath, in it there shall be none."

And on the sixth day they gathered twice as much. And they laid it up till the morning, as Moses bade; and it did not stink, neither was there any worm therein.

And there went out some of the people on the seventh day for to gather, and they found none.

Manna was like coriander-seed, white; and the taste of it was like wafers made with honey.

And Moses said to Aaron, "Take a potful of manna and lay it up before the Lord to be kept for your generations."

And the children of Israel did eat manna forty years until they came unto the borders of the land of Canaan.

Water from the Rock. And Israel journeyed from the wilderness of Sin [4] and pitched in Rephidim. And there was

---

4) The Wilderness of Sin, extending twenty-five miles along the shore of the Red Sea, is barren, but has some vegetation.

no water. Wherefore the people did chide with Moses and said, "Give us water that we may drink."

And Moses cried unto the Lord, saying, "What shall I do unto this people? They be almost ready to stone me."

And the Lord said unto Moses, "Thy rod, wherewith thou smotest the river,[5)] take in thine hand and go. Behold, I will stand before thee there upon the rock in Horeb; and thou shalt smite the rock, and there shall come water out of it that the people may drink." And Moses did so.

And he called the name of the place Massah and Meribah because of the chiding of the children of Israel and because they tempted the Lord, saying, "Is the Lord among us or not?"

Battle with the Amalekites. Then came Amalek and fought with Israel in Rephidim.

And Moses said unto Joshua, "Choose us out men and go out, fight with Amalek. To-morrow I will stand on the top of the hill with the rod of God in mine hand."

So Joshua did as Moses had said to him, and Moses, Aaron, and Hur went up to the top of the hill.

And when Moses held up his hand, Israel prevailed; and when he let down his hand, Amalek prevailed. But Moses' hands were heavy; and Aaron and Hur stayed up his hands, the one on the one side and the other on the other side; and his hands were steady until the going down of the sun.

And Joshua discomfited[6)] Amalek with the edge of the sword.

Fourth Petition.

Ps. 145, 15. 16. The eyes of all wait upon Thee, and Thou givest them their meat in due season. Thou openest Thine hand and satisfiest the desire of every living thing.

<table>
<tr><td>Riven the Rock for me
Thirst to relieve,
Manna from heaven falls
Fresh every eve.</td><td>Never a want severe
Causeth my eye a tear
But Thou dost whisper near,
"Only believe." (422, 2.)</td></tr>
</table>

---

5) The Nile.   6) Subdued, routed.

THE GIVING OF THE LAW

30. The Giving of the Law on Sinai
Ex. 19—24

The Preparation. In the third month, when the children of Israel were gone forth out of the land of Egypt, they came into the Wilderness of Sinai [1] and camped there before Mount Sinai.

And Moses went up, and the LORD called unto him, saying, "Thus shalt thou say to Israel, 'Ye have seen what I did unto the Egyptians and how I bare you on eagles' wings and brought you unto Myself. If ye will obey My voice and keep My covenant, then ye shall be a peculiar treasure unto Me above all people; for all the earth is Mine; and ye shall be unto Me a kingdom of priests and an holy nation.'"

And Moses called the elders of the people and laid before them all these words which the LORD commanded him. And all the people answered together and said, "All that the LORD hath spoken we will do."

And Moses returned the words of the people unto the LORD. And the LORD said, "Sanctify the people to-day and to-morrow and let them wash their clothes and be ready against the third day; for the LORD will come down in the sight of all the people upon Mount Sinai. And thou shalt set bounds round about, saying, 'Take heed to yourselves that ye go not up into the mount; whosoever toucheth the mount shall be surely put to death.'"

The Ten Commandments. And on the third day, in the morning, there were thunders and lightnings and a thick cloud upon the mount and the voice of the trumpet exceeding loud, so that all the people that was in the camp trembled.

---

[1] The plain at the foot of Mount Sinai. Mount Horeb and Mount Sinai are in the southern portion of the Sinai Peninsula.

And Moses brought the people out of the camp to meet with God; and they stood at the nether [2] part of the mount.

And Mount Sinai was altogether on a smoke, because the LORD descended upon it in fire; and the smoke thereof ascended as the smoke of a furnace, and the whole mount quaked greatly.

The Giving of the Law

And the voice of the trumpet sounded long and waxed louder and louder. And God spake all these words, saying: —

"I am the LORD, thy God, which have brought thee out of the land of Egypt, out of the house of bondage. Thou shalt have no other gods before Me. Thou shalt not make unto thee any graven image or any likeness of anything that is in heaven above or that is in the earth beneath or that is in the

---

2) Lower.

water under the earth; thou shalt not bow down thyself to them nor serve them; for I, the Lord, *thy God, am a jealous God, visiting the iniquity of the fathers upon the children unto the third and fourth generation of them that hate Me and showing mercy unto thousands of them that love Me and keep My commandments.*

"Thou shalt not take the name of the Lord, *thy God, in vain; for the* Lord *will not hold him guiltless that taketh His name in vain.*

"Remember the Sabbath-day to keep it holy. Six days shalt thou labor and do all thy work; but the seventh day is the Sabbath of the Lord, *thy God; in it thou shalt not do any work, thou, nor thy son, nor thy daughter, thy man-servant, nor thy maid-servant, nor thy cattle, nor thy stranger that is within thy gates; for in six days the* Lord *made heaven and earth, the sea, and all that in them is, and rested the seventh day; wherefore the* Lord *blessed the Sabbath-day and hallowed it.*

"Honor thy father and thy mother that thy days may be long upon the land which the Lord, *thy God, giveth thee.*

"Thou shalt not kill.

"Thou shalt not commit adultery.

"Thou shalt not steal.

"Thou shalt not bear false witness against thy neighbor.

"Thou shalt not covet thy neighbor's house.

"Thou shalt not covet thy neighbor's wife, nor his man-servant, nor his maid-servant, nor his ox, nor his ass, nor anything that is thy neighbor's."

Effect on the People. And when the people heard and saw this, they fled and said unto Moses, "Speak thou with us, and we will hear; but let not God speak with us lest we die."

And Moses said, "Fear not; for God is come that His fear may be before your faces that ye sin not."

And the people stood afar off, and Moses drew near unto the thick darkness where God was. And the LORD spake unto Moses, and Moses told the people all the words of the LORD and all the judgments; and all the people answered with one voice, "All the words which the LORD hath said will we do."

The Covenant Made. And Moses wrote all the words of the LORD and rose up early in the morning and builded an altar under the hill and twelve pillars, according to the twelve tribes of Israel. And he sent young men to offer sacrifices.

And Moses took half of the blood of the sacrifices and put it in basins, and the other half he sprinkled on the altar.

And he took the book of the covenant [3] and read in the audience [4] of the people.

And when they said, "All that the LORD hath said will we do," Moses took the blood and sprinkled it on the people and said, "Behold the blood of the covenant which the LORD hath made with you concerning all these words."

And the LORD said unto Moses, "Come up to Me into the mount." And Moses was in the mount forty days and forty nights.

First Chief Part: "What are the Ten Commandments?"

Deut. 6, 6. 7. These words which I command thee this day shall be in thine heart; and thou shalt teach them diligently unto thy children.

>   The Law of God is good and wise
>   And sets His will before our eyes,
>   Shows us the way of righteousness,
>   And dooms to death when we transgress. (295, 1.)

---

[3] The book in which Moses had written the above-mentioned laws, which formed the covenant, or solemn agreement, between God and Israel.

[4] Within hearing.

31. The Golden Calf
Ex. 32—34

Early Violation of the Covenant. And when the people saw that Moses delayed to come down out of the mount, they said unto Aaron, "Up, make us gods which shall go before us; for as for this Moses, the man that brought us up out of the land of Egypt, we wot not what is become of him."

And Aaron said unto them, "Break off the golden earrings of your wives, sons, and daughters and bring them unto me." And he received them and made it a molten calf.

And they said, "These be thy gods, O Israel, which brought thee up out of the land of Egypt."

And Aaron built an altar before it and made proclamation, "To-morrow is a feast to the LORD."

And they rose up early on the morrow and offered burnt offerings; and the people sat down to eat and to drink and rose up to play.

The Lord's Anger. And the LORD said unto Moses, "Go, get thee down; for thy people have corrupted themselves; they have turned aside quickly out of the way which I commanded them.

"I see this people is a stiff-necked people; now, therefore, let Me alone that My wrath may wax hot against them and that I may consume them; and I will make of thee a great nation."

Moses Intercedes. And Moses besought the LORD, his God, and said, "LORD, why doth Thy wrath wax hot? Wherefore should the Egyptians say, 'For mischief did He bring them out to slay them in the mountains'? Remember Abraham, Isaac, and Israel, to whom Thou swarest, I will multiply your seed as the stars of heaven, and all this land that I have spoken of will I give unto your seed, and they shall inherit it forever."

And the LORD repented[1] of the evil which He thought to do unto His people.

Moses' Zeal. And Moses went down from the mount, and the two tables of the testimony were in his hand.

The tables were written on both their sides and were

"He cast the tables out of his hands"

the work of God, and the writing was the writing of God, graven upon the tables.

And as soon as he came nigh unto the camp, he saw the calf and the dancing. And Moses' anger waxed hot, and he cast the tables out of his hands and brake them beneath the mount.

And he took the calf and burned it in the fire, and ground

---

1) Not in the sense in which we sinners repent of a wrong deed, but in the sense of holding up His punishment and showing mercy.

it to powder, and strewed it upon the water, and made the children of Israel drink of it.

Then Moses stood in the gate of the camp and said, "Who is on the Lord's side? Let him come unto me." And all the sons of Levi gathered themselves together unto him.

And he said unto them, "Thus saith the Lord, 'Put every man his sword by his side and go in and out from gate to gate throughout the camp and slay every man his brother, his companion, and his neighbor.'"

And the children of Levi did according to the word of Moses; and there fell of the people that day about three thousand men.

The Two Tables Renewed. The Lord spake unto Moses face to face, as a man speaketh unto his friend. And the Lord said unto Moses, "Hew thee two tables of stone like unto the first; and I will write upon these tables the words that were in the first tables, which thou brakest."

And Moses hewed two tables of stone like unto the first; and rose up early in the morning and went up unto Mount Sinai, as the Lord had commanded him, and took in his hand the two tables of stone.

And the Lord descended in the cloud and passed by before him and proclaimed, "The Lord, The Lord God, merciful and gracious, long-suffering and abundant in goodness and truth, keeping mercy for thousands, forgiving iniquity and transgression and sin, and that will by no means clear the guilty."

And Moses bowed his head and worshiped, and said, "O Lord, pardon our iniquity and our sin and take us for Thine inheritance."

And the Lord made a covenant that He would lead them into the land. And Moses was there with the Lord forty days and forty nights; he did neither eat bread nor drink water.

And the LORD wrote upon the tables the words of the covenant, the Ten Commandments.

Moses' Shining Face. And when Moses came down from Mount Sinai with the two tables in his hand, the skin of his face shone, and he knew it not.

And Aaron and the people were afraid to come nigh him. And Moses called unto them; and Aaron and all the rulers returned unto him.

And Moses put a veil on his face when speaking with them. And he commanded them all that the LORD had spoken with him. But when Moses went in before the LORD to speak with Him, he took the veil off until he came out.

First Commandment.

Is. 42, 8. I am the Lord: that is My name; and My glory will I not give to another, neither My praise to graven images.

> Ye who confess Christ's holy name,
> To God give praise and glory!
> Ye who the Father's power proclaim,
> To God give praise and glory!
> All idols under foot be trod,
> The Lord is God! The Lord is God!
> To God all praise and glory! (19, 5.)

---

32. Public Worship and Discipline
Ex. 35—40. Lev. 24. Num. 6 and 15

God Commands Sabbath Worship. And Moses gathered all the congregation of the children of Israel together and said unto them, "These are the words which the LORD hath commanded that ye should do them.

"'Six days shall work be done, but on the seventh day there shall be to you an holy day, a Sabbath of rest to the LORD; whosoever doeth work therein shall be put to death.'"

The Place of Worship. And Moses said, "This is the thing which the LORD commanded, saying, 'Take ye from among you an offering unto the LORD and make the Tabernacle.'"

And they came, every one whose heart stirred him up and every one whom his spirit made willing; and they brought the LORD's offering to the work of the Tabernacle.

The Tabernacle and Court

And all the wise men that wrought all the work of the sanctuary spake unto Moses, saying, "The people bring much more than enough for the service of the work which the LORD commanded to make."

And Moses gave commandment, saying, "Let neither man nor woman make any more work for the offering of the sanctuary."

So the people were restrained from bringing. For the stuff they had was sufficient for all the work to make it, and too much.

And it came to pass in the first month in the second year, on the first day of the month, that the Tabernacle was reared up. Then a cloud covered the tent of the congregation, and the glory of the LORD filled the Tabernacle.

BRIEF DESCRIPTION OF THE TABERNACLE

The Tabernacle stood in a court of 150×75 feet, surrounded by a fence of canvas screens, about 8 feet high. This court, or yard, had only one entrance, 30 feet wide, on the east end, closed by a curtain of fine linen, embroidered with figures of cherubim. The Tabernacle

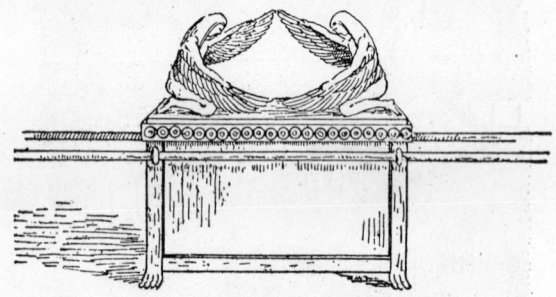

Ark of the Covenant

measured 45×15×15 feet. It stood in the west half of the court, with only one entrance at the east end, and faced the brazen altar (for burnt offerings), which stood in the yard. Near this altar was the brazen laver, which contained water for the priests to wash their hands and feet.

The Tabernacle was divided into the Holy Place and the Most Holy Place. In the Most Holy Place stood the Ark of the Covenant, which contained the two tables of the Law and the pot of manna. The top of this Ark of God, on which were two golden cherubim, was called the mercy-seat. In the Holy Place stood the altar of incense, the golden candlestick, and the table of showbread.

The people of Israel observed the Sabbath, the Passover, Pentecost, the Day of Atonement, and the Feast of Tabernacles. They also brought sacrifices and had a high priest, priests, and Levites. Aaron was consecrated as high priest and his sons as priests. The children of Levi were appointed to the service of the Tabernacle.

The children of Israel remained at Mount Sinai about one year. During this time the Tabernacle was built.

The Aaronitic Blessing. And the LORD spake unto Moses, saying, "Speak unto Aaron and unto his sons, saying, 'Ye shall put My name upon [1] the children of Israel, and I will bless them, and thus shall ye bless them, saying unto them: —

"*'The* LORD *bless thee and keep thee.*

"*'The* LORD *make His face shine upon thee and be gracious unto thee.*

"*'The* LORD *lift up His countenance upon thee and give thee peace.*'"

Punishment of a Blasphemer. And the son of an Israelitish woman, whose father was an Egyptian, went out among the children of Israel; and this son of the Israelitish woman and a man of Israel strove together in the camp; and the Israelitish woman's son blasphemed the name of the LORD and cursed.

And they brought him unto Moses. And they put him in ward [2] that the mind of the LORD might be showed them.

And the LORD spake unto Moses, saying, "Bring forth him that cursed without the camp, and let all that heard him lay their hands upon his head, and let all the congregation stone him.

"And thou shalt speak unto the children of Israel, saying, 'Whosoever curseth his God shall bear his sin. And he that blasphemeth the name of the LORD, he shall surely be put to death, and all the congregation shall certainly stone him; as

---

1) The name of God is placed upon the people like a beautiful garment, covering their faults and sins and protecting them from danger. This threefold blessing refers to Father, Son, and Holy Ghost.

2) Imprisoned him.

well the stranger as he that is born in the land, when he blasphemeth the name of the LORD, shall be put to death.'"

Punishment of a Sabbath-Breaker. When the children of Israel were in the wilderness, they found a man that gathered sticks upon the Sabbath-day.

And they that found him gathering sticks brought him unto Moses and Aaron and unto all the congregation. And they put him in ward because it was not declared what should be done to him.

And the LORD said unto Moses, "The man shall be surely put to death, all the congregation shall stone him with stones without the camp."

And all the congregation brought him without the camp and stoned him with stones, and he died, as the LORD commanded Moses.

Second and Third Commandments.

Jas. 3, 9. 10. With the tongue bless we God, even the Father; and therewith curse we men, which are made after the similitude of God. Out of the same mouth proceedeth blessing and cursing. My brethren, these things ought not so to be.

> O King of Glory, come
> And with Thy favor crown
> This temple as Thy home,
> This people as Thine own.
> Beneath this roof vouchsafe to show
> How God can dwell with men below. (638, 2.)

33. Mutiny and Rebellion
Num. 13—16

NOTE. — The first part of this story happened about one year after the departure from Egypt, soon after the building of the Tabernacle and the celebration of the Passover, when Israel moved in a northerly direction into the Wilderness of Paran. (Map 2.) The people were making ready to enter Canaan. — Korah's rebellion happened some twenty years later, when the people lived in the wilderness, very likely in Kadesh-barnea. (Map 2.)

Canaan Investigated. The LORD said unto Moses, "Send thou men to search the land of Canaan; of every tribe send one of the chief men."

And Moses said to them, "Go up and see the land, what it is, and the people that dwelleth therein, whether they be strong or weak, few or many."

So they went up and searched the land from Zin unto Rehob.

And they came to the brook of Eshcol [1] and cut down from thence a branch with one cluster of grapes; [2] and they bare it between two upon a staff. And they brought of the pomegranates [3] and of the figs.

Fear and Mutiny. And they returned from searching of the land after forty days and said, "We came unto the land; and surely it floweth with milk and honey; and this is the fruit of it.

"Nevertheless, the people be strong that dwell in the land, and the cities are walled and very great; and, moreover, we saw the children of Anak [4] there."

And Caleb stilled the people before Moses and said, "Let

---

1) Most likely between Bethlehem and Hebron.

2) Even to-day bunches of grapes weighing from twelve to eighteen pounds are said to be found in Southern Palestine.

3) A beautiful fruit of the size of a large apple, having an acid flavor; wine was made of its juice.

4) Giants.

us go up at once and possess it, for we are well able to overcome it."

But the men that went up with him said, "We be not able to go up against the people, for they are stronger than we." And they brought up an evil report of the land.

And all the congregation lifted up their voice, and cried, and murmured against Moses and Aaron, and said, "Would

"They bare it upon a staff"

God that we had died in the land of Egypt or in this wilderness!" And they said one to another, "Let us make a captain, and let us return into Egypt."

Then Moses and Aaron fell on their faces before all the assembly of the congregation of the children of Israel.

Joshua's and Caleb's Report. And Joshua and Caleb, which were of them that searched the land, rent their clothes and said, "The land which we passed through to search it is an exceeding good land. If the LORD delight in us, then He will bring us into this land. Only rebel not ye against the

Lord, neither fear ye the people of the land; the Lord is with us."

But all the congregation bade stone them with stones.

A Forty-Year Sentence. And the glory of the Lord appeared in the Tabernacle of the congregation before all the children of Israel. And the Lord said unto Moses, "How long will this people provoke Me, and how long will it be ere they believe Me, for all the signs which I have showed among them?

"But as truly as I live, all the earth shall be filled with the glory of the Lord. Because all those men which have seen My glory and My miracles which I did in Egypt and in the wilderness and have tempted Me now these ten times and have not hearkened to My voice: from twenty years old and upward they shall not see the land which I sware unto their fathers, save Caleb and Joshua.

"But your little ones, them will I bring in, and they shall know the land which ye have despised. And your children shall wander in the wilderness forty years, after the number of the forty days in which ye searched the land. I, the Lord, have said; I will surely do it."

The Jealousy of Korah and His Mob. Now Korah, of the tribe of Levi, and Dathan and Abiram, of the tribe of Reuben, with two hundred and fifty princes of the congregation, gathered themselves together against Moses and against Aaron and said unto them, "Ye take too much upon you; wherefore lift ye up yourselves above the congregation of the Lord?" [5]

And when Moses heard it, he fell upon his face and spake unto Korah and unto all his company, saying, "Even to-morrow the Lord will show who are His and who is holy.

---

[5] Jealousy against Moses and Aaron and rebellion against God Himself.

Thou and all thy company are gathered together against the LORD; and what is Aaron that ye murmur against him?"

And Moses sent to call Dathan and Abiram, which said, "We will not come up. Is it a small thing that thou hast brought us up out of a land that floweth with milk and honey to kill us in the wilderness, except thou make thyself altogether a prince over us?"

And the LORD spake unto Moses and unto Aaron, saying, "Separate yourselves from among this congregation that I may consume them in a moment."

And they fell upon their faces and said, "O God, shall one man sin, and wilt Thou be wroth with all the congregation?"

The Mob Destroyed. And the LORD spake unto Moses, saying, "Speak unto the congregation, saying, 'Get you up from about the tabernacle of Korah, Dathan, and Abiram.'"

And Moses rose up and spake unto the congregation saying, "Depart, I pray you, from the tents of these wicked men and touch nothing of theirs lest ye be consumed in all their sins."

And Moses said, "Hereby ye shall know that the LORD hath sent me: If these men die the common death of all men, then the LORD hath not sent me. But if the LORD make a new thing and the earth open her mouth and swallow them up, with all that appertain unto t!... and they go down alive into the pit,[6] then ye shall under....d that these men have provoked the LORD."

And when he had said these words, the ground clave asunder that was under them; and the earth opened her mouth and swallowed them up and their houses, and all the men that appertained unto Korah, and all their goods.

And all Israel that were round about them fled at the

---

6) Into hell.

cry of them; for they said, "Lest the earth swallow us up also."

And there came out a fire from the LORD and consumed the two hundred and fifty men.

And in proof that God had chosen Aaron, his rod budded and blossomed and yielded almonds. And the rod was kept in the Ark of God.

The Aftermath. But on the morrow all the congregation murmured against Moses and Aaron, saying, "Ye have killed the people of the LORD."

And the LORD sent a plague among the people, and they that died in the plague were fourteen thousand and seven hundred, beside them that died about the matter of Korah.

Conclusion of the Ten Commandments.

Gal. 6, 7. Be not deceived; God is not mocked; for whatsoever a man soweth, that shall he also reap.

> Righteous Judge, for sin's pollution
> Grant Thy gift of absolution
> Ere that day of retribution! (607, 11.)

---

34. The Water of Meribah and the Brazen Serpent
Num. 20. 21

The Sin of Moses and Aaron. Then came the children of Israel into the Desert of Zin in the first month.[1] And the people abode in Kadesh; and Miriam died there and was buried there.

And there was no water for the congregation; and they chode[2] with Moses, saying, "Would God that we had died when our brethren died before the LORD! And why have ye

---

1) Of the fortieth year of the wilderness journey.
2) Found fault with, or reproached.

brought up the congregation of the LORD into this wilderness that we and our cattle should die there?"

And Moses and Aaron fell upon their faces. And the glory of the LORD appeared; and the LORD said unto Moses, "Take the rod and gather thou the assembly together, thou and Aaron, thy brother, and speak ye unto the rock before their eyes; and it shall give forth his water."

And Moses and Aaron gathered the congregation together before the rock, and he said unto them, "Hear now, ye rebels, must we fetch you water out of this rock?"

And Moses lifted up his hand, and with his rod he smote the rock twice. And the water came out abundantly, and the congregation drank and their beasts also.

And the LORD spake unto Moses and Aaron, "Because ye believed Me not and rebelled against My word at the water of Meribah,[3] therefore ye shall not bring this congregation into the land which I have given them."[4]

Aaron's Death. And the LORD said unto Moses, "Aaron shall not enter into the land which I have given unto the children of Israel. Take Aaron up unto Mount Hor, and he shall die there."

And they went up into Mount Hor in the sight of all the congregation. And Aaron died there in the top of the mount. And all the congregation mourned for Aaron thirty days.

The Brazen Serpent. And they journeyed from Mount Hor by the way of the Red Sea to compass the land of Edom; and the soul of the people was much discouraged because of the way.

And they spake against God and against Moses, "Wherefore have ye brought us up out of Egypt to die in the wilder-

---

[3] Meaning contention or strife.
[4] Note that God Himself here characterizes the sin committed by Moses and Aaron: "Ye believed Me not and rebelled against My word." Even Moses and Aaron became weak among this rebellious people.

THE WATER OF MERIBAH AND THE BRAZEN SERPENT 123

ness? For there is no bread, neither water, and our soul loatheth [5] this light bread."

And the LORD sent fiery [6] serpents among the people, and they bit the people; and many died.

Therefore they came to Moses and said, "We have sinned, for we have spoken against the LORD and against thee; pray

"And Moses made a serpent of brass"

unto the LORD that He may take the serpents from us." And Moses prayed for the people.

And the LORD said unto Moses, "Make thee a brazen serpent and set it upon a pole; every one that is bitten, when he looketh upon it, shall live."

And Moses made a serpent of brass; and if a serpent had bitten any man, when he beheld the serpent of brass, he lived.

5) We are disgusted with this bread from heaven, the manna.
6) Dangerous, venomous; called fiery probably from the burning which followed their deadly bite.

Second Article.

John 3, 14. 15. And as Moses lifted up the serpent in the wilderness, even so must the Son of Man be lifted up, that, whosoever believeth in Him, should not perish, but have everlasting life.

> My faith looks up to Thee,
> Thou Lamb of Calvary,
>   Savior divine!
> Now hear me while I pray;
> Take all my guilt away;
> Oh, let me from this day
>   Be wholly Thine! (394, 1.)

35. Balaam
Num. 22—24

Balaam Asked to Curse Israel. The children of Israel pitched in the Plain of Moab. And Moab was sore afraid of the people.

And Balak was king of the Moabites at that time. He sent messengers therefore unto Balaam, saying, "Come, curse me this people; for they are too mighty for me; for I wot that he whom thou blessest is blessed and he whom thou cursest is cursed."

And the elders of Moab and Midian came to Balaam and spake the words of Balak.

And God said unto Balaam, "Thou shalt not go with them; thou shalt not curse the people, for they are blessed."

And Balaam said to the princes of Balak, "Get you into your land; for the LORD refuseth to give me leave to go with you."

The Request Renewed. And Balak sent yet again princes, more, and more honorable.

And Balaam said, "If Balak would give me his house full of silver and gold, I cannot go beyond the word of the

LORD, my God. Tarry ye here this night that I may know what the LORD will say unto me more." [1]

And God came to Balaam and said, "Go with them; [2] but the word which I shall say unto thee, that shalt thou do."

And Balaam went with the princes of Moab.

The Animal's Rebuke. And God's anger was kindled because he went, and the Angel of the LORD stood in the way against him.

Now, he was riding upon his ass. And the ass saw the Angel, [3] and His sword drawn in His hand, and turned aside out of the way. And Balaam smote the ass to turn her into the way.

But the Angel of the LORD stood in the path of the vineyard, a wall being on this side and a wall on that side. And when the ass saw the Angel, she thrust herself unto the wall and crushed Balaam's foot against the wall; and he smote her again.

And the Angel of the LORD stood in a narrow way, where was no way to turn either to the right hand or to the left. And when the ass saw the Angel of the LORD, she fell down under Balaam; and he smote the ass with a staff.

And the LORD opened the mouth of the ass, and she said unto Balaam, "What have I done unto thee that thou hast smitten me these three times?"

Then the LORD opened the eyes of Balaam, and he saw the Angel of the LORD standing in the way. And Balaam said, "I have sinned. I will get me back again."

---

1) The men had brought a rich reward, and Balaam hoped that God might permit him to go.

2) Spoken in anger, as though God meant to say: "Go if you do not want to hear Me."

3) A dumb brute was made to see what the prophet failed to see. This was a rebuke to Balaam for his disobedience and covetousness.

And the Angel of the LORD said, "Go with the men; but only the word that I shall speak unto thee, that thou shalt speak."

Balaam's Prophecy. And on the morrow Balak took Balaam and brought him up into the high place of Baal that he might see the utmost part of the people.

And the LORD put a word into Balaam's mouth; and he took up his parable and said, "How shall I curse whom God hath not cursed? God is not a man that He should lie, neither the son of man that He should repent. Hath He said, and shall He not do it? Or hath He spoken, and shall He not make it good?

"Behold, I have received commandment to bless; and He hath blessed, and I cannot reverse it. *There shall come a Star out of Jacob, and a Scepter shall rise out of Israel and shall smite the corners of Moab. Out of Jacob shall come He that shall have dominion.*"

And Balaam rose up and went and returned to his place; and Balak also went his way.

Table of Duties: To Bishops.

Jer. 23, 31. Behold, I am against the prophets, saith the Lord, that use *their* tongues and say, He saith.

> So God His own is shielding
> And help to them is yielding.
> When need and woe distress them,
> His loving arms caress them. (122, 5.)

36. Moses' Last Days and Death
Deut. 1—34. Num. 27

Joshua Appointed Successor to Moses. And the children of Israel encamped in the Plains of Moab, by Jordan.

And the LORD said unto Moses, "Get thee up into this mount and see the land which I have given unto the children of Israel. And when thou hast seen it, thou also shalt be gathered unto thy people as Aaron was."

And Moses spake unto the LORD, saying, "Let the LORD set a man over the congregation that it be not as sheep which have no shepherd."

And the LORD said unto Moses, "Take thee Joshua, the son of Nun, a man in whom is the Spirit, and lay thine hand upon him; and set him before all the congregation and give him a charge in their sight that all the congregation of the children of Israel may be obedient." And Moses did so.

Moses' Farewell. And in the fortieth year, on the first day of the eleventh month, Moses spake unto the children of Israel, saying, *"Hear, O Israel: The* LORD, *our God, is one* LORD. *And thou shalt love the* LORD, *thy God, with all thine heart and with all thy soul and with all thy might.*

"And these words which I command thee this day shall be in thine heart; and thou shalt teach them diligently unto thy children and shalt talk of them when thou sittest in thine house, and when thou walkest by the way, and when thou liest down, and when thou risest up.

"And if thou shalt hearken diligently unto the voice of the LORD, thy God, to observe and to do all His commandments, His blessings shall come on thee.

"But if thou wilt not obey the voice of the LORD, thy God, His curses shall come upon thee. Cursed shalt thou be when thou comest in, and cursed shalt thou be when thou goest out.

And the LORD shall scatter thee among all people, from the one end of the earth even unto the other.

"*The* LORD, *thy God, will raise up unto thee a Prophet from the midst of thee, of thy brethren, like unto me; unto Him ye shall hearken.*"

Moses' Death. And Moses went up unto the mountain of Nebo, that is over against Jericho; and the LORD showed

Moses' Farewell

him all the land unto the utmost sea [1]) and said unto him, "This is the land which I sware unto Abraham, unto Isaac, and unto Jacob, saying, 'I will give it unto thy seed.' I have caused thee to see it with thine eyes, but thou shalt not go over thither."

So Moses, the servant of the LORD, died according to the word of the LORD. And He buried him in a valley in the land of Moab; but no man knoweth of his sepulcher unto this day.

---

1) The Mediterranean Sea.

And Moses was an hundred and twenty years old when he died; his eye was not dim nor his natural force abated.

And the children of Israel wept for Moses thirty days.

And Joshua, the son of Nun, was full of the spirit of wisdom; for Moses had laid his hands upon him; and the children of Israel hearkened unto him.

And there arose not a prophet since in Israel like unto Moses, whom the LORD knew face to face.

Seventh Petition: "Grant us a blessed end."

Rev. 14, 13. Blessed are the dead which die in the Lord from henceforth; yea, saith the Spirit, that they may rest from their labors; and their works do follow them.

> Jerusalem, thou city fair and high,
> Would God I were in thee!
> My longing heart fain, fain, to thee
> would fly,
> It will not stay with me.
> Far over vale and mountain,
> Far over field and plain,
> It hastes to seek its Fountain
> And leave this world of pain. (619, 1.)

37. Israel Enters Canaan
Josh. 1—5

God's Command to Joshua. Now, after the death of Moses, the servant of the LORD, it came to pass that the LORD spake unto Joshua, saying, "Moses, My servant, is dead; now, therefore, arise, go over this Jordan, unto the land which I do give to the children of Israel.

"Only be thou strong and very courageous that thou mayest do according to all the Law which Moses, My servant, commanded thee.

"This Book of the Law shall not depart out of thy mouth;

but thou shalt meditate therein day and night; then thou shalt make thy way prosperous, and then thou shalt have good success."

Then Joshua commanded the officers of the people, saying, "Within three days ye shall pass over this Jordan to go in to possess the land which the Lord, your God, giveth you."

And they said, "As we hearkened unto Moses, so will we hearken unto thee."

Spies Sent to Jericho. And Joshua sent out two men to spy secretly. And they came to Jericho and went into the house of Rahab and lodged there.

And it was told the king of Jericho, saying, "Behold, there came men in hither of the children of Israel to search out the country."

And the king sent unto Rahab, saying, "Bring forth the men."

And the woman had hid them on the roof of the house under the stalks of flax. And she said, "I wist not whence they were; and when it was dark, they went out. Pursue after them quickly, for ye shall overtake them." And the men pursued after them.

And she came up to the men upon the roof and said, "I know that the Lord hath given you the land. Now, therefore, I pray you, swear unto me, since I have showed you kindness, that ye will also show kindness unto my father's house; that ye will save alive my father, my mother, my brethren, and my sisters, and all that they have."

And the men did so. Then she let them down by a cord through the window; for her house was upon the town wall.

Passing over Jordan. So the two men returned to Joshua and said, "Truly, the Lord hath delivered into our hands all the land; for even all the inhabitants do faint because of us."

And Joshua rose early in the morning, and the people

came to Jordan. And the priests that bare the Ark of the Covenant went before the people.

And when the feet of the priests that bare the Ark were dipped in the brim of the water, the waters which came down from above stood and rose up upon a heap and those that went down toward the Salt Sea failed.

"The waters stood"

And the people passed over right against Jericho. And the priests that bare the Ark of the Covenant stood firm on dry ground in the midst of Jordan, until all the Israelites passed over on dry ground.

And when the priests that bare the Ark of the Covenant of the LORD were come up out of the midst of Jordan, and the soles of the priests' feet were lifted up unto the dry land, the waters of Jordan returned unto their place and flowed over all his banks as they did before.

And the people came up out of the Jordan on the tenth

day of the first month and encamped in Gilgal, in the east border of Jericho.

And twelve stones which they took out of Jordan did Joshua pitch in Gilgal, saying, "When your children shall ask their fathers, 'What mean those stones?' then ye shall let your children know, saying, 'Israel came over this Jordan on dry land,' that all the people of the earth might know the hand of the LORD, that it is mighty; that ye might fear the LORD, your God, forever."

And the manna ceased; but they did eat of the fruit of the land of Canaan.

First Article: God is faithful.

Ps. 33, 4. The Word of the Lord is right, and all His works are done in truth.

> The Lord forsaketh not His flock,
>   His chosen generation;
> He is their Refuge and their Rock,
>   Their Peace and their Salvation,
> And with a mother's tender hand
> He leads His own, His chosen band,—
>   To God all praise and glory! (19, 4.)

38. The Fall of Jericho
Josh. 6. 7

Jericho Taken. And the LORD said unto Joshua, "See, I have given into thine hand Jericho. All your men of war shall go round about the city once. Thus shalt thou do six days.

"And seven priests shall bear before the Ark seven trumpets; and the seventh day ye shall compass the city seven times, and the priests shall blow with the trumpets. And when ye hear the sound of the trumpet, all the people shall shout with a great shout; and the wall of the city shall fall down flat."

And when Joshua had spoken unto the people, the seven priests bearing the seven trumpets passed on before the Lord. So they did six days.

And on the seventh day they rose early, about the dawning of the day, and compassed the city seven times. And at the seventh time, when the priests blew with the trumpets,

"And the wall fell down flat"

Joshua said unto the people, "Shout; for the Lord hath given you the city.

"And the city shall be accursed, and all that are therein, to the Lord; only Rahab shall live, and all that are with her in the house, because she hid the messengers that we sent. And ye, in any wise keep yourselves from the accursed thing lest ye make yourselves accursed."

So the people shouted with a great shout, and the wall

fell down flat, so that the people went up into the city and took it.

Achan's Theft. But Achan, of the tribe of Judah, took of the accursed thing. And the anger of the Lord was kindled against Israel.

And Joshua sent men from Jericho to Ai. And the men of Ai smote of them about thirty and six men; wherefore the hearts of the people melted and became as water.

And Joshua rent his clothes and fell to the earth upon his face before the Ark of the Lord until the eventide, he and the elders of Israel, and put dust upon their heads.

And the Lord said unto Joshua, "Get thee up; wherefore liest thou thus upon thy face? Up, sanctify the people and say, 'Sanctify yourselves against to-morrow; for thus saith the Lord God of Israel, "There is an accursed thing in the midst of thee, O Israel. Thou canst not stand before thine enemies until ye take away the accursed thing from among you."

" 'In the morning therefore ye shall be brought according to your tribes; and it shall be that the tribe that the Lord taketh shall come according to the families thereof; and the family which the Lord shall take shall come by households; and the household which the Lord shall take shall come man by man.' "

And Achan, of the tribe of Judah, was taken.

And Joshua said, "My son, give glory to the Lord and tell me now what thou hast done; hide it not from me."

And Achan answered Joshua and said, "Indeed, I have sinned against the Lord. I saw among the spoils a goodly Babylonish garment and two hundred shekels of silver and a wedge of gold; then I coveted them and took them; and, behold, they are hid in the earth in my tent."

So Joshua sent messengers, and they brought them to Joshua.

And Joshua said, "Why hast thou troubled us? The LORD shall trouble thee."

And all Israel stoned him and raised over him a great heap of stones.

Seventh Commandment.

Jas. 1, 14. 15. But every man is tempted when he is drawn away of his own lust and enticed. Then, when lust hath conceived, it bringeth forth sin; and sin, when it is finished, bringeth forth death.

> Stand, then, in His great might,
> With all His strength endued;
> But take, to arm you for the fight,
> The panoply of God.   (450, 3.)

39. Joshua's Victories and Last Days
Josh. 10—24

Sun and Moon Stand Still. And five kings gathered themselves together and encamped before Gibeon.

So Joshua ascended from Gilgal and came unto them suddenly. And the LORD discomfited them before Israel and slew them with a great slaughter at Gibeon and chased them.

And as they fled from before Israel, the LORD cast down great hailstones from heaven upon them, and they died.

Then spake Joshua and said, "Sun, stand thou still upon Gibeon, and thou, Moon, in the valley of Ajalon."

And the sun stood still, and the moon stayed, about a whole day, until the people had avenged themselves upon their enemies. And there was no day like that before it or after it that the LORD hearkened unto the voice of a man; for the LORD fought for Israel.

Division of the Land. So Joshua took all the land according to all that the LORD had said unto Moses; and Joshua gave it for an inheritance unto Israel according to their divisions by their tribes. And the land rested of war.

But unto the tribe of Levi, Moses gave not any inheritance; the Lord God of Israel was their inheritance, as He said unto them. And the children of Israel gave unto the Levites out of their inheritance, at the commandment of the Lord, forty-eight cities and their suburbs.

And the whole congregation of the children of Israel assembled together at Shiloh and set up the Tabernacle of the congregation there.

And the bones of Joseph, which the children of Israel had brought up out of Egypt, buried they in Shechem.

Joshua's Exhortation. And after the Lord had given rest unto Israel from all their enemies, Joshua called for all Israel and said unto them, "I am old and stricken in age; and ye have seen all that the Lord, your God, hath done unto all these nations; for He hath fought for you. Take good heed therefore unto yourselves that ye love the Lord, your God.

"Else, if ye do go back and cleave unto the remnant of these nations, they shall be snares and traps unto you and scourges in your sides until ye perish from off this good land.

"And, behold, this day I am going the way of all the earth; and ye know that not one thing hath failed of all the good things which the Lord spake concerning you; all are come to pass, and not one thing hath failed thereof.

"Therefore, as all good things are come upon you, so shall the Lord bring upon you all evil things when ye transgress the covenant of the Lord, your God. Now, therefore, fear the Lord and serve Him in sincerity and in truth; and if it seem evil unto you to serve the Lord, choose you this day whom ye will serve. *But as for me and my house, we will serve the Lord.*"

And the people answered and said, "God forbid that we

should forsake the LORD to serve other gods; we also will serve the LORD; for He is God."

So Joshua made a covenant with the people that day and set them a statute and an ordinance in Shechem.

And Joshua, the servant of the LORD, died, being an hundred and ten years old. And they buried him in Mount Ephraim.

Conclusion of the Commandments.

Deut. 27, 26. Cursed be he that confirmeth not all the words of this Law to do them. And all the people shall say, Amen.

> Then here will I and mine today
> A solemn covenant make and say:
> Though all the world forsake Thy Word,
> I and my house will serve the Lord. (625, 5.)

NOTE. — Six cities of refuge were appointed, to which any one who had accidentally killed another could flee for protection and a fair trial.

SUMMARY STUDY OF THE THIRD PERIOD

Recall how Israel came to be in Egypt.

Write or relate a short biography of Moses; of Joshua.

Enumerate the miracles which God performed during this period. What was the object of these miracles?

Discuss the general conduct of the children of Israel on the way from Egypt to Canaan.

Tell why Israel had to wander in the desert forty years; why Moses and Aaron did not enter Canaan.

Name the types of Christ that occur in this period. What direct prophecy concerning Christ was made?

Show how the promises of God were fulfilled in this period?

Draw comparisons between our own lives as Christians and that of the children of Israel: their delivery from Egypt, their way through the desert, and their settlement in Canaan.

"THERE REMAINETH THEREFORE A REST TO THE PEOPLE OF GOD. . . . LET US LABOR THEREFORE TO ENTER INTO THAT REST." Heb. 4, 9. 11.

FOURTH PERIOD

THE TIME OF THE JUDGES
(Ca. 1426—1095 B. C.)

This period covers three hundred thirty-one years, in which the children of Israel could have lived at peace and prospered, but during which they time and again forsook the Lord, worshiped false gods, and lived after the manner of the surrounding heathen. The Lord then gave them into the hands of their enemies to bring them to repentance. Whenever they repented, God sent them a deliverer, such as Gideon and Samson, or a more permanent leader and judge, such as Samuel. This continued until Israel finally asked for, and received, a king. In this period falls the story of Ruth, the Moabite daughter-in-law of Naomi, who became the great-grandmother of David and therefore a direct ancestor of our Savior Jesus Christ.

40. Gideon
Judg. 2—7

The Judges. And Joshua, the servant of the LORD, died; and there arose another generation, which knew not the LORD nor the works which He had done for Israel.

And the children of Israel did evil in the sight of the LORD and followed other gods. And the LORD delivered them into the hand of their enemies.

And when the LORD raised them up judges, the LORD was with the judge and delivered them out of the hand of their enemies.

Gideon Called. And when the children of Israel cried unto the LORD because of the Midianites, the Angel of the LORD appeared to Gideon. And Gideon threshed wheat by the wine-press to hide it from the Midianites.

And the Angel said unto him, "The LORD is with thee, thou mighty man of valor. Go, and thou shalt save Israel from the Midianites."

Divine Assurance Given Gideon. And Gideon said unto God, "If Thou wilt save Israel by mine hand, behold, I will put a fleece of wool in the floor; and if the dew be on the fleece only and it be dry upon all the earth besides, then shall I know that Thou wilt save Israel by mine hand."

And it was so; for he rose up early on the morrow and wringed the dew out of the fleece, a bowlful of water.

And Gideon said unto God, "Let me prove, I pray Thee, but this once with the fleece; let it now be dry only upon the fleece, and upon all the ground let there be dew."

And God did so that night; for it was dry upon the fleece only, and there was dew on all the ground.

Selection of an Army. Then Gideon rose up early in the morning and all the people with him.

And the LORD said unto Gideon, "The people that are with thee are too many for Me to give the Midianites into their hands lest Israel vaunt themselves [1] against Me, saying, 'Mine own hand hath saved me.' Now, therefore, proclaim in the ears of the people, saying, 'Whosoever is afraid, let him return.'"

And there returned of the people twenty and two thousand, and there remained ten thousand.

And the LORD said unto Gideon, "The people are yet too many; bring them down unto the water. Every one that lappeth of the water with his tongue as a dog lappeth, him shalt thou set by himself; likewise every one that boweth down upon his knees to drink."

And the number of them that lapped, putting their hand to their mouth, were three hundred men. And the LORD said unto Gideon, "By the three hundred men that lapped will I save you, and let all the other people go every man unto his place."

---

[1] Pride themselves on the victory instead of giving all glory to Me.

Preparing to Meet the Enemy. And the same night the LORD said unto him, "Arise, get thee down unto the host,[2)] and hear what they say."

Then went he down with his servant. And the Midianites and the Amalekites lay along in the valley like grasshoppers

"The sword of the Lord and of Gideon"

for multitude; and their camels were without number, as the sand by the seaside for multitude.

And there was a man that told a dream unto his fellow and said, "Behold, I dreamed, and, lo, a cake of barley bread tumbled into the host of Midian and came unto a tent and smote it that it fell."

And his fellow answered and said, "This is nothing else

---

2) The army.

save the sword of Gideon, a man of Israel; into his hand hath God delivered Midian."

And Gideon worshiped and returned to the host of Israel and said, "Arise; for the LORD hath delivered into your hand the host of Midian."

Gideon Defeats the Midianites. And he divided the three hundred men into three companies; and he put a trumpet in every man's hand, with empty pitchers, and lamps within the pitchers. And he said unto them, "Look on me, and as I do, so shall ye do."

So Gideon and the hundred men that were with him came to the newly set watch; and they blew the trumpets and brake the pitchers that were in their hands.

And the three companies blew the trumpets, and brake the pitchers, and held the lamps in their left hands, and cried, "The sword of the LORD and of Gideon."

Then all the host of Midian ran and cried and fled; and the LORD set every man's sword against his fellow. Thus Midian was subdued before the children of Israel.

Then the men of Israel said unto Gideon, "Rule thou over us."

But Gideon said, "I will not rule over you; the LORD shall rule over you."

And the country was in quietness forty years in the days of Gideon.

Conclusion of the Commandments.

Ps. 37, 5. Commit thy way unto the Lord, trust also in Him; and He shall bring it to pass.

> With might of ours can naught be done,
>   Soon were our loss effected;
> But for us fights the Valiant One,
>   Whom God Himself elected. (262, 2a.)

41. Samson

(Part I)

Judg. 13—15

Samson's Birth. And the children of Israel did evil again in the sight of the Lord; and the Lord delivered them into the hand of the Philistines [1] forty years.

And there was a man of the Danites whose name was Manoah. And the Angel of the Lord appeared unto his wife and said unto her, "Behold now, thou shalt bear a son. And no razor shall come on his head: for the child shall be a Nazarite [2] unto God, and he shall begin to deliver Israel out of the hand of the Philistines."

And the woman bare a son and called his name Samson; and the child grew, and the Lord blessed him.

Marriage to a Philistine Woman. And Samson went down to Timnath and saw a woman in Timnath of the daughters of the Philistines. And he came up and told his father and his mother and said, "I have seen a woman in Timnath of the daughters of the Philistines; now, therefore, get her for me to wife."

Then his father and his mother said unto him, "Is there never a woman among the daughters of thy brethren that thou goest to take a wife of the uncircumcised Philistines?"

---

[1] The Philistines were a strong tribe, dwelling southwest of the land of Israel. The principal towns of Philistia were Gaza, Ashkelon, Ekron, Ashdod, and Gath.

[2] One bound to God by a solemn vow. (See Num. 6, 2—21.) A Nazarite was a man (or a woman) who had made a vow to abstain from wine and strong drink; he was to "eat nothing of the vine-tree, from the kernels even to the husks." Nor was a razor to come upon his head all the time of his vow. He was not to enter a house containing a dead body. This vow lasted from eight days to a lifetime. Those who were consecrated to be Nazarites by their parents from their birth were Perpetual Nazarites.

But they knew not that it was of the Lord that He sought an occasion against the Philistines.

And as he went down with his father and mother, behold, a young lion roared against him. And the Spirit of the Lord

"And he rent the lion"

came upon him, and he rent the lion as he would have rent a kid.

And after a time he returned that way; and, behold, there was a swarm of bees and honey in the carcass of the lion. And he took thereof and went on eating.

The Riddle at the Wedding-Feast. And Samson made a feast and said unto the guests, "I will now put forth a riddle unto you; if ye can within the seven days of the feast find it out, then I will give you thirty sheets and thirty change of garments; but if ye cannot, then shall ye give me thirty sheets and thirty change of garments."

And they said unto him, "Put forth thy riddle that we may hear it."

And he said unto them, "Out of the eater came forth meat, and out of the strong came forth sweetness." And they could not expound the riddle.

Betrayed by His Wife. And they said unto Samson's wife, "Entice thy husband that he may declare unto us the riddle lest we burn thee and thy father's house with fire."

And Samson's wife wept before him and said, "Thou dost but hate me and lovest me not; thou hast put forth a riddle unto the children of my people and hast not told it me."

And she wept before him the seven days; and on the seventh day he told her. And she told the riddle to the children of her people.

And the men said unto him, "What is sweeter than honey? and what is stronger than a lion?"

And he said unto them, "If ye had not plowed with my heifer, ye had not found out my riddle."

And the Spirit of the Lord came upon him, and he went down to Ashkelon, and slew thirty men of them, and took their spoil, and gave change of garments unto them which expounded the riddle.

The Marriage Broken Up, Samson Takes Revenge. But in the time of the wheat-harvest Samson visited his wife. And her father said, "I verily thought that thou hadst hated her; therefore I gave her to thy companion."

And Samson went and caught three hundred foxes and turned tail to tail and put a firebrand in the midst between two tails. And when he had set the brands on fire, he let them go into the standing corn of the Philistines and burned up both the shocks and also the standing corn, with the vineyards and olives.

Then the Philistines said, "Who hath done this?" And they answered, "Samson."

Then the Philistines went up and pitched in Judah. And the men of Judah bound Samson and brought him to the Philistines. And when he came, the Philistines shouted against him.

And the Spirit of the LORD came upon him, and the cords that were upon his arms became as flax that was burned with fire, and his bands loosed from off his hands. And he found a new jawbone of an ass and took it and slew a thousand men therewith.

The Sixth Commandment: Betrothal, Marriage.

Ps. 79, 10. Wherefore should the heathen say, Where is their God? Let Him be known among the heathen in our sight by the revenging of the blood of Thy servants which is shed.

O my Savior, help afford By Thy Spirit and Thy Word!
When my wayward heart would stray, Keep me in the
  narrow way;
Grace in time of need supply While I live and when I die. (342, 5.)

42. Samson
(PART II)
Judg. 16

Samson Carries the Gate of the City Away. Then Samson went to Gaza. And the Gazites laid wait for him all night to kill him. And he arose at midnight, and took the doors of the gate of the city and the two posts, and went away with them, bar and all, and put them upon his shoulders, and carried them up to the top of a hill that is before Hebron.

Unfaithful Delilah. And it came to pass afterward that he loved a woman whose name was Delilah.

Advanced Bible History.

And the lords of the Philistines came up unto her and said unto her, "Entice him and see wherein his great strength lieth, and we will give thee, every one of us, eleven hundred pieces of silver."

And Delilah said to Samson, "Tell me, I pray thee, wherein thy great strength lieth."

And Samson said unto her, "If they bind me with seven green withes,[1] then shall I be weak and be as another man."

Then the lords of the Philistines brought up to her seven green withes, and she bound him with them.

Now, there were men lying in wait, abiding with her in the chamber. And she said unto him, "The Philistines be upon thee, Samson." And he brake the withes as a thread of tow[2] is broken when it toucheth the fire.

And Delilah said unto Samson, "Behold, thou hast mocked me and told me lies; now tell me, I pray thee, wherewith thou mightest be bound."

And he said unto her, "If they bind me with new ropes that never were occupied,[3] then shall I be weak."

Delilah therefore took new ropes and bound him therewith and said unto him, "The Philistines be upon thee, Samson." And he brake them off from his arms like a thread.

And Delilah said unto him, "Hitherto thou hast mocked me and told me lies; tell me wherewith thou mightest be bound."

And he said unto her, "If thou weavest the seven locks of my head with the web."[4]

And she fastened it with the pin and said unto him, "The Philistines be upon thee, Samson." And he awaked out of

---

[1] Seven new ropes made of tough green twigs or of the flexible bark of the twigs. [2] Thin string. [3] Never used.
[4] If she would weave his locks into the web of her loom and fasten his hair to the loom with a nail.

his sleep and went away with the pin of the beam and with the web.

And she said unto him, "How canst thou say, 'I love thee,' when thine heart is not with me? Thou hast mocked me these three times and hast not told me wherein thy great strength lieth."

Samson is Overcome. And when she pressed him daily

"And he bowed himself with all his might"

with her words, his soul was vexed that he told her all his heart and said unto her, "There hath not come a razor upon mine head; for I have been a Nazarite unto God; if I be shaven, then my strength will go from me."

Then Delilah sent for the lords of the Philistines. And she made him sleep upon her knees; and she called for a man, and she caused him to shave off the seven locks of his head; and his strength went from him.

But the Philistines took him and put out his eyes and bound him with fetters of brass; and he did grind in the prison-house.

Samson's End. Howbeit the hair of his head began to grow again. Then the lords of the Philistines gathered them together to offer a great sacrifice unto Dagon, their god. And they called for Samson, and he made them sport;[5] and they set him between the pillars.

Now, the house was full of men and women; and all the lords of the Philistines were there; and there were upon the roof about three thousand men and women that beheld while Samson made sport.

And Samson called unto the LORD and said, "O LORD God, remember me, I pray thee, and strengthen me only this once."

And Samson took hold of the two middle pillars upon which the house stood and said, "Let me die with the Philistines." And he bowed himself with all his might; and the house fell upon the lords and upon all the people that were therein. So the dead which he slew at his death were more than they which he slew in his life.

Then his brethren and all the house of his father came down and took him and buried him in the burying-place of his father. And he judged Israel twenty years.

First and Sixth Commandments.

Ps. 147, 10. 11. He delighteth not in the strength of the horse; He taketh not pleasure in the legs of a man. The Lord taketh pleasure in them that fear Him, in those that hope in His mercy.

A mighty Fortress is our God,	Now means deadly woe;
A trusty Shield and Weapon;	Deep guile and great might
He helps us free from every need	Are his dread arms in fight;
That hath us now o'ertaken.	On earth is not his equal.
The old evil Foe	(262, 1.)

---

5) Entertained them, probably with music.

43. Ruth
Book of Ruth 1—4

A Family from Bethlehem Goes to the Land of Moab. In the days when the judges ruled there was a famine in the land. And a man of Bethlehem named Elimelech went into the country of Moab with his wife Naomi and two sons. And Elimelech died there.

But his sons took them wives of the women of Moab;

"Whither thou goest, I will go"

the name of the one was Orpah and the name of the other Ruth. And when they had dwelt there about ten years, the sons both died.

Naomi Returns with Ruth. Then Naomi arose with her daughters-in-law that she might return from the country of Moab. And on the way she said to them, "Go, return; the LORD deal kindly with you as ye have dealt with the dead and with me."

And they lifted up their voice and wept. And Orpah kissed her mother-in-law and returned; but Ruth clave unto her.[1)]

And Naomi said, "Return thou also."

And Ruth said, "Entreat me not to leave thee; for whither thou goest, I will go, and where thou lodgest, I will lodge; thy people shall be my people and thy God my God; where thou diest, will I die, and there will I be buried; naught but death shall part thee and me."

And when they came to Bethlehem, all the city was moved about them and said, "Is this Naomi?"

And she said unto them, "Call me not Naomi; call me Mara; for the Almighty hath dealt very bitterly with me. I went out full, and the LORD hath brought me home again empty."

Ruth, the Gleaner. And they came to Bethlehem in the beginning of the barley-harvest. And Ruth went and gleaned ears; and the field belonged to Boaz, who was of the kindred of Elimelech, the husband of Naomi.

And, behold, Boaz came from Bethlehem and said unto the reapers, "The LORD be with you." And they answered him, "The LORD bless thee."

Then said Boaz, "Whose damsel is this?"

And the servant that was set over the reapers said, "It is the Moabitish damsel that came back with Naomi."

Then said Boaz unto Ruth, "Go not to glean in another field, but abide here fast by my maidens. On the field that they reap, go thou after them; and when thou art athirst, go unto the vessels and drink; and at meal-time come thou hither and eat of the bread."

Then she fell on her face and said, "Why have I found grace in thine eyes, seeing I am a stranger?"

---

1) Clung to her; would not leave her.

And Boaz said, "It hath been showed me all that thou hast done unto thy mother-in-law. A full reward be given thee of the LORD."

And when she was risen up to glean, Boaz commanded his men, saying, "Let her glean even among the sheaves. And let fall also some of the handfuls on purpose for her that she may glean them, and rebuke her not."

So she gleaned in the field until evening and came to her mother-in-law.

And her mother-in-law said, "Where hast thou gleaned to-day?"

And she said, "The man's name is Boaz."

And Naomi said, "Blessed be he of the LORD. The man is one of our next kinsmen."

So Ruth gleaned unto the end of the harvest.

Ruth the Foremother of David. And Naomi said, "Boaz winnoweth barley to-night in the threshing-floor; put thy raiment upon thee and get thee down to the floor."

And she went down unto the floor and did according to all that her mother-in-law bade her and said to Boaz, "Spread thy skirt over thine handmaid;[2] for thou art a near kinsman."

And Boaz said, "It is true that I am thy near kinsman; howbeit, there is a kinsman nearer than I. If he will not do the part of a kinsman to thee, then will I do it, as the LORD liveth."

And she came to her mother-in-law and told her all.

Then went Boaz and said to the kinsman, "Wilt thou redeem Elimelech's parcel of land?"

And he said, "I cannot redeem it; buy it for thee."

So Boaz bought the land and took Ruth, and she was

---

[2] This was a marriage proposal, which included the redeeming of a parcel of land that had belonged to Naomi's husband.

his wife. And the Lord gave her a son, and they called his name Obed. He is the father of Jesse, the father of David.

Fourth Commandment.

Eph. 6, 2. 3. Honor thy father and mother; which is the first commandment with promise. That it may be well with thee and thou mayest live long on the earth.

> If thou but suffer God to guide thee
> And hope in Him through all thy ways,
> He'll give thee strength, whate'er betide thee
> And bear thee through the evil days.
> Who trusts in God's unchanging love
> Builds on the Rock that naught can move. (518, 1.)

Note. — Bethlehem is six miles south of Jerusalem and is called Bethlehem-Judah, or Bethlehem-Ephratah (the fruitful), to distinguish it from another Bethlehem in Zebulun.

Jesus was born in Bethlehem-Ephratah and was a descendant of Boaz and Ruth.

44. Samuel

1 Sam. 1—7

Hannah Prays for a Son. Now, there was a certain man, and his name was Elkanah. But Hannah, his wife, had no children. And she went up to the house of the Lord.

Now, Eli, the priest, sat by a post of the Temple. And she was in bitterness of soul and prayed unto the Lord, and wept sore, and said, "O Lord of hosts, if Thou wilt give unto Thine handmaid a man child, then I will give him unto the Lord all the days of his life."

And as she continued praying before the Lord, Eli marked her mouth. Now, Hannah spake in her heart; only her lips moved. Therefore Eli thought she had been drunken and said unto her, "How long wilt thou be drunken?"

And Hannah answered and said, "I have drunk neither wine nor strong drink, but have poured out my soul before the Lord."

Then Eli said, "Go in peace, and the God of Israel grant thee thy petition."

Samuel Born and Given to the Lord. And the LORD remembered her. Wherefore it came to pass that she bare a son and called his name Samuel. And when she had

"She took him up unto the house of the Lord"

weaned him, she took him up unto the house of the LORD, to Eli.

And Samuel ministered before the LORD, being a child, girded with a linen ephod.[1]

Moreover his mother made him a little coat and brought it to him from year to year when she came up with her husband to offer the yearly sacrifice.

---

1) A garment worn by priests and servants of the priests as a sign of their calling.

And the child Samuel grew on and was in favor both with the Lord and also with men.

And the Lord visited Hannah, so that she bare three sons and two daughters.

The Wicked Sons of Eli. Now, the sons of Eli were sons of Belial;[2] they knew not the Lord. Eli was very old and heard all that his sons did. And he said unto them, "Why do ye such things? Nay, my sons; for it is no good report that I hear."[3]

Notwithstanding they hearkened not unto the voice of their father.

The Punishment Foretold. And there came a man of God unto Eli and said unto him, "Thus saith the Lord, 'Wherefore kick ye at My sacrifice and at Mine offering which I have commanded in My habitation, and honorest thy sons above Me?[4] Them that honor Me I will honor, and they that despise Me shall be lightly esteemed.

"'There shall not be an old man in thine house forever. And this shall be a sign unto thee that shall come upon thy two sons, on Hophni and Phinehas: in one day they shall die, both of them.'"

God Reveals Himself to Samuel. And it came to pass when, in the Temple, Samuel was laid down to sleep, that the Lord called, "Samuel!"

And he ran unto Eli and said, "Here am I; for thou calledst me." And he said, "I called thee not; lie down again." And he went.

---

2) An expression meaning ungodly, wicked persons. (Eli's sons were priests.)

3) Far too lenient. The sons were not fit to be priests at all. This lenience as father and chief priest was the grievous sin of Eli.

4) They had caused people to "abhor the offering of the Lord." 1 Sam. 2, 17.

And the Lord called yet again, "Samuel!"

And Samuel arose and went to Eli and said, "Here am I; for thou didst call me." And he answered, "I called not, my son; lie down again."

And the Lord called Samuel again the third time. And

"Here am I"

he arose and went to Eli and said, "Here am I; for thou didst call me."

And Eli perceived that the Lord had called the child. Therefore Eli said, "Go, lie down; and if He call thee, thou shalt say, 'Speak, Lord, for Thy servant heareth.'" So Samuel went and lay down in his place.

And the Lord called as at other times, "Samuel! Samuel!" Then Samuel answered, "Speak; for Thy servant heareth."

God's Threat against Eli Repeated. And the LORD said to Samuel, "Behold, I will perform against Eli all things which I have spoken concerning his house, for the iniquity which he knoweth; because his sons made themselves vile and he restrained them not." [5]

And Samuel feared to show Eli the vision. Then Eli called Samuel and said, "What is the thing that the LORD hath said unto thee?"

And Samuel told him every whit. And he said, "It is the LORD; let Him do what seemeth Him good."

God's Threats Carried Out. Now, Israel went out against the Philistines to battle. And the two sons of Eli, Hophni and Phinehas, were there with the Ark of the Covenant of God.[6] And the Philistines fought, and Israel was smitten; and the Ark of God was taken; and the two sons of Eli were slain.

And there ran a man of the army and came to Shiloh, with his clothes rent and with earth upon his head, and told it to Eli; and all the city cried out.

And when he made mention of the Ark of God, Eli fell from off his seat backward, and his neck brake, and he died. Now, he was ninety and eight years old and had judged Israel forty years.

Defeat of the Philistines. And the LORD visited the Philistines with many plagues on account of the Ark of the Covenant, so that they sent it back to the children of Israel. And it was taken to Kirjath-jearim.

And Samuel spake unto all the house of Israel, saying, "If ye do return unto the LORD with all your hearts, then

---

5) Hebrew: Did not scold, rebuke them.
6) Containing the two tables of the Ten Commandments, Aaron's rod, and a golden pot, in which three quarts of manna were preserved. The Ark was often taken into battle because it was a symbol of God's gracious presence.

put away the strange gods and serve the Lord only; and He will deliver you out of the hand of the Philistines."

Then they put away the strange gods and served the Lord only.

And Samuel gathered all Israel together to Mizpeh and cried unto the Lord for Israel; and the Lord heard him.

And the Lord thundered with a great thunder upon the Philistines, and they were smitten; and they came no more into the coast of Israel.

Then Samuel took a stone and set it up and called it Ebenezer, saying, "Hitherto hath the Lord helped us."

Third and Fourth Commandments.

Prov. 30, 17. The eye that mocketh at his father and despiseth to obey his mother, the ravens of the valley shall pick it out, and the young eagles shall eat it.

> He knows and He approves
> The way the righteous go;
> But sinners and their works shall meet
> A dreadful overthrow. (414, 6.)

Note. — At the time of Eli the Tabernacle stood at Shiloh; later it was at Bethel, Nob, and Gibeon.

SUMMARY STUDY OF THE FOURTH PERIOD

How were the people of Israel governed during this period?

Name some of the judges of Israel and state what they did for Israel.

What caused the repeated downfall of the Israelites? What was the common punishment employed by the Lord?

How close is the end of this period to the coming of Christ? What ancestors of Christ are mentioned in this period?

Discuss the sin of Eli and give several reasons why it drew such a heavy punishment.

Name the women mentioned in this period and tell briefly their part in the accounts given.

State some important lessons which should be derived from the accounts in this section. Name also evils that should be shunned.

"THOU HAST BROKEN THE YOKE OF HIS BURDEN AND THE STAFF OF HIS SHOULDER, THE ROD OF HIS OPPRESSOR, AS IN THE DAY OF MIDIAN," Is. 9, 4.

FIFTH PERIOD
THE FIRST THREE KINGS
(Ca. 1095—975 B. C.)

The kings here referred to are Saul, David, and Solomon. During their reign the twelve tribes remained united in a single kingdom, while after Solomon's death Judah and Benjamin formed the Kingdom of Judah and the rest of the tribes the Kingdom of Israel.

Beginning with this period, we find the children of Israel turning away from the form of government which obtained in the time of the Judges and before, to a kingdom, which was common among the surrounding heathen lands. Samuel continued to live through the reign of Saul and anointed David as the second king. Outwardly the people of Israel grew in prosperity and power, reaching their greatest time of peace and glory under Solomon. This period ushered in a long era of prophet activity. Samuel established a school of prophets, so that the people had regular teachers of religion. David, a prophet, poet, and musician himself, greatly improved the worship in the Tabernacle and wrote numerous psalms, in which he expressed the hopes, joys, and sorrows of his people and prophesied of the Savior. Solomon built the Temple and wrote several books of the Bible.

45. Saul, the First King of Israel
1 Sam. 8—15

Israel Desires a King. And when Samuel was old, he made his sons judges over Israel. And his sons walked not in his ways, but turned aside after lucre and took bribes and perverted judgment.[1]

Then all the elders of Israel gathered themselves together and said unto him, "Behold, thou art old, and thy sons walk not in thy ways; now make us a king to judge us like all the nations."

But the thing displeased Samuel, and he prayed unto the LORD.

---

1) Did not judge rightly.

And the Lord said unto Samuel, "Hearken unto the voice of the people, for they have not rejected thee, but they have rejected Me that I should not reign over them."

Saul Anointed. Now, there was a man of Benjamin whose name was Kish, and he had a son whose name was Saul, a choice young man and a goodly; from his shoulders and upward he was higher than any of the people.

And the asses of Kish were lost. And he said to Saul, his son, "Take one of the servants with thee and go seek the asses."

And he passed through Mount Ephraim, but found them not. And the servant said, "Behold, now, there is in this city a man of God; all that he saith cometh surely to pass. Let us go thither; peradventure he can show us our way that we should go."

And when they were come into the city, behold, Samuel came out against them. Now, the Lord had told Samuel a day before Saul came, "To-morrow about this time I will send thee a man, and thou shalt anoint him to be captain over My people Israel."

And when Samuel saw Saul, the Lord said unto him, "Behold, this man shall reign over My people."

Then Saul said to Samuel, "Tell me, I pray thee, where the seer's house is."

And Samuel answered, "I am the seer. As for thine asses that were lost, set not thy mind on them; for they are found. And on whom is all the desire of Israel? Is it not on thee and on all thy father's house?"

And Saul remained with him overnight. And the next day they arose early and went out. Then Samuel took a vial of oil, and poured it upon his head, and kissed him, and said, "The Lord hath anointed thee to be captain over His inheritance."

And when Saul had turned his back to go from Samuel, God gave him another heart.

Saul Selected and Declared King. And Samuel called the people to Mizpeh and said, "Present yourselves before the LORD by your tribes and by your thousands."

"The Lord hath anointed thee"

And when Samuel had caused all the tribes of Israel to come near, the tribe of Benjamin was taken. When he had caused the tribe of Benjamin to come near by their families, Saul was taken.

And they sought him. And, behold, he had hid himself among the stuff.[2] And they fetched him thence; and when he stood among the people, he was higher than any of the people, from his shoulders and upward.

---

2) The baggage of the large assembly.

And Samuel said, "See ye him whom the Lord hath chosen, that there is none like him among all the people?"

And all the people shouted and said, "God save the king!" But the children of Belial said, "How shall this man save us?" But Saul held his peace.

The King's First Heroic Deed. Then Nahash, the Ammonite, came up and encamped against Jabesh-gilead,[3] and said, "On this condition will I make a covenant with you that I may thrust out all your right eyes."

And the elders of Jabesh said unto him, "Give us seven days respite."

And messengers came to Gibeah, to Saul, who came after the herd out of the field. And when they told him the tidings of Jabesh, the Spirit of God came upon him, and he took a yoke of oxen and hewed them in pieces and sent them throughout all the coasts of Israel, saying, "Whosoever cometh not forth after Saul and after Samuel, so shall it be done unto his oxen."

And the people came out with one consent and slew the Ammonites, so that two of them were not left together.

And the people said unto Samuel, "Who is he that said, 'Shall Saul reign over us?' Bring the men that we may put them to death."

And Saul said, "There shall not a man be put to death this day; for to-day the Lord hath wrought salvation in Israel."

Saul's Disobedience. Samuel said to Saul, "Go and smite Amalek and utterly destroy all that they have and spare them not." And Saul smote the Amalekites and took Agag, their king, alive.

---

[3] A city in Gilead, east of the Jordan, in the borders of the tribe of Manasseh, and about 50 miles from Gibeah, where Saul was when he heard of the siege. (Map 3.)

But Saul spared Agag and the best of the sheep, and of the oxen, and of the fatlings, and the lambs, and all that was good, and would not utterly destroy them; but everything that was vile and refuse, that they destroyed utterly.

Rejected as King of Israel. Then came the word of the LORD unto Samuel, saying, "It repenteth Me that I have

"The Lord hath rent the kingdom from thee"

set up Saul to be king, for he hath not performed My commandments."

And Samuel came to Saul. And Saul said unto him, "Blessed be thou of the LORD; I have performed the commandment of the LORD."

And Samuel said, "What meaneth, then, this bleating of the sheep in mine ears and the lowing of the oxen which I hear?"

And Saul said, "The people spared the best of the sheep and of the oxen to sacrifice unto the Lord, thy God; and the rest we have utterly destroyed."

Then Samuel said, "Wherefore didst thou not obey the voice of the Lord? *Behold, to obey is better than sacrifice* and to hearken, than the fat of rams. Because thou hast rejected the word of the Lord, He hath rejected thee from being king."

And as Samuel turned about to go away, he laid hold upon the skirt of his mantle, and it rent. And Samuel said unto him, "The Lord hath rent the kingdom of Israel from thee this day, and hath given it to a neighbor of thine that is better than thou."

Then Samuel went to Ramah and came no more to see Saul until the day of his death. Nevertheless Samuel mourned for Saul.

Sixth Petition.

1 John 2, 17. And the earth passeth away and the lust thereof; but he that doeth the will of God abideth forever.

> I need Thy presence every passing hour:
> What but Thy grace can foil the Tempter's power?
> Who like Thyself my guide and stay can be?
> Through cloud and sunshine, oh, abide with me! (552, 6.)

---

46. David Anointed King
1 Sam. 16

Samuel Sent to Jesse. And the Lord said unto Samuel, "How long wilt thou mourn for Saul, seeing I have rejected him? Fill thine horn with oil and go to Jesse, the Bethlehemite; for I have provided Me a king among his sons. And thou shalt anoint unto Me him whom I name unto thee."

And Samuel did that which the Lord spake and came to Bethlehem and called Jesse and his sons to a sacrifice.

And when they were come, he looked on Eliab, Jesse's eldest son, and said, "Surely the LORD's anointed is before Him." [1)]

But the LORD said unto Samuel, "Look not on his countenance or on the height of his stature, because I have refused

"Then Samuel anointed him"

him; for the LORD seeth not as man seeth; for man looketh on the outward appearance, but the LORD looketh on the heart."

David is Chosen. And Jesse made seven of his sons to pass before Samuel. And Samuel said unto Jesse, "The LORD hath not chosen these. Are here all thy children?"

And he said, "There remaineth yet the youngest, and, behold, he keepeth the sheep."

---

1) Before God now stands the chosen king.

And Samuel said unto Jesse, "Send and fetch him." And he sent and brought him in.

Now, David was ruddy and of a beautiful countenance and goodly to look to. And the LORD said, "Arise, anoint him; for this is he."

Then Samuel took the horn of oil and anointed him in the midst of his brethren. And the Spirit of the LORD came upon David from that day forward.

David Made the Servant of Saul. But the Spirit of the LORD departed from Saul, and an evil spirit troubled him. And Saul said unto his servants, "Provide me now a man that can play well and bring him to me."

Then answered one of the servants and said, "Behold, I have seen a son of Jesse that is cunning in playing."

Then Saul sent messengers unto Jesse and said, "Send me David, thy son."

And David came to Saul and stood before him; and he loved him greatly; and he became his armor-bearer.

And when the evil spirit was upon Saul, David took a harp and played; so Saul was refreshed and was well, and the evil spirit departed from him.

Table of Duties: To the Young in General.

Luke 1, 52. He hath put down the mighty from their seats and exalted them of low degree.

> Oh, come, Thou Key of David, come
> And open wide our heav'nly home;
> Make safe the way that leads on high
> And close the path to misery.
> Rejoice! Rejoice! Emmanuel
> Shall come to thee, O Israel. (62, 4.)

47. David and Goliath
1 Sam. 17

Goliath's Boast. Now, the Philistines gathered together their armies to battle and stood on a mountain on the one side, and Israel stood on a mountain on the other side; and there was a valley between them.

And there went out of the camp of the Philistines a giant named Goliath, whose height was six cubits and a span.[1] And he had a helmet of brass upon his head, and he was armed with a coat of mail;[2] and he had greaves of brass[3] upon his legs and a target of brass[4] between his shoulders. And the staff of his spear was like a weaver's beam; and one bearing a shield went before him.

And he stood and cried unto the armies of Israel and said, "Why are ye come out to battle? Choose you a man for you and let him come down to me. If he be able to kill me, then will we be your servants; but if I kill him, then shall ye be our servants. I defy the armies of Israel this day!"

When Saul and all Israel heard those words of the Philistine, they were dismayed and greatly afraid. And the Philistine drew near morning and evening and presented himself forty days.

David Learns of Goliath. And the three eldest sons of Jesse went and followed Saul to the battle. But David went and returned from Saul to feed his father's sheep at Bethlehem.

---

1) *Cubit:* The distance from the elbow to the end of the middle finger (18 to 21 inches). *Span:* The distance between the end of the thumb and the end of the little finger when the fingers are spread; also known as a half cubit. The height of Goliath was about ten feet.

2) A short coat of iron plates to protect the chest and back. It weighed about 150 pounds.   3) Plates of brass.   4) A shield.

And Jesse said unto David, his son, "Take, now, for thy brethren these ten loaves and run to the camp and look how thy brethren fare." And David rose up early in the morning and ran to the army and saluted his brethren.

And as he talked with them, behold, there came up Goliath and spake as before. And all the men of Israel, when they saw the man, fled from him and were sore afraid.

The Brave Spirit of David. And David spake to the men, saying, "What shall be done to the man that killeth this Philistine and taketh away the reproach from Israel? For who is this uncircumcised Philistine that he should defy the armies of the living God?"

And the people answered him after this manner, saying, "The man who killeth him, the king will enrich him with great riches and will give him his daughter."

David Sent for by Saul. And when the words were heard which David spake, they rehearsed them before Saul; and he sent for him.

And David said to Saul, "Let no man's heart fail because of him; thy servant will go and fight with this Philistine."

And Saul said to David, "Thou art not able to go; for thou art but a youth and he a man of war from his youth."

And David said unto Saul, "Thy servant kept his father's sheep, and there came a lion and a bear and took a lamb out of the flock; and I went out after him and slew him. Thy servant slew both the lion and the bear. The LORD that delivered me from the lion and the bear, He will deliver me out of the hand of this Philistine."

Saul Puts His Armor on David. And Saul said unto David, "Go, and the LORD be with thee."

And Saul armed David with his armor, and he put a helmet of brass upon his head; also he armed him with a coat of mail. And David girded his sword upon his armor, and he essayed to go.

And David said unto Saul, "I cannot go with these; for I have not proved them." 5) And David put them off him.

"He took his sword"

The Shepherd Boy Challenges the Warrior. And he took his staff in his hand and chose him five smooth stones out of the brook and put them in a shepherd's bag, and his sling was in his hand; and he drew near to the Philistine.

And when the Philistine saw David, he disdained him and said, "Am I a dog that thou comest to me with staves?" And he cursed David and said, "Come to me, and I will give

---

5) Not tried them; no experience with armor.

thy flesh unto the fowls of the air and to the beasts of the field."

Then said David to the Philistine, "Thou comest to me with a sword, a spear, and a shield; but I come to thee in the name of the LORD of hosts, the God of the armies of Israel, whom thou hast defied.

"This day will the LORD deliver thee into mine hand; and I will smite thee and take thine head from thee; and I will give the carcasses of the host of the Philistines this day unto the fowls of the air and to the wild beasts of the earth, that all the earth may know that there is a God in Israel."

David's Victory. And when the Philistine drew nigh, David hasted and ran toward the Philistine. And he put his hand in his bag and took thence a stone, and slang it, and smote the Philistine in his forehead, that the stone sunk into his forehead; and he fell upon his face to the earth.

But there was no sword in the hand of David. Therefore he ran, and stood upon the Philistine, and took his sword, and cut off his head therewith.

And when the Philistines saw their champion was dead, they fled. And the men of Israel arose and pursued them and slew them.

First and Second Commandments.

Jer. 17, 5. Cursed be the man that trusteth in man and maketh flesh his arm and whose heart departeth from the Lord.

> With might of ours can naught be done,
>   Soon were our loss effected;
> But for us fights the Valiant One,
>   Whom God Himself elected.
> Ask ye, Who is this?
> Jesus Christ it is,
> Of Sabaoth Lord,
> And there's none other God;
>   He holds the field forever. (262, 2.)

48. David and Jonathan
1 Sam. 17—20

Jonathan's Friendship. And as David returned from the slaughter of the Philistine, the soul of Jonathan, the son of Saul, was knit with the soul of David; and Jonathan loved him as his own soul.

And Saul took him that day and would let him go no more home to his father's house.

Then Jonathan and David made a covenant because he loved him as his own soul.

Saul's Jealousy. And it came to pass that the women came out of all the cities, singing and with instruments of music, to meet King Saul. And they said, "Saul hath slain his thousands and David his ten thousands."

And Saul was very wroth, and the saying displeased him; and he said, "They have ascribed unto David ten thousands and to me but thousands; and what can he have more but the kingdom?" And Saul eyed David from that day and forward.

And on the morrow the evil spirit from God came upon Saul, and David played with his hand as at other times; and there was a javelin in Saul's hand. And he cast the javelin; for he said, "I will smite David even to the wall with it." And David avoided out of his presence twice.

And Saul was afraid of David because the LORD was with him and was departed from Saul. Therefore Saul removed him from him and made him his captain over a thousand.

And David behaved himself wisely in all his ways; and the LORD was with him. And Saul gave him Michal, his daughter, to wife.

Jonathan Intercedes for David. And Saul spake to

Jonathan, his son, and to all his servants that they should kill David.

And Jonathan spake good of David unto Saul, his father, and said unto him, "Let not the king sin against his servant David, because he hath not sinned against thee and because his works have been to thee-ward very good; for he did put his life in his hand and slew the Philistine. Thou sawest it and didst rejoice; wherefore, then, wilt thou sin against innnocent blood?"

And Saul sware, "As the LORD liveth, he shall not be slain."

And the evil spirit from the LORD was upon Saul as he sat in his house with his javelin in his hand; and David played with his hand. And Saul sought to smite David even to the wall with the javelin; but he slipped away out of Saul's presence, and he smote the javelin into the wall. And David fled and escaped that night.

David Lays His Case before Jonathan. And David came and said before Jonathan, "What have I done? What is mine iniquity, and what is my sin before thy father that he seeketh my life? Truly, as the LORD liveth, there is but a step between me and death."

And Jonathan said, "When I have sounded my father if there be good toward thee or evil, then I will show it thee.

"In three days come to the place where thou didst hide thyself; and I will shoot three arrows as though I shot at a mark. And I will send a lad, saying, 'Go, find out the arrows.' If I say unto the lad, 'Behold, the arrows are on this side of thee,' then come thou; for there is peace to thee and no hurt.

"But if I say, 'Behold, the arrows are beyond thee,' go thy way; for the LORD hath sent thee away.

"And as touching the matter which thou **and I have**

spoken of, behold, the LORD be between thee and me forever." So David hid himself in the field.

Jonathan Risks His Own Life for David. And when the new moon [1] was come, the king sat him down to eat meat. And David's place was empty.

"And he shot an arrow"

And Saul said unto Jonathan, his son, "Wherefore cometh not the son of Jesse to meat?" And Jonathan sought to excuse David.

Then Saul's anger was kindled against Jonathan, and he

---

[1] According to the Law of Moses the first day of every month was observed by a special sacrifice. The priests proclaimed the feast by the sound of the trumpet. All members of the family would gather for the solemn celebration. David, the king's son-in-law, was expected to be present, and Saul considered his absence a sign of disrespect.

said unto him, "Thou son of the perverse, rebellious woman,[2] do not I know that thou hast chosen the son of Jesse to thine own confusion? [3] For as long as the son of Jesse liveth upon the ground, thou shalt not be established nor thy kingdom. Wherefore, now send and fetch him unto me, for he shall surely die."

And Jonathan answered, "Wherefore shall he be slain? What hath he done?"

And Saul cast a javelin at him to smite him, whereby Jonathan knew that it was determined of his father to slay David.

Parting of David and Jonathan. And in the morning Jonathan went out into the field at the time appointed with David, and a little lad with him. And as the lad ran, he shot an arrow beyond him and said, "Is not the arrow beyond thee? Make speed, haste, stay not."

And Jonathan's lad gathered up the arrows and came to his master; but he knew not anything of the matter.

And Jonathan gave his artillery [4] unto his lad and said unto him, "Go, carry them to the city."

And as soon as the lad was gone, David arose; and they kissed one another and wept one with another, but David most of all.

And Jonathan said to David, "Go in peace, forasmuch as we have sworn both of us in the name of the LORD, saying, 'The LORD be between me and thee and between my seed and thy seed forever.'"

And he arose and departed; and Jonathan went into the city.

---

[2] The queen, who no doubt, like Jonathan, feared and loved the Lord.
[3] To your own ruin and disgrace.
[4] Weapons — bow, quiver, and arrows.

Eighth Commandment.

Prov. 31, 8. 9. Open thy mouth for the dumb in the cause of all such as are appointed to destruction. Open thy mouth, judge righteously, and plead the cause of the poor and needy.

Blest be the tie that binds	We share our mutual woes,
Our hearts in Christian love;	Our mutual burdens bear;
The fellowship of kindred minds	And often for each other flows
Is like to that above.	The sympathizing tear. (464, 1. 3.)

49. Persecution of David and Saul's Death
1 Sam. 21—31. 2 Sam. 1

David Aided by Ahimelech, the Priest. Then came David to Nob,[1] to Ahimelech, the priest. And, being hungry, the priest gave him the showbread, for there was no other bread there.

And David said, "Is there not here under thine hand spear or sword?"

And the priest said, "The sword of Goliath, the Philistine, whom thou slewest, is here; if thou wilt take that, take it."

And David said, "There is none like that; give it me."

And David arose and fled from Saul. And about four hundred men gathered themselves unto him; and he became a captain over them.

Doeg the Traitor. And Saul said unto his servants, "All of you have conspired against me, and there is none that showeth me that my son hath made a league with the son of Jesse."

---

[1] Nob was a city in the tribe of Benjamin, in the vicinity of Jerusalem, belonging to the priests, and the place where the Tabernacle was stationed in the time of Saul. In the Tabernacle twelve unleavened loaves were placed upon a table. The number of twelve loaves represented the twelve tribes of Israel. Fresh loaves were placed on the table every Sabbath-day, and the old loaves were eaten by the priests.

Then answered Doeg, the Edomite, "I saw the son of Jesse coming to Ahimelech. And he enquired the LORD for him and gave him victuals and the sword of Goliath."

Then the king sent to call Ahimelech and the priests that were with him. And the king commanded his footmen to slay the priests. But they would not lay their hand upon the priests of the LORD.

And the king said to Doeg, "Turn thou and fall upon the priests." And Doeg slew the priests, fourscore and five persons.

David Spares Saul. And it was told Saul, "Behold, David is in the wilderness of Engedi."

And Saul took three thousand chosen men and went to seek David. And he came by the way where was a cave; and Saul went in; and David and his men remained in the sides of the cave.

And the men of David said, "Behold, this is the day in which the LORD will deliver thine enemy into thine hand."

Then David arose and cut off the skirt of Saul's robe privily. And he said unto his men, "The LORD forbid that I should stretch forth mine hand against my master, seeing he is the anointed of the LORD."

And when Saul rose up out of the cave, David also went out and cried after Saul, saying, "My lord the king! Behold, this day thine eyes have seen how that the LORD had delivered thee to-day into mine hand. Yea, see the skirt of thy robe in my hand. The LORD judge between me and thee; but mine hand shall not be upon thee."

And Saul wept and said, "My son David, thou art more righteous than I. The LORD reward thee good for that thou hast done unto me this day." And Saul went home.

At this time Samuel died; and all the Israelites lamented him and buried him at Ramah.

Saul's Fear. And it came to pass that the Philistines gathered their armies together to fight with Israel. And when Saul saw the host of the Philistines, he was afraid, and his heart greatly trembled. And when Saul inquired of the LORD, the LORD answered him not.

The Witch of Endor. Then said Saul unto his servants, "Seek me a woman that hath a familiar spirit,[2] that I may go to her and enquire of her."

And his servant said to him, "Behold, there is a woman that hath a familiar spirit at Endor."

And Saul disguised himself and came to the woman by night. And the woman said unto him, "Whom shall I bring up unto thee?"

And he said, "Bring me up Samuel."

And Samuel[3] said to Saul, "The LORD hath rent the kingdom out of thine hand and given it to thy neighbor, even to David; and to-morrow shalt thou and thy sons be with me."

The Shameful Death of Saul. Now, the Philistines fought against Israel; and the men of Israel fled from before the Philistines and fell down slain in Mount Gilboa. And the Philistines slew Saul's three sons.

And the battle went sore against Saul, and the archers hit him; and he was sore wounded.

Then said Saul unto his armor-bearer, "Draw thy sword and thrust me through therewith lest the Philistines come and thrust me through and abuse me."

But his armor-bearer would not, for he was sore afraid. Therefore Saul took a sword and fell upon it. And when his

---

[2] An evil spirit, familiar with things that will happen; a fortune-telling spirit.

[3] Not the real Samuel, but an evil spirit who had taken the form of Samuel.

DAVID BRINGING THE ARK INTO JERUSALEM

armor-bearer saw that Saul was dead, he fell likewise upon his sword and died with him.

And it came to pass on the morrow, when the Philistines came to strip the slain, that they found Saul and his three sons fallen. And they cut off his head and fastened his body to the wall of Bethshan.

Saul Yet Honored. And when the inhabitants of Jabesh-gilead heard of that which the Philistines had done to Saul, they arose and took the bodies of Saul and his sons from the wall of Bethshan and came to Jabesh and burned them there. And they took their bones and buried them under a tree at Jabesh and fasted seven days.

And David lamented over Saul and Jonathan, saying, "Ye daughters of Israel, weep over Saul. How are the mighty fallen in the midst of the battle! O Jonathan, thou wast slain in thine high places. I am distressed for thee, my brother Jonathan; very pleasant hast thou been unto me; thy love to me was wonderful."

Second, Fifth, and Eighth Commandments. — Fifth Petition.

Matt. 5, 44. 45. Love your enemies, bless them that curse you, do good to them that hate you, and pray for them which despitefully use you and persecute you, that ye may be the children of your Father which is in heaven.

> In God, my faithful God,
> I trust when dark my road;
> Though many woes o'ertake me,
> Yet He will not forsake me;
> His love it is doth send them
> And, when 'tis best, will end them. (526, 1.)

50. David Becomes King
2 Sam. 1—9

David King of Judah; Later of All Israel. And David went up to Hebron. And the men of Judah came, and there they anointed David king over the house of Judah.

But Abner, the captain of Saul's host, took Ishbosheth, the son of Saul, and made him king over Israel.

Now, there was long war between the house of Saul and the house of David. And when Abner and Ishbosheth had died, then came all the tribes of Israel to David unto Hebron and anointed David king over Israel.

Enemies Conquered; Jerusalem Made Capital City. And the king and his men went to Jerusalem against the Jebusites, and took the stronghold of Zion, and dwelt in the fort, and called it the City of David.

But when the Philistines heard that, they came up to seek David. And David came and smote them, for the LORD delivered them into his hand.

And after this he smote Moab and the children of Ammon, so that they became his servants and brought gifts.

And David gat him a name when he returned from the smiting of the Syrians, and all they of Edom became David's servants; for the LORD preserved David whithersoever he went.

The Ark Brought to Jerusalem. And David gathered together all the chosen men of Israel, thirty thousand, and went with all the people to bring up the Ark of God from Kirjathjearim. And they brought up the Ark of the LORD with shouting and with the sound of the trumpet, and set it in his place, in the midst of the Tabernacle that David had pitched for it; and David offered burnt offerings and peace-offerings before the LORD.

Jonathan's Friendship Rewarded. And David said, "Is there yet any that is left of the house of Saul that I may show him kindness for Jonathan's sake?"

And it was said unto the king, "Jonathan hath yet a son, which is lame on both his feet." Then King David sent and fetched him.

Now, when Mephibosheth, the son of Jonathan, was come

"And they brought up the Ark"

unto David, he fell on his face and did reverence. And David said unto him, "Fear not; for I will surely show thee kindness for Jonathan thy father's sake and will restore thee all the land of Saul, thy father; and thou shalt eat bread at my table continually."

So Mephibosheth dwelt in Jerusalem; for he did eat continually at the king's table.

Length of David's Reign. David was thirty years old

when he began to reign, and he reigned forty years. In Hebron he reigned over Judah seven years and six months, and in Jerusalem he reigned thirty and three years over all Israel and Judah.

David Plans to Build a Temple. And it came to pass, when the king sat in his house and the LORD had given him rest round about from all his enemies, that the king said unto Nathan, the prophet, "See, now, I dwell in a house of cedar, but the Ark of God dwelleth within curtains." [1)]

And Nathan said to the king, "Go, do all that is in thine heart; for the LORD is with thee."

Prophecy Concerning the Son of David, Jesus Christ. And it came to pass that night that the word of the LORD came unto Nathan, saying, "Go and tell My servant David, 'Thus saith the LORD, "Shalt thou build Me a house for Me to dwell in? *When thy days be fulfilled and thou shalt sleep with thy fathers, I will set up thy seed after thee, and I will establish His kingdom. He shall build a house for My name, and I will stablish the throne of His kingdom forever. I will be His Father, and He shall be My Son.*"'"

Table of Duties: Of Government.

Matt. 22, 42. What think ye of Christ? Whose son is He? They say unto Him, The son of David.

> Hail to the Lord's Anointed,
>   Great David's greater Son!
> Hail, in the time appointed
>   His reign on earth begun!
> He comes to break oppression,
>   To set the captive free,
> To take away transgression,
>   And rule in equity. (59, 1.)

---

1) Goatskins, with which the Tabernacle was **covered.**

51. David's Fall and Repentance
2 Sam. 11. 12

Adultery. David sent Joab, and his servants with him, and all Israel; and they destroyed the children of Ammon and besieged Rabbah.

But David tarried at Jerusalem. And it came to pass that he walked upon the roof of his house and saw Bathsheba, the wife of Uriah. And the woman was very beautiful to look upon. So he sent messengers and took her.

Murder. And David wrote a letter to Joab, saying, "Set ye Uriah in the forefront of the hottest battle and retire ye from him that he may be smitten and die."

And it came to pass, when Joab observed the city, that he assigned Uriah unto a place where he knew that valiant men were. And the men of the city went out and fought, and there fell some of the servants of David; and Uriah died also.

Then Joab sent and told David. And the wife of Uriah mourned for her husband. And when the mourning was past, she became David's wife.

Nathan Pronounces God's Sentence upon David. But the thing displeased the LORD. And the LORD sent Nathan unto David. And he came unto him and said unto him, "There were two men in one city, the one rich and the other poor. The rich man had exceeding many flocks and herds; but the poor man had nothing save one little ewe lamb, which he had bought and nourished up; and it grew up together with him and with his children; it did eat of his own meat, and drank of his own cup, and lay in his bosom, and was unto him as a daughter.

"And there came a traveler unto the rich man, and he spared to take of his own flock and of his own herd, but took the poor man's lamb and dressed it for the man that was come to him."

And David's anger was greatly kindled, and he said, "As the LORD liveth, the man that hath done this thing shall surely die."

And Nathan said to David, "Thou art the man. Thus

"Thou art the man"

saith the LORD God of Israel, 'I anointed thee king over Israel, and I delivered thee out of the hand of Saul; wherefore hast thou despised the commandment of the LORD to do evil in His sight? Thou hast taken Uriah's wife to be thy wife and hast slain him with the sword of the children of Ammon. Now, therefore, the sword shall never depart from thine house. Behold, I will raise up evil against thee out of thine own house.'"

David's Repentance. And David said unto Nathan, "I have sinned against the LORD."

And Nathan said unto David, "The LORD also hath put away thy sin; thou shalt not die. But the child that is born unto thee shall surely die." And Nathan departed unto his house.

And the LORD struck the child of the wife of Uriah, and it was very sick and died.

And Bathsheba bare another son, and he called his name Solomon; and the LORD loved him.

Fifth and Sixth Commandments. — Confession.

Ps. 51, 10. Create in me a clean heart, O God; and renew a right spirit within me.

> Destroy in me the lust of sin,
> From all impureness make me clean;
> Oh, grant me power and strength, my God,
> To strive against my flesh and blood. (398, 2.)

---

52. Absalom's Rebellion
2 Sam. 14—19

The Person of Absalom. In all Israel there was none to be so much praised as Absalom for his beauty; from the sole of his foot even to the crown of his head there was no blemish in him. And when he polled his head, the hair of his head weighed two hundred shekels.[1]

Absalom Steals the Hearts of the People. And Absalom prepared him chariots and horses and fifty men to run before him.

And he rose up early and stood beside the way of the gate; and when any man that had a controversy came to the king for judgment, then Absalom called unto him and said,

---

1) Six pounds.

"Of what city art thou? See, thy matters are good and right; but there is no man deputed of the king [2] to hear thee. Oh, that I were made judge in the land, that every man which hath any suit or cause might come unto me, and I would do him justice!"

And when any man came nigh to him to do him obeisance, he put forth his hand and took him and kissed him. And on this manner did Absalom to all Israel and so stole the hearts of the men of Israel.

The Rebellion. And Absalom went to Hebron and sent spies throughout all the tribes of Israel, saying, "As soon as ye hear the sound of the trumpet, then ye shall say, 'Absalom reigneth in Hebron.'"

And the conspiracy was strong; for the people increased continually with Absalom.

And there came a messenger to David, saying, "The hearts of the men of Israel are after Absalom." [3]

David's Flight. And David said unto his servants, "Arise and let us flee; for we shall not else escape from Absalom."

And the king went forth and all his household after him. And all the country wept with a loud voice, and all the people passed over.

And David passed over the brook Kidron,[4] and went up Mount Olivet, and wept as he went up, and had his head covered, and he went barefoot.

But Shimei, a man of the house of Saul, came forth, and cursed David, and cast stones at him, and said, "Come out, come out, thou bloody man and thou man of Belial!"

---

2) No one appointed by the king.
3) God had said to David through Nathan, "Behold, I will raise up evil against thee out of thine own house."
4) The brook Kidron, flowing through the valley of Kidron, is a winter torrent; that is, it is dry in summer. The valley of Kidron lies between Jerusalem and Mount Olivet.

But David said, "Let him curse, for the LORD hath bidden him."

And Absalom and all the men of Israel came to Jerusalem.

Absalom Slain. And David numbered the people that were with him and set captains over them. And the king

"And his head caught"

commanded them, saying, "Deal gently with the young man, even with Absalom."

So the people went out into the field against Israel; and the battle was in the wood of Ephraim, where the people of Israel were slain before the servants of David.

And Absalom met the servants of David. And he rode upon a mule; and the mule went under the thick boughs of a great oak, and his head caught hold of the oak, and he was taken up between the heaven and the earth; and the mule that was under him went away.

And a certain man told Joab. Then Joab took three darts and thrust them through the heart of Absalom.

And Joab blew the trumpet, and the people returned from pursuing after Israel; for Joab held back the people.

And when David heard that Absalom was dead, he wept and said, "O my son Absalom! my son, my son Absalom! Would God I had died for thee! O Absalom, my son, my son!"

Fourth Commandment.

Prov. 30, 17. The eye that mocketh at his father and despiseth to obey his mother, the ravens of the valley shall pick it out, and the young eagles shall eat it.

>Oh, that the Lord would guide my ways
>   To keep His statutes still!
>Oh, that my God would grant me grace
>   To know and do His will! (416, 1.)

---

53. Solomon
1 Kings 1—11. 1 Chron. 28. 29

Solomon Anointed. Now, when King David was old and stricken in years, he caused Zadok, the priest, and Nathan, the prophet, to anoint Solomon as king over Israel.

And they blew the trumpet; and all the people said, "God save King Solomon!"

David's Final Instructions to Solomon. Now, the days of David drew nigh that he should die, and he charged Solomon, his son, saying, "I go the way of all the earth; be thou strong therefore and show thyself a man; and walk in the ways of the Lord, thy God, to keep His statutes, commandments, judgments, and testimonies, that thou mayest prosper in all that thou doest.

"Take heed now; for the Lord hath chosen thee to build a house for the sanctuary." Then David gave to Solomon the pattern of the house of the Lord and of the chambers.

Then the princes of Israel gave for the house of God gold, silver, brass, iron, and precious stones; with perfect heart they offered willingly to the LORD. And David rejoiced with great joy and blessed the LORD.

So David slept with his fathers and was buried in the city of David. Then sat Solomon upon the throne of David, his father; and his kingdom was established greatly.

Solomon's Prayer. And Solomon loved the LORD, walking in the statutes of David, his father. And he went to Gibeon to sacrifice there.

In Gibeon the LORD appeared to Solomon in a dream by night; and God said, "Ask what I shall give thee."

And Solomon said, "Thou hast showed unto David, my father, great mercy and hast given him a son to sit on his throne. And now, O LORD, my God, Thou hast made Thy servant king, and I am but a little child; I know not how to go out or come in. Give therefore Thy servant an understanding heart to judge Thy people that I may discern between good and bad."

And the speech pleased the LORD that Solomon had asked this thing. And God said, "Because thou hast asked this thing and hast not asked for long life, neither riches, behold, I have done according to thy word. Lo, I have given thee a wise and an understanding heart. And I have also given thee that which thou hast not asked, both riches and honor. And if thou wilt walk in My ways, as thy father David did walk, then I will lengthen thy days."

And Solomon awoke; and, behold, it was a dream. And he came to Jerusalem and offered burnt offerings.

Solomon's Judgment. Then came there two harlots unto the king. And the one said, "O my lord, I and this woman dwell in one house; and her child died in the night because she overlaid it. And she arose at midnight and took my son from beside me while thine handmaiden slept and laid her dead child in my bosom. And when I rose in the morning to give my child suck, behold, it was dead; but when I had considered it in the morning, behold, it was not my son."

"Give her the living child"

And the other woman said, "Nay; but the living is my son, and the dead is thy son."

And the king said, "Bring me a sword." And they brought a sword before the king.

And he said, "Divide the living child in two and give half to the one and half to the other."

Then spake the woman whose the living child was, for her bowels yearned [1] upon her son, and she said, "O my lord, give her the living child and in no wise slay it."

But the other said, "Let it be neither mine nor thine, but divide it."

Then the king answered and said, "Give her the living child and in no wise slay it; she is the mother thereof."

And all Israel heard of the judgment, and they saw that the wisdom of God was in him to do judgment.

Prayer. Fourth Petition: Good Government.

Matt. 6, 33. Seek ye first the kingdom of God and His righteousness, and all these things shall be added unto you.

The powers ordained by Thee With heavenly wisdom bless;
May they Thy servants be And rule in righteousness!
O Lord, stretch forth Thy mighty hand And guard and bless
    our Fatherland.   (580, 4.)

---

54. The Building of the Temple and Solomon's Death
1 Kings 5—8. 11

Solomon Prepares to Build the Temple. And Solomon sent to Hiram, king of Tyre, saying, "Behold, I purpose to build an house unto the name of the LORD. Therefore command thou that they hew me cedar-trees out of Lebanon; and unto thee will I give hire for thy servants." And Hiram gave Solomon cedar- and fir-trees.

And Solomon sent thirty thousand men to Lebanon. And Solomon had threescore and ten thousand that bare burdens and fourscore thousand hewers in the mountains, beside the chief of Solomon's officers, three thousand and three hundred, which ruled over the people that wrought in the work. And

---

[1] She yearned with the strongest feeling for her child.

they brought great stones and costly stones and hewed stones to lay the foundation.

The Building of the Temple. In the four hundred and eightieth year after the children of Israel were come out of Egypt, Solomon began to build the house of the Lord.

The length thereof was threescore cubits, the breadth twenty cubits, and the height thirty cubits.

The porch before the Temple, twenty cubits was the length and ten cubits the breadth thereof.

And against the wall of the house he built chambers round about.

And the house was built of stone made ready before it was brought thither, so that there was neither hammer nor ax nor any tool of iron heard in the house while it was in building.

The Most Holy Place. And he built twenty cubits on the side of the house with boards of cedar for the Most Holy Place to set there the Ark of the Covenant. And the whole house he overlaid with gold. Seven years was he in building it.

The Dedication. And all the men of Israel assembled themselves unto King Solomon; and the priests brought in the Ark of the Covenant of the Lord unto his place, to the Most Holy Place. And when the priests were come out of the Holy Place, the glory of God filled the house of the Lord.

And Solomon stood before the altar of the Lord and spread forth his hands toward heaven, and he said, "Lord God of Israel, behold, the heaven and heaven of heavens cannot contain Thee; how much less this house! Yet have Thou respect unto the prayer of Thy servant that Thine eyes may be open toward this house night and day.

"When Thy people be smitten down before the enemy; when heaven is shut up and there is no rain; if there be in the land famine; if there be pestilence, whatsoever plague, whatsoever sickness, there be; what prayer and supplication soever be made in this house, hear Thou in heaven and forgive Thy people that have sinned against Thee."

And Solomon arose from before the altar of the LORD and blessed all the congregation of Israel.

"And Solomon stood before the altar"

And Solomon offered a sacrifice unto the LORD, two and twenty thousand oxen and an hundred and twenty thousand sheep. At that time Solomon held a feast and all Israel with him.[1]

---

[1] The Temple was begun in the fourth year of Solomon's reign. There were 183,000 Jews and strangers employed on it. The arrangements of the Temple were identical with those of the Tabernacle, but the dimensions of every part were exactly double those of the Tabernacle. It was the most magnificent edifice in the world at that time. (1005 B. C.)

Solomon's Last Days. But Solomon loved many strange women. When he was old, his wives turned away his heart after other gods. And Solomon did evil in the sight of the Lord.

And the Lord was angry and said, "Forasmuch as thou hast not kept My covenant, I will rend the kingdom from thee. Notwithstanding in thy days I will not do it for David thy father's sake."

And it came to pass at that time when Jeroboam went out of Jerusalem that the prophet Ahijah found him in the way; and he had clad himself with a new garment; and they two were alone in the field.

And Ahijah caught the new garment that was on him and rent it in twelve pieces. And he said to Jeroboam, "Take thee ten pieces; for thus saith the Lord, the God of Israel, 'Behold, I will rend the kingdom out of the hand of Solomon and will give ten tribes to thee.'"

Solomon's Death. And the time that Solomon reigned over all Israel was forty years. And Solomon slept with his fathers and was buried in the city of David. And Rehoboam reigned in his stead.

First and Third Commandments.

Ps. 26, 6—8. So will I compass Thine altar, O Lord, that I may publish with the voice of thanksgiving and tell of all Thy wondrous works. Lord, I have loved the habitation of Thy house and the place where Thine honor dwelleth.

> To this temple, where we call Thee,
> Come, O Lord of hosts, to-day;
> With Thy wonted loving-kindness
> Hear Thy servants as they pray
> And Thy fullest benediction
> Shed within these walls alway. (466, 2.)

SUMMARY STUDY OF THE FIFTH PERIOD

How long did each of the three kings of this period reign over Israel?

Give a short biography of each, touching upon such topics as ancestry, youth, training, personal fitness, main incidents in life, weaknesses, benefits to the people, and so on.

What was done during this period to improve public worship? (Think of the Tabernacle, the Temple, and the inspired writings of David and Solomon.)

What direct prophecy concerning Christ occurred in this period? Show by a few psalms that David prophesied very clearly of Christ during this period. What was the purpose of the Psalms?

Name some incidents from the lives of Saul, David, and Solomon that should be either a warning or a good example to us, supporting your statement in each case, if possible, with some other word of God.

"THINE HOUSE AND THY KINGDOM SHALL BE ESTABLISHED FOREVER BEFORE THEE; THY THRONE SHALL BE ESTABLISHED FOREVER." 2 Sam. 7, 16.

Advanced Bible History.

SIXTH PERIOD

FROM THE DIVISION OF THE KINGDOM TO THE CAPTIVITY AT BABYLON

(Ca. 975—606 B. C.)

"When Rehoboam, Solomon's son, succeeded to the throne of Israel, ten of the twelve tribes revolted and elected their own king, Jeroboam; and from that time on there were two kingdoms, the tribes of Judah and Benjamin being ruled by kings from the house of David, while the kings of Israel ruled the ten tribes. Of the latter, nineteen in number (not counting Tibni), not one was a godly man; of the former, Asa, Jehoshaphat, Joash, Amaziah, Uzziah, Jotham, Hezekiah, and Josiah upheld the worship of the true God more or less."—Rupprecht, *Bible History References.*

In this period fall the activities of the prophets Elijah, Elisha, and Jonah. In general, it is one of the darkest periods of Israel's history. Idolatry and ungodly life were common, until finally God in His just wrath had both the ten tribes and Judah led into captivity, the former never to return, the latter to return after seventy years. The time of Christ was approaching.

55. The Division of the Kingdom
1 Kings 12—14

Rehoboam's Folly. Rehoboam went to Shechem; for all Israel were come to Shechem to make him king.

And Jeroboam and all the congregation of Israel came and spake unto Rehoboam, saying, "Thy father made our yoke grievous; now, therefore, make thou the grievous service and the heavy yoke lighter, and we will serve thee."

And King Rehoboam consulted with the old men that stood before Solomon and said, "How do ye advise that I may answer this people?"

And they spake unto him, "If thou wilt grant the request of this people this day, then they will be thy servants forever."

But he forsook the counsel of the old men which they had given him and consulted with the young men that were grown up with him.

And the young men answered, "Thus shalt thou speak unto this people, 'My father did lade you with a heavy yoke, I will add to your yoke; my father hath chastised you with whips, but I will chastise you with scorpions.' " 1)

So Rehoboam, the king, answered the people roughly, after the counsel of the young men.

So when Israel saw that the king hearkened not unto

"Behold thy gods, O Israel"

them, the people answered, "What portion have we in David? To your tents, O Israel!"

So Israel rebelled against the house of David and made Jeroboam king over Israel. There was none that followed the house of David but the tribe of Judah with the tribe of Benjamin.2)

---

1) A whip with knots or small stones was called a scorpion because, like the sting of the scorpion, this whip would cause great pain.

2) The Kingdom of Israel had nineteen kings and was destroyed by Shalmaneser; the Kingdom of Judah had twenty kings and was destroyed by Nebuchadnezzar.

Jeroboam's Idolatry. And Jeroboam said in his heart, "Now shall the kingdom return to the house of David if this people go up to do sacrifice in the house of the LORD at Jerusalem."

And he made two calves of gold and said unto the people, "It is too much for you to go up to Jerusalem; behold thy gods, O Israel, which brought thee up out of the land of Egypt." And he set the one in Bethel, and the other put he in Dan.

And this thing became a sin; for the people went to worship before the one, even unto Dan. And Jeroboam offered upon the altar which he had made at Bethel.

Jeroboam's Punishment Foretold. At that time Abijah, the son of Jeroboam, fell sick. And Jeroboam said to his wife, "Arise and disguise thyself that thou be not known to be the wife of Jeroboam; and get thee to Shiloh. Behold, there is Ahijah, the prophet, which told me that I should be king over this people. He shall tell thee what shall become of the child." And Jeroboam's wife did so.

But Ahijah could not see by reason of his age. And the LORD said unto Ahijah, "Behold, the wife of Jeroboam cometh; thus and thus shalt thou say unto her."

And as she came in at the door, Ahijah said, "Come in, thou wife of Jeroboam; why feignest thou thyself to be another? For I am sent to thee with heavy tidings. Go, tell Jeroboam, 'Thus saith the LORD God of Israel, "I exalted thee from among the people, and made thee prince over My people Israel, and rent the kingdom away from the house of David, and gave it thee; and yet thou hast not been as My servant David, who kept My commandments and who followed Me with all his heart. Thou hast made thee other gods; therefore, behold, I will bring evil upon the house of Jeroboam till it be all gone. Him that dieth of Jeroboam in the city

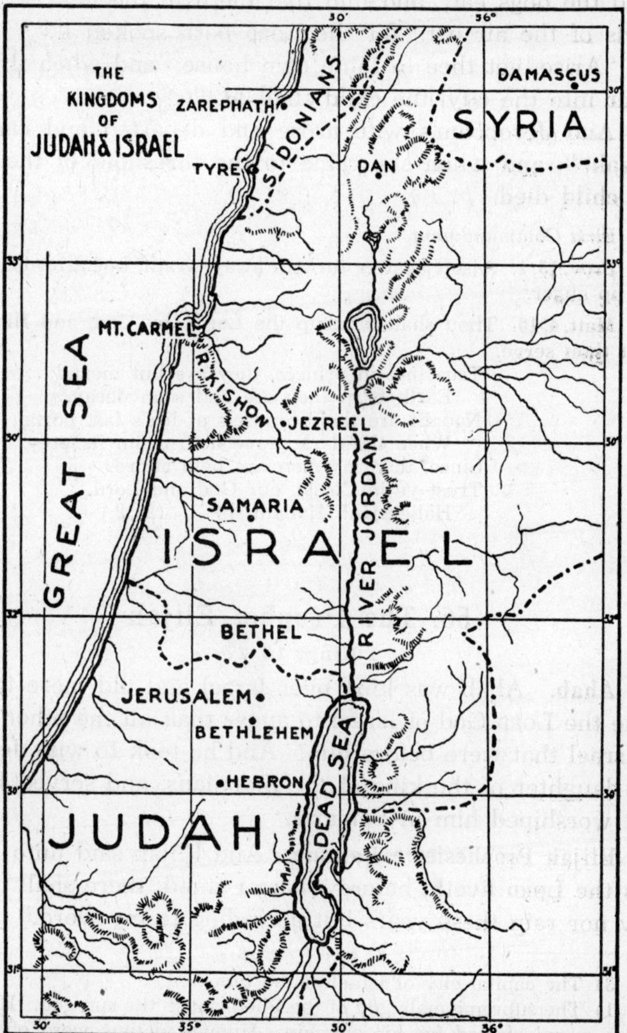
THE
KINGDOMS
OF
JUDAH & ISRAEL
ZAREPHATH
SIDONIANS
DAMASCUS
SYRIA
TYRE
DAN
MT. CARMEL
R. KISHON
JEZREEL
GREAT SEA
SAMARIA
RIVER JORDAN
ISRAEL
BETHEL
JERUSALEM
BETHLEHEM
HEBRON
DEAD SEA
JUDAH
30'
35°
36°
33°
32°
31°

shall the dogs eat; and him that dieth in the field shall the fowls of the air eat; for the Lord hath spoken it."'

"Arise, get thee to thine own house; and when thy feet enter into the city, the child shall die."

And Jeroboam's wife arose and departed and came to Tirzah;[3] and when she came to the threshold of the door, the child died.

First Commandment.

Prov. 15, 1. A soft answer turneth away wrath, but grievous words stir up anger.

Matt. 4, 10. Thou shalt worship the Lord, thy God, and Him only shalt thou serve.

> Trust not in princes, they are but mortal;
>   Earth-born they are and soon decay.
> Naught are their counsels at life's last portal,
>   When the dark grave doth claim its prey.
> Since, then, no man can help afford,
> Trust ye in Christ, our God and Lord.
>   Hallelujah! Hallelujah!   (26, 2.)

56. The Prophet Elijah
1 Kings 16. 17

Ahab. Ahab was king over Israel and did more to provoke the Lord God of Israel to anger than all the other kings of Israel that were before him. And he took to wife Jezebel, the daughter of the king of the Zidonians, and served Baal[1] and worshiped him in Samaria.

Elijah Prophesies a Famine. And Elijah said unto Ahab, "As the Lord liveth, before whom I stand, there shall not be dew nor rain these years but according to my word."

---

3) The capital city of Israel at the time.
1) The supreme male god of the Phenicians; the sun god. Elevated places were selected for his worship. Human victims were offered to him. Ahab erected a temple in honor of this idol in his capital, **Samaria**.

And the word of the Lord came unto him, saying, "Get thee hence and hide thyself by the brook Cherith, that is before Jordan. And thou shalt drink of the brook; and I have commanded the ravens to feed thee there."

"And the ravens brought him bread and flesh"

So Elijah went and did according unto the word of the Lord and dwelt by the brook Cherith. And the ravens brought him bread and flesh in the morning and in the evening; and he drank of the brook.

And after a while the brook dried up because there had been no rain in the land.

Elijah at Zarephath. And the word of the Lord came unto him, saying, "Arise, get thee to Zarephath, which belongeth to Zidon; behold, I have commanded a widow woman there to sustain thee."

So Elijah arose and went to Zarephath. And, behold, the widow woman was there gathering sticks.

And he called to her and said, "Fetch me, I pray thee, a little water that I may drink and a morsel of bread."

And she said, "As the LORD liveth, I have not a cake but a handful of meal in a barrel and a little oil in a cruse;[2] and, behold, I am gathering sticks that I may go in and dress it for me and my son that we may eat it and die."

And Elijah said unto her, "Fear not; go and do as thou hast said; but make me a little cake first and bring it unto me and after make for thee and for thy son.

"For thus saith the LORD, 'The barrel of meal shall not waste, neither shall the cruse of oil fail.'"

And she went and did according to the saying of Elijah; and she and he and her house did eat many days. And the barrel of meal wasted not, neither did the cruse of oil fail, according to the word of the LORD which the LORD spake to Elijah.

The Widow's Son Restored. And the widow's son fell sick; and his sickness was so sore that there was no breath left in him.

And she said unto Elijah, "O thou man of God, art thou come unto me to call my sin to remembrance and to slay my son?"

And he said unto her, "Give me thy son."

And he took him out of her bosom and carried him up in the loft and laid him upon his own bed. And Elijah cried unto the LORD and said, "O LORD, my God, I pray Thee, let this child's soul come into him again."

---

2) A bottle, probably of earthenware, to hold olive-oil.

And the Lord heard the voice of Elijah; and the soul of the child came into him again, and he revived.

And Elijah took the child and brought him down out of the chamber and delivered him unto his mother; and Elijah said, "See, thy son liveth."

And the woman said to Elijah, "Now by this I know that thou art a man of God and that the word of the Lord in thy mouth is truth."

First Article.

1 Pet. 5, 7. Cast all your care upon Him; for He careth for you.

> Give us this day our daily bread
> And let us all be clothed and fed.
> From war and strife be our Defense,
> From famine and from pestilence,
> That we may live in godly peace,
> Free from all care and avarice. (458, 5.)

---

57. Elijah and the Prophets of Baal

1 Kings 18

Elijah Sent to Ahab. And the word of the Lord came to Elijah in the third year, saying, "Go, show thyself unto Ahab; and I will send rain upon the earth." And there was a sore famine in Samaria.

And Elijah went; and when Ahab saw Elijah, Ahab said unto him, "Art thou he that troubleth Israel?"

And he answered, "I have not troubled Israel, but thou and thy father's house, in that ye have forsaken the commandments of the Lord and thou hast followed Baalim.

"Now, therefore, send and gather to me all Israel unto Mount Carmel and the four hundred and fifty prophets of Baal and the four hundred prophets of the groves which eat at Jezebel's table."

And Ahab gathered all the children of Israel and the prophets of Baal together unto Mount Carmel.

The Challenge. And Elijah came unto all the people and said, "How long halt ye between two opinions? If the Lord be God, follow Him; but if Baal, then follow him."

And the people answered him not a word.

Then said Elijah, "I, even I only, remain a prophet of the Lord; but the prophets of Baal are four hundred and fifty men.

"Give us two bullocks, and let them choose one bullock for themselves, and cut it in pieces, and lay it on wood, and put no fire under; and I will dress the other bullock and lay it on wood and put no fire under; and call ye on the name of your gods, and I will call on the name of the Lord; and the God that answereth by fire, let him be God."

And all the people answered and said, "It is well spoken."

The Prophets of Baal. And the prophets of Baal took the bullock and dressed it and called on the name of Baal from morning even until noon, saying, "O Baal, hear us." But there was no voice nor any that answered. And they leaped upon the altar which was made.

And at noon Elijah mocked them and said, "Cry aloud, for he is a god; either he is talking, or he is pursuing, or he is in a journey, or peradventure he sleepeth and must be awaked."

And they cried aloud and cut themselves after their manner with knives and lancets till the blood gushed out upon them. And they cried until the time of the evening sacrifice; and there was neither voice nor any to answer nor any that regarded.

"The Lord Is God." And Elijah said unto all the people, "Come near unto me." And all the people came near unto him.

And he repaired the altar of the LORD that was broken down. And Elijah took twelve stones, according to the number of the tribes of the sons of Jacob, and built an altar in the name of the LORD.

And he made a trench about the altar and laid the bullock on the wood and said, "Fill four barrels with water

"The Lord, He is the God"

and pour it on the sacrifice and on the wood." And the water ran round about the altar; and he filled the trench also with water.

And Elijah came near and said, "LORD God of Abraham, Isaac, and of Israel, let it be known this day that Thou art God in Israel and that I am Thy servant. Hear me, O LORD, hear me, that this people may know that Thou art the LORD God and that Thou hast turned their heart back again."

Then the fire of the LORD fell and consumed the burnt

sacrifice, and the wood, and the stones, and the dust and licked up the water that was in the trench.

And when all the people saw it, they fell on their faces; and they said, "The LORD, He is the God; the LORD, He is the God."

And Elijah said unto them, "Take the prophets of Baal; let not one of them escape." And they took them. And Elijah brought them down to the brook Kishon and slew them there.

The Famine Ended. And Elijah said unto Ahab, "Get thee up, eat and drink, for there is a sound of abundance of rain. Prepare thy chariot and get thee down that the rain stop thee not."

And in the mean while the heaven was black with clouds and wind, and there was a great rain. And Ahab rode and went to Jezreel.

First Commandment. — Second Petition.

Ps. 115, 3. 4. But our God is in the heavens; He hath done whatsoever He hath pleased. Their idols are silver and gold, the work of man's hands.

   Ye who confess Christ's holy name,
    To God give praise and glory!
   Ye who the Father's power proclaim,
    To God give praise and glory!
   All idols under foot be trod,
   The Lord is God! The Lord is God!
    To God all praise and glory! (19, 5.)

58. Elijah in the Wilderness
1 Kings 19

Elijah Weary and Discouraged. And Ahab told Jezebel all that Elijah had done. And Jezebel sought to take his life. Then Elijah arose and came into the wilderness of Beer-

"He lay and slept"

sheba and sat down under a juniper-tree;[1] and he requested for himself that he might die and said, "It is enough; now, O Lord, take away my life, for I am not better than my fathers."

And as he lay and slept, behold, then an angel touched him and said unto him, "Arise and eat."

---

[1] A much-branched bush of the broom family, growing in the desert.

And he looked, and, behold, there was a cake baken on the coals, and a cruse of water at his head. And he did eat and drink and went in the strength of that meat forty days and forty nights unto Horeb, the mount of God.

Why Elijah was Discouraged. And he came unto a cave and lodged there; and, behold, the word of the Lord came to him, and He said unto him, "What doest thou here, Elijah?"

And he said, "I have been very jealous for the Lord;[2] for the children of Israel have forsaken Thy covenant, thrown down Thine altars, and slain Thy prophets with the sword; and I, even I only, am left; and they seek my life to take it away."

God Instils New Hope. And He said, "Go forth and stand upon the mount before the Lord."

And, behold, the Lord passed by, and a great and strong wind rent the mountains and brake in pieces the rocks before the Lord; but the Lord was not in the wind: and after the wind an earthquake; but the Lord was not in the earthquake: and after the earthquake a fire; but the Lord was not in the fire: and after the fire a still, small voice.

And it was so, when Elijah heard it, that he wrapped his face in his mantle and went out and stood in the entering-in of the cave. And the Lord said unto him, "Go, return on thy way and anoint Hazael to be king over Syria and Jehu to be king over Israel and Elisha to be prophet in thy room. Yet I have left Me seven thousand in Israel, all the knees which have not bowed unto Baal."

Elisha. So Elijah departed thence and found Elisha plowing and cast his mantle upon him.[3] And Elisha arose and went after Elijah and ministered unto him.

---

2) Very earnest about defending the honor of the Lord.
3) To designate Elisha as his successor.

Third Article: The Church.

Luke 17, 20. 21. The kingdom of God cometh not with observation; neither shall they say, Lo, here! or, Lo, there! For, behold, the kingdom of God is within you.

> "Fear not, I am with thee, oh, be not dismayed;
> For I am thy God and will still give thee aid;
> I'll strengthen thee, help thee, and cause thee to stand,
> Upheld by My righteous, omnipotent hand." (427, 3.)

59. Naboth's Vineyard
1 Kings 21. 22. 2 Kings 9

Ahab's Covetousness. Naboth had a vineyard in Jezreel, hard by the palace of Ahab, the king.

And Ahab said, "Give me thy vineyard that I may have it for a garden, and I will give thee for it a better vineyard or the worth of it in money."

And Naboth said, "The LORD forbid it me that I should give the inheritance of my fathers unto thee." [1]

And Ahab came into his house heavy and displeased and laid him down upon his bed and would eat no bread.

Jezebel. But Jezebel, his wife, came to him and said, "Arise, eat bread, and be merry; I will give thee the vineyard."

So she wrote letters in Ahab's name and sealed them with his seal and sent the letters unto the elders and to the nobles in his city. And she wrote: "Set two men, sons of Belial, before Naboth to bear witness against him, saying, 'Thou didst blaspheme God and the king.' [2] And then carry him out and stone him, that he may die."

---

[1] It was forbidden by God to sell the inheritance permanently out of the family, Lev. 25, 23—28; Num. 36, 7 ff. For this reason Ahab later also had to make it appear lawful that he took Naboth's property.

[2] This was the "show of right." A blasphemer had to be stoned.

And the men of his city did as Jezebel had sent unto them. Then Jezebel said to Ahab, "Arise, take possession[3] of the vineyard; for Naboth is dead."

God's Judgment. And the word of the LORD came to Elijah, saying, "Arise, go down to meet Ahab in the vineyard of Naboth, whither he is gone down to possess it.

"Hast thou killed and also taken possession?"

"And thou shalt speak unto him, saying, 'Thus saith the LORD, "Hast thou killed and also taken possession?" Thus saith the LORD, "In the place where dogs licked the blood of Naboth shall dogs lick thy blood, even thine. And the dogs shall eat Jezebel by the wall of Jezreel."'"

And after three years Ahab went to war against the king

---

3) The sons of Naboth also were killed; hence there were no heirs, and Ahab took possession, 2 Kings 9, 26.

of Syria, at Ramoth-gilead. And a certain man drew a bow at a venture and smote the king of Israel; and the blood ran out of the wound into the chariot.

So the king died and was brought to Samaria; and they buried the king in Samaria. And one washed the chariot, and the dogs licked up his blood, according to the word of the LORD.

Jezebel's Punishment. And when Jehu was come to Jezreel, Jezebel heard of it; and she painted her face and tired her head and looked out at a window.

And he said, "Throw her down." So they threw her down; and some of her blood was sprinkled on the wall and on the horses; and he trod her under foot.

And when he was come in, he did eat and drink and said, "Go, see now this cursed woman and bury her; for she is a king's daughter."

And they went to bury her; but they found no more of her than the skull and the feet and the palms of her hands. Wherefore they came again and told him.

And he said, "This is the word of the LORD which He spake by His servant Elijah the Tishbite, saying, 'In the portion of Jezreel shall dogs eat the flesh of Jezebel, and the carcass of Jezebel shall be as dung upon the face of the field in the portion of Jezreel, so that they shall not say, "This is Jezebel." ' "

Ninth Commandment.

Hab. 2, 6. Woe to him that increaseth that which is not his! How long? and to him that ladeth himself with thick clay!

And let me with all men,	Great wealth and honor fair,
As far as in me lieth,	Then this refuse me not,
In peace and friendship live;	That naught be mingled there
And if Thy gift supplieth	Of goods unjustly got. (395, 5.)

Advanced Bible History.

60. Elijah and Elisha
2 Kings 2—4

The Walk to Jordan. And when the Lord would take Elijah into heaven by a whirlwind, Elijah went with Elisha from Gilgal.

And Elijah said unto Elisha, "Tarry here, I pray thee; for the Lord hath sent me to Bethel."

And Elisha said, "As the Lord liveth, I will not leave thee."

And when they came to Bethel, the sons of the prophets said unto Elisha, "Knowest thou that the Lord will take away thy master from thy head to-day?" And he said, "Yea, I know it; hold ye your peace."

And Elijah said unto him, "Elisha, tarry here, I pray thee; for the Lord hath sent me to Jericho."

And he said, "As the Lord liveth, I will not leave thee."

So they came to Jericho. And the sons of the prophets that were at Jericho came to Elisha and said unto him, "Knowest thou that the Lord will take away thy master from thy head to-day?" And he answered, "Yea, I know it; hold ye your peace."

And Elijah said unto him, "Tarry, I pray thee, here; for the Lord hath sent me to Jordan."

And he said, "As the Lord liveth, I will not leave thee."

And they two went on. And fifty men of the sons of the prophets went and stood to view afar off; and they two stood by Jordan.

Elijah's Translation into Heaven. And Elijah took his mantle and wrapped it together and smote the waters; and they were divided, so that they two went over on dry ground.

And Elijah said unto Elisha, "Ask what I shall do for thee before I be taken away from thee."

And Elisha said, "I pray thee, let a double portion of thy spirit be upon me."

And he said, "Thou hast asked a hard thing; nevertheless, if thou see me when I am taken from thee, it shall be so unto thee; but if not, it shall not be so."

And as they still went on and talked, behold, there appeared a chariot of fire and horses of fire and parted them

"My father, my father"

both asunder; and Elijah went up by a whirlwind into heaven.

And Elisha saw it, and he cried, "My father, my father, the chariot of Israel, and the horsemen thereof!" And he saw him no more.

And he took up the mantle of Elijah that fell from him and went back and stood by the bank of Jordan; and he took the mantle and smote the waters and said, "Where is the LORD God of Elijah?"

And when he had smitten the waters, they parted hither and thither; and Elisha went over.

And when the sons of the prophets which were to view at Jericho saw him, they said, "The spirit of Elijah doth rest on Elisha." And they came to meet him and bowed themselves to the ground before him.

Elisha Mocked. And Elisha went up unto Bethel; and as he was going up by the way, there came forth little children out of the city and mocked him and said unto him, "Go up, thou bald head; go up, thou bald head."

And he turned back and looked on them and cursed them in the name of the LORD. And there came forth two she-bears out of the wood and tare forty and two children of them.

The Flowing Oil. And he went from thence to Mount Carmel, and from thence he returned to Samaria.

Now, there cried a certain woman of the wives of the sons of the prophets unto Elisha, saying, "My husband is dead, and the creditor is come to take unto him my two sons to be bondmen."

And Elisha said, "What hast thou in the house?"

And she said, "Thine handmaid hath not anything in the house save a pot of oil."

Then he said, "Go, borrow thee vessels of all thy neighbors, even empty vessels; borrow not a few and pour out into all those vessels, and thou shalt set aside that which is full."

And she poured out until the vessels were full. And she said unto her son, "Bring me yet a vessel." And he said unto her, "There is not a vessel more." And the oil stayed.

Then she came and told the man of God. And he said,

"Go, sell the oil, and pay thy debt, and live thou and thy children of the rest."

Fourth Commandment.

Heb. 13, 17. Obey them that have the rule over you and submit yourselves; for they watch for your souls as they that must give account, that they may do it with joy and not with grief; for that is unprofitable for you.

Draw us to Thee,	That we may be
Lord, lovingly;	Forever free
Let us depart with gladness	From sorrow, grief, and sadness.

(215, 2.)

---

61. Naaman and Elisha
2 Kings 5

Naaman's Leprosy. Naaman, the captain of the host of the king of Syria, was a great man and honorable, but he was a leper.[1]

And the Syrians had gone out and had brought away captive out of the land of Israel a little maid; and she waited on Naaman's wife. And she said unto her mistress, "Would God my lord were with the prophet that is in Samaria! For he would recover him of his leprosy."

And one went in and told his lord, saying, "Thus and thus said the maid that is of the land of Israel."

The Royal Letter of Introduction. And the king of Syria said, "Go, and I will send a letter unto the king of Israel."

And Naaman departed and took with him ten talents of silver and six thousand pieces of gold and ten changes of raiment. And he brought the letter to the king of Israel,

---

1) Leprosy is a disease that no man can cure and is still found in the East. The leper was excluded from the Temple and Tabernacle. He had no social intercourse with his fellow-men unless they were also lepers. A house for lepers was built outside Jerusalem on a hill. The Syrians had no such restrictions for the lepers. So Naaman remained in office though afflicted with this dreadful malady.

saying, "Now, when this letter is come unto thee, behold, I have sent Naaman, my servant, to thee that thou mayest recover him of his leprosy."

And when the king of Israel had read the letter, he rent his clothes and said, "Am I God, to kill and to make alive, that this man doth send unto me to recover a man of his leprosy? Consider and see how he seeketh a quarrel against me."

And when Elisha, the man of God, heard this, he sent to the king, saying, "Wherefore hast thou rent thy clothes? Let him come now to me, and he shall know that there is a prophet in Israel."

Naaman's Disappointment. So Naaman came with his horses and chariot and stood at the door of the house of Elisha.

And Elisha sent a messenger unto him saying, "Go and wash in Jordan seven times, and thy flesh shall come again to thee, and thou shalt be clean."

But Naaman was wroth and went away and said, "Behold, I thought he will surely come out to me, and stand, and call on the name of the LORD, his God, and strike his hand over the place, and recover the leper. Are not the rivers of Damascus better than all the waters of Israel? May I not wash in them and be clean?"

Naaman Healed. And his servants spake unto him and said, "My father, if the prophet had bid thee do some great thing, wouldst thou not have done it? How much rather, then, when he saith to thee, 'Wash and be clean'?"

Then went he down and dipped himself seven times in Jordan; and he was clean.

And he returned to the man of God and said, "Behold, now I know that there is no God in all the earth but in Israel. Now, therefore, I pray thee, take a blessing of thy servant."

But he said, "As the LORD liveth, before whom I stand, I will receive none. Go in peace."

Gehazi's Unfaithfulness. But Gehazi, the servant of Elisha, said, "I will run after him and take somewhat of him."

So Gehazi followed after Naaman and said, "My master

"Take a blessing of thy servant"

hath sent me, saying, 'Behold, even now there be come to me two young men of the sons of the prophets; give them, I pray thee, a talent of silver and two changes of garments.'"

And Naaman said, "Take two talents." And he urged him and laid them upon two of his servants; and they bare them before him.

But he went in and stood before his master. And Elisha said, "Whence comest thou, Gehazi?"

And he said, "Thy servant went nowhither."

And he said unto him, "Went not mine heart with thee when the man turned again from his chariot to meet thee? Is it a time to receive money and garments? The leprosy of Naaman shall cleave unto thee and unto thy seed forever."

And he went out from his presence a leper as white as snow.

Baptism. — The Seventh and Eighth Commandments.

1 Tim. 6, 10. But they that will be rich fall into temptation and a snare and into many foolish and hurtful lusts, which drown men in destruction and perdition.

>See heathen nations bending
>Before the God we love
>And thousand hearts ascending
>In gratitude above. (497, 2 a.)

62. The Prophet Jonah
Jonah 1—4

Jonah's Flight. The word of the Lord came unto Jonah, saying, "Arise, go to Nineveh, that great city,[1] and cry against it; for their wickedness is come up before Me."

But Jonah rose up to flee from the presence of the Lord and went to Joppa,[2] and he found a ship, and went down into it to go with them unto Tarshish.[3]

But the Lord sent out a great wind into the sea, so that the ship was like to be broken. Then the mariners were afraid and cried every man unto his god.

---

1) A famous city of the ancient world, capital of the great Assyrian Empire, which stood on the eastern bank of the river Tigris. It contained one hundred and twenty thousand young children and probably six hundred thousand souls.

2) A seaport on the coast of Palestine, about forty miles northwest of Jerusalem.

3) A city in Spain, in those days "the end of the world." (Map 1.)

But Jonah was gone down into the sides of the ship and was fast asleep. So the shipmaster came to him and said, "What meanest thou, O sleeper? Arise, call upon thy God, if so be that God will think upon us that we perish not."

The Cause of the Tempest Discovered. And they said every one to his fellow, "Come and let us cast lots that we may know for whose cause this evil is upon us." So they cast lots, and the lot fell upon Jonah.

"The Lord had prepared a great fish"

Then said they unto him, "Tell us for whose cause this evil is upon us. Whence comest thou, and of what people art thou?"

And he said unto them, "I am a Hebrew; and I fear the Lord, the God of heaven, which hath made the sea and the dry land."

Then said they unto him, "What shall we do unto thee that the sea may be calm unto us?" And he said unto them, "Cast me forth into the sea, so shall the sea be calm; for I know that for my sake this great tempest is upon you."

Jonah Cast into the Sea. So they took up Jonah and

cast him forth into the sea; and the sea ceased from her raging. Then the men feared the Lord exceedingly and offered a sacrifice unto the Lord and made vows.

Now, the Lord had prepared a great fish to swallow up Jonah. And Jonah was in the belly of the fish three days and three nights.

Then Jonah prayed unto the Lord, his God, out of the fish's belly. And the Lord spake unto the fish, and it vomited out Jonah upon the dry land.

Nineveh's Repentance. And the word of the Lord came unto Jonah the second time, saying, "Arise, go unto Nineveh, that great city, and preach unto it the preaching that I bid thee." So Jonah went unto Nineveh.

Now, Nineveh was an exceeding great city of three days' journey. And Jonah began to enter into the city a day's journey; and he cried and said, "Yet forty days, and Nineveh shall be overthrown."

So the people of Nineveh believed God and proclaimed a fast. And the king of Nineveh arose from his throne, and laid his robe from him, and covered him with sackcloth, and sat in ashes.

And he caused it to be proclaimed and published, saying, "Let neither man nor beast taste anything, but cry mightily unto God; yea, let every one turn from his evil way. Who can tell if God will turn away from His fierce anger that we perish not?"

And God saw that they turned from their evil way; and He repented of the evil that He had said that He would do unto them; and He did it not.

Jonah's Displeasure. But it displeased Jonah exceedingly, and he was very angry. And he said unto the Lord, "O Lord, was not this my saying when I was yet in my country? Therefore I fled before unto Tarshish; for I knew that Thou art a gracious God and merciful, slow to anger, and of great kindness and repentest Thee of the evil."

And Jonah went out of the city and sat on the east side of the city and there made him a booth till he might see what would become of the city.

Jonah and the Gourd. And the LORD God prepared a gourd,[4] and made it to come up over Jonah that it might be a shadow over his head. So Jonah was exceeding glad of the gourd.

But God prepared a worm when the morning rose, and it smote the gourd that it withered. And it came to pass, when the sun did arise, that God prepared a vehement east wind; and the sun beat upon the head of Jonah that he fainted and wished in himself to die.

And God said to Jonah, "Doest thou well to be angry for the gourd?"

And he said, "I do well to be angry, even unto death."

Then said the LORD, "Thou hast had pity on the gourd, for the which thou hast not labored, neither madest it grow; which came up in a night and perished in a night; and should not I spare Nineveh, that great city, wherein are more than sixscore thousand persons that cannot discern between their right hand and their left hand,[5] and also much cattle?"

Fifth Petition. — Third Article.

Ps. 139, 7—10. Whither shall I go from Thy Spirit, or whither shall I flee from Thy presence? If I ascend up into heaven, Thou art there; if I make my bed in hell, behold, Thou art there; if I take the wings of the morning and dwell in the uttermost parts of the sea, even there shall Thy hand lead me, and Thy right hand shall hold me.

> O Christ, our true and only Light,
> Enlighten those who sit in night;
> Let those afar now hear Thy voice
> And in Thy fold with us rejoice. (512, 1.)

---

4) A castor-oil plant, which grows quickly and has large leaves.
5) Children.

63. Overthrow of the Kingdom of Israel. Hezekiah
2 Kings 17—20. 2 Chron. 30

Israel Sins. The children of Israel sinned against the LORD, their God, and walked in the statutes of the heathen and served idols, whereof the LORD had said unto them, "Ye shall not do this thing."

Yet the LORD testified against Israel by all the prophets and by all the seers, saying, "Turn ye from your evil ways." Notwithstanding they would not hear, but left all the commandments of the LORD, their God, and made them molten images, even two calves, and made a grove,[1] and worshiped all the host of heaven, and served Baal.

And they caused their sons and their daughters to pass through the fire [2] and used divination and enchantments [3] and sold themselves to do evil in the sight of the LORD to provoke Him to anger.

Israel Led into Captivity. Therefore the LORD was very angry with Israel and removed them out of His sight, as He had said by all His servants, the prophets. For in the ninth year of Hoshea, Shalmaneser, king of Assyria, went up to Samaria and besieged it three years, and after taking it, he carried Israel away into Assyria.

Reform in the House of Judah. In the third year of Hoshea, king of Israel, Hezekiah, king of Judah, began to reign and did that which was right in the sight of the LORD. He opened again the doors of the house of the LORD and

---

[1] Image of a heathen goddess, whose worship in groves was connected with shameful immoralities.

[2] Making burnt offerings of their children by laying them on the red-hot iron arms of Molech, an idol so constructed that a fire could be built inside.

[3] "Divination," fortune-telling. "Enchantments," magic spells and charms produced by magicians.

commanded the priests and Levites to sanctify it. And he sent to all Israel and Judah that they should turn again unto the Lord and serve Him in His sanctuary.

And there assembled at Jerusalem much people, and took away the altars that were in Jerusalem, and cast them into the brook Kidron, and kept the Feast of Unleavened Bread [4)]

"He opened again the doors of the house of the Lord"

with great gladness. For since the time of Solomon there was not the like in Jerusalem.

Jerusalem Besieged. In the fourteenth year of King Hezekiah did Sennacherib, king of Assyria, come up against all the fenced cities of Judah and took them and sent Rabshakeh with a great host against Jerusalem. And they went up and came to Jerusalem.

Then Rabshakeh stood and cried with a loud voice, "Let

---

4) The Passover.

not Hezekiah make you trust in the Lord, saying, 'The Lord will surely deliver us.' Hath any of the gods of the nations delivered at all his land out of the hand of the king of Assyria?"

And it came to pass, when King Hezekiah heard it, he rent his clothes and covered himself with sackcloth and went into the house of the Lord.

And he sent to Isaiah. And Isaiah said, "Thus saith the Lord, 'Be not afraid of the words which thou hast heard. Sennacherib shall not come into this city nor shoot an arrow there nor cast a bank against it. By the way that he came, by the same shall he return and shall not come into this city. For I will defend this city.'"

Sennacherib's Army Destroyed. And it came to pass that night that the angel of the Lord went out and smote in the camp of the Assyrians a hundred fourscore and five thousand. And when they arose early in the morning, behold, they were all dead corpses.

So Sennacherib, king of Assyria, departed, and went, and returned, and dwelt at Nineveh. And it came to pass, as he was worshiping in the house of his god, his sons smote him with the sword.

Hezekiah's Life Lengthened. In those days was Hezekiah sick unto death. And the prophet Isaiah came to him and said unto him, "Thus saith the Lord, 'Set thine house in order; for thou shalt die and not live.'"

Then he turned his face to the wall and prayed unto the Lord, saying, "I beseech Thee, O Lord; remember now how I have walked before Thee in truth and with a perfect heart." And Hezekiah wept sore.

And it came to pass, afore Isaiah was gone out into the middle court, that the word of the Lord came to him, saying, "Turn again and tell Hezekiah, the captain of My people,

'Thus saith the LORD, "I have heard thy prayer, I have seen thy tears. Behold, I will heal thee; on the third day thou shalt go up unto the house of the LORD. And I will add unto thy days fifteen years." ' "

And Isaiah said, "Take a lump of figs." And they took and laid it on the boil, and he recovered.

First Commandment. — Conclusion of the Commandments.

Jer. 17, 5. 7. Thus saith the Lord, Cursed be the man that trusteth in man and maketh flesh his arm and whose heart departeth from the Lord. Blessed is the man that trusteth in the Lord and whose hope the Lord is.

> Though destruction walk around us,
> Though the arrows past us fly,
> Angel guards from Thee surround us;
> We are safe if Thou art nigh. (565, 2.)

NOTE. — The Kingdom of Israel existed two hundred and fifty-three years and had nineteen kings, all of whom were ungodly. These were their names: Jeroboam, Nadab, Baasha, Elah, Zimri, Omri, Ahab, Ahaziah, Jehoram, Jehu, Jehoahaz, Jehoash, Jeroboam II, Zachariah, Shallum, Menahem, Pekahiah, Pekah, and Hoshea. The Kingdom of Israel was destroyed by Shalmaneser, king of the Assyrians, about seven hundred and twenty-two years before Christ. He led the ten tribes into the Assyrian Captivity. This kingdom was never restored.

The Kingdom of Judah was in existence three hundred and eighty-seven years and was governed by twenty kings. These were their names: Rehoboam, Abijam, Asa, Jehoshaphat, Jehoram, Ahaziah, Athaliah, Joash, Amaziah, Uzziah, Jotham, Ahaz, Hezekiah, Manasseh, Amon, Josiah, Jehoahaz, Jehoiakim, Jehoiachin, and Zedekiah. The Kingdom of Judah was overthrown by Nebuchadnezzar, king of the Chaldeans. He appeared before Jerusalem three times. The third time he utterly destroyed Jerusalem and carried the Jews into the Babylonian Captivity. The Jews were in exile seventy years.

64. The Babylonian Captivity
(606 B. C.)

2 Kings 23—25. 2 Chron. 36. Jer. 34—39

The Wicked Kings. Jehoahaz was twenty and three years old when he began to reign, and he reigned three months in Jerusalem. And the king of Egypt put him down at Jerusalem and condemned the land in a hundred talents of silver and a talent of gold.[1)]

---

1) Compelled them to pay a fine amounting to over $200,000.

And the king of Egypt made Jehoiakim, his brother, king over Judah; and he did that which was evil in the sight of the Lord, his God. Against him came up Nebuchadnezzar, king of Babylon, and bound him in fetters to carry him to Babylon.

And Jehoiachin, his son, reigned in his stead and did that which was evil in the sight of the Lord. And when the year was expired, King Nebuchadnezzar sent and brought him to Babylon, with the goodly vessels of the house of the Lord and ten thousand captives, and made Zedekiah, his brother, king over Judah and Jerusalem.

And he did that which was evil in the sight of the Lord, his God, and humbled not himself before Jeremiah, the prophet, speaking from the mouth of the Lord. And he also rebelled against King Nebuchadnezzar, who had made him swear by God.

The Captivity Foretold. The word of the Lord came unto Jeremiah, "Go and speak to Zedekiah, king of Judah, and tell him, 'Thus saith the Lord, "Behold, I will give this city into the hand of the king of Babylon, and he shall burn it with fire. And thou shalt not escape out of his hand, but shalt surely be taken and delivered into his hand."'"

Judah Overthrown. And it came to pass that Nebuchadnezzar and all his host came against Jerusalem and pitched against it; and they built forts against it round about. And famine prevailed in the city, and there was no bread for the people of the land. And the city was broken up, and all the men of war fled by night; and the king went the way toward the plain.

And the army of the Chaldees pursued after the king and overtook him in the plains of Jericho; and all his army were scattered from him. So they took the king and brought him up to the king of Babylon.

And they slew the sons of Zedekiah before his eyes, and put out the eyes of Zedekiah, and bound him with fetters of brass, and carried him to Babylon.

And the captain of the guard, a servant of the king of Babylon, burned the house of the LORD; and the king's house and all the houses of Jerusalem and every great man's house burned he with fire. And all the army of the Chaldees that were with the captain of the guard brake down the walls of Jerusalem round about.

"Nebuchadnezzar and all his host came against Jerusalem"

The Captivity. Now, the rest of the people that were left in the city and the fugitives that fell away to the king of Babylon, with the remnant of the multitude, did the captain of the guard carry away to fulfil threescore and ten years. But the captain of the guard left of the poor of the land to be vine-dressers and husbandmen.

And the pillars of brass that were in the house of the LORD and the bases and the brazen sea that was in the house of the LORD did the Chaldees break in pieces and carried the brass of them to Babylon. And the pots, and the shovels, and the snuffers, and the spoons, and all the vessels of brass wherewith they ministered, took they away. And the firepans and the bowls and such things as were of gold, in gold, and of silver, in silver, the captain of the guard took away. The two pillars, one sea, and the bases which Solomon had made for the house of the LORD; the brass of all these vessels was without weight.[2]

Conclusion of the Commandments.

Hos. 13, 9. O Israel, thou hast destroyed thyself; but in Me is thine help.

Acts 7, 51. Ye stiff-necked and uncircumcised in heart and ears, ye do always resist the Holy Ghost; as your fathers did, so do ye.

> O Lord, look down from heav'n, behold
> And let Thy pity waken;
> How few are we within Thy fold,
> Thy saints by men forsaken!
> True faith seems quenched on ev'ry hand,
> Men suffer not Thy Word to stand;
> Dark times have us o'ertaken. (260, 1.)

SUMMARY STUDY OF THE SIXTH PERIOD

State the origin and the general differences between the Kingdom of Israel and the Kingdom of Judah.

What became of each in the end?

Name the kings of Israel and the kings of Judah mentioned in the stories of this period.

What was the cause of the downfall of both kingdoms?

Give a brief description of the life and work of Elijah; of Elisha; of Jonah.

What occurrences in the New Testament were foreshadowed, or typified, by incidents in the lives of Elijah and Jonah?

Recount a number of the practical lessons which this period offers for our personal faith and life.

---

2) An expression like "a pearl without price," meaning too much to figure.

"OH, THAT THE SALVATION OF ISRAEL WERE COME OUT OF ZION!" Ps. 14, 7.

SEVENTH PERIOD

FROM THE BABYLONIAN CAPTIVITY TO THE BIRTH OF CHRIST

(606 B. C. to the Birth of Christ)

You will recall that the Messiah was to come out of the tribe of Judah, the house of David. The tribe of Judah had been led into the Babylonian Captivity, where it was scattered throughout the great Babylonian Empire. There it remained for seventy years, and there occurred the incidents of which our last six stories of the Old Testament in this book treat, except that the very last one speaks of the return. For the first hundred years after their return the Lord gave His people three more prophets: Haggai, Zechariah, and Malachi. In the remaining four hundred years before Christ no prophet's voice was heard, none until John the Baptist appeared to prepare the people for the Messiah.

65. The Prophet Daniel

Dan. 1. 2

Daniel at the Court. And Nebuchadnezzar spake unto the master of his eunuchs [1] that he should bring certain of the children of Israel and of the king's seed and of the princes, children in whom was no blemish, but well favored, and skilful in all wisdom, and cunning in knowledge, and understanding science, and such as had ability in them to stand in the king's palace, and whom they might teach the learning and the tongue of the Chaldeans.

And the king appointed them a daily provision of the king's meat and of the wine which he drank, so nourishing them three years that at the end thereof they might stand before the king. Now, among these were Daniel, Shadrach, Meshach, and Abednego.

---

[1] The chief of the king's staff of officers. Eunuch: officer of the king.

Daniel Refuses to Defile Himself. But Daniel purposed in his heart that he would not defile himself with the portion of the king's meat [2] nor with the wine which he drank; therefore he requested of the prince of the eunuchs that he might not defile himself.

And the prince of the eunuchs said unto Daniel, "I fear my lord, the king, who hath appointed your meat and your drink; for why should he see your faces worse liking than the children which are of your sort? Then shall ye make me endanger my head to the king."

Then said Daniel, "Prove thy servants, I beseech thee, ten days; and let them give us pulse [3] to eat and water to drink."

So he consented to them in this matter and proved them ten days. And at the end of ten days their countenances appeared fairer and fatter in flesh than all the children which did eat the portion of the king's meat. Thus he took away the portion of their meat and the wine that they should drink and gave them pulse.

God's Blessing. As for these four children, God gave them knowledge and skill in all learning and wisdom; and Daniel had understanding in all visions and dreams.

Now, at the end of the days that the king had said he should bring them in, then the prince of the eunuchs brought them in before Nebuchadnezzar. And the king found them ten times better than all the magicians and astrologers that were in all his realm.

Nebuchadnezzar's Dream. And in the second year of the reign of Nebuchadnezzar, Nebuchadnezzar dreamed dreams wherewith his spirit was troubled, and his sleep brake from him.

---

[2] Food forbidden in the Ceremonial Law.
[3] Vegetables of the bean family; here, vegetables of all kinds.

Then the king commanded to call the magicians and the astrologers and said unto them, "I have dreamed a dream, and my spirit was troubled to know the dream. But the thing is gone from me. Therefore show me the dream and the interpretation thereof."

The Chaldeans answered before the king and said, "There is not a man upon the earth that can show the king's matter."

"The king found them ten times better —"

For this cause the king was angry and very furious and commanded to destroy all the wise men of Babylon. And the decree went forth that the wise men should be slain; and they sought Daniel and his fellows to be slain.

Then Daniel went in and desired of the king that he would give him time and that he would show the king the interpretation.

Daniel went to his house and made the thing known

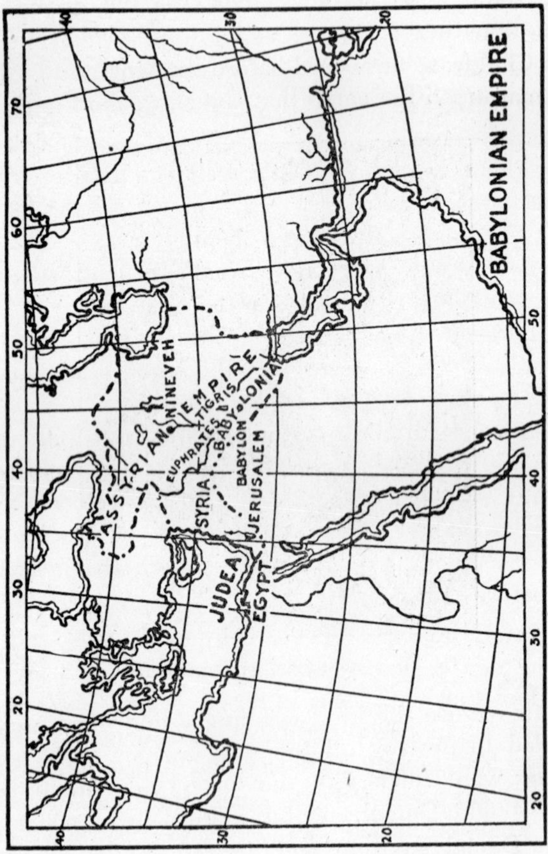
BABYLONIAN EMPIRE
ASSYRIAN EMPIRE
NINEVEH
EUPHRATES
TIGRIS
BABYLONIA
BABYLON
SYRIA
JERUSALEM
JUDEA
EGYPT

to his companions that they would desire mercies of the God of heaven concerning this secret;[4] that Daniel and his fellows should not perish with the rest of the wise men of Babylon.

Then was the secret revealed unto Daniel in a night vision, and Daniel blessed the God of heaven.

Daniel Tells the King's Dreams. Therefore Daniel went in and said, "There is a God in heaven that revealeth secrets and maketh known to the King Nebuchadnezzar what shall be in the latter days.

"Thou, O king, sawest, and, behold, a great image. The great image, whose brightness was excellent, stood before thee; and the form thereof was terrible.

"This image's head was of fine gold, his breast and his arms of silver, his belly and his thighs of brass, his legs of iron, his feet part of iron and part of clay.

"Thou sawest till that a stone was cut out without hands, which smote the image upon his feet that were of iron and of clay and brake them to pieces. And the stone that smote the image became a great mountain and filled the whole earth.

"This is the dream; and we will tell the interpretation thereof before the king.

The Interpretation. "Thou, O king, art this head of gold. And after thee shall rise another kingdom, inferior to thee, and another third kingdom of brass, which shall bear rule over all the earth. And the fourth kingdom shall be strong as iron and shall break in pieces and bruise all things

"And in the days of these kings shall the God of heaven set up a kingdom which shall never be destroyed; and the kingdom shall not be left to other people, but it shall break

---

4) That they would unite with him in prayer for this unusual mercy of finding out the secret, which would save their lives.

in pieces and consume all these kingdoms, and it shall stand forever.

"Forasmuch as thou sawest that the stone was cut out of the mountain without hands and that it brake in pieces the iron, the brass, the clay, the silver, and the gold: the great God hath made known to the king what shall come to pass hereafter; and the dream is certain and the interpretation thereof sure."

The King Confesses the True God. Then the King Nebuchadnezzar fell upon his face and said, "Of a truth it is that your God is a God of gods and a Lord of kings and a Revealer of secrets, seeing thou couldest reveal this secret."

Then the king made Daniel a great man and gave him many great gifts and made him ruler over the whole province of Babylon and chief of the governors over all the wise men of Babylon.

Daniel requested of the king, and he set Shadrach, Meshach, and Abednego over the affairs of the province of Babylon, but Daniel sat in the gate of the king.

First Commandment. First Article: Confessing, serving God.

Ps. 139, 1. 2. O Lord, Thou hast searched me and known me. Thou knowest my downsitting and mine uprising; Thou understandest my thought afar off.

    May every heart confess Thy name
     And ever Thee adore
    And, seeking Thee, itself inflame
     To seek Thee more and more. (361, 4.)

66. The Three Men in the Fiery Furnace
Dan. 3

The Golden Image. Nebuchadnezzar,[1] the king, made an image of gold [2] in the province of Babylon and then sent to gather all the rulers of the provinces to come to the dedication of the image. And they stood before the image.

Then a herald cried aloud, "O people, at what time ye hear the sound of the cornet, ye shall fall down and worship the golden image. And whoso falleth not down shall the same hour be cast into the midst of a burning fiery furnace."

Therefore, when the people heard the sound of the cornet, all fell down and worshiped the golden image.

Wherefore, at that time certain Chaldeans came near and accused the Jews. They spake, "O king, Shadrach, Meshach, and Abednego have not regarded thee; they serve not nor worship the golden image."

The Fiery Furnace. Then Nebuchadnezzar in his rage commanded to bring them before him and said, "If ye worship it not, ye shall be cast into the midst of a burning fiery furnace; and who is that God that shall deliver you out of my hands?"

Shadrach, Meshach, and Abednego answered, "Our God is able to deliver us. But if not, be it known unto thee that we will not worship the golden image."

---

1) Nebuchadnezzar was the founder of the great Babylonian Empire and reigned forty-three years. The capital of this great empire was Babylon. The Chaldeans, as the Babylonians are also called, destroyed the Assyrian Empire with its capital, Nineveh. Some time after the death of Nebuchadnezzar his son or grandson Belshazzar became king of Babylon. He was the last king of this powerful nation. Darius, the Median, the son of Ahasuerus, took Babylon from Belshazzar, who was slain.

2) A statue which, standing on a base thirty to forty feet, was ninety feet high and nine feet wide. Probably not solid gold, but gold-plated.

Then was Nebuchadnezzar full of fury and commanded that they should heat the furnace seven times more than it was wont to be heated.

Then these men were bound and cast into the midst of the burning fiery furnace. Therefore, because the furnace was

"Lo, I see four men"

exceeding hot, the flame of the fire slew those men that took up Shadrach, Meshach, and Abednego.

The Men Delivered. Then Nebuchadnezzar, the king, was astonished and said, "Did not we cast three men bound into the midst of the fire? Lo, I see four men loose, walking in the midst of the fire, and they have no hurt; and the form of the fourth is like the son of God." [3]

Then Nebuchadnezzar came near to the mouth of the

---

3) Like a son of the gods.

burning fiery furnace and said, "Ye servants of the most high God, come forth."

Then Shadrach, Meshach, and Abednego came forth. Nor was an hair of their head singed, nor the smell of fire had passed on them.

Then Nebuchadnezzar spake and said, "Blessed be the God of Shadrach, Meshach, and Abednego, who hath delivered His servants that trusted in Him. There is no other god that can deliver after this sort."

Then the king promoted Shadrach, Meshach, and Abednego in the province of Babylon.

First Commandment.

Matt. 10, 28. Fear not them which kill the body, but are not able to kill the soul; but rather fear Him which is able to destroy both soul and body in hell.

Matt. 10, 32. 33. Whosoever shall confess Me before men, him will I also confess before My Father which is in heaven. But whosoever shall deny Me before men, him will I also deny before My Father which is in heaven.

>Sing, pray, and keep His ways unswerving,
> Perform thy duties faithfully,
>And trust His Word; though undeserving,
> Thou yet shalt find it true for thee.
>God never yet forsook in need
>The soul that trusted Him indeed. (518, 7.)

67. Belshazzar
Dan. 5

Belshazzar's Feast. Belshazzar, the king, made a feast to a thousand of his lords. And while he drank wine, he commanded to bring the golden and silver vessels which his father, Nebuchadnezzar, had taken out of the Temple which was in Jerusalem. And the king, his princes, and his wives drank wine in them and praised the gods of gold and of silver, of brass, of iron, of wood, and of stone.

The Handwriting on the Wall. In the same hour came forth fingers of a man's hand and wrote over against the candlestick upon the plaster of the wall of the king's palace. And the king saw the part of the hand that wrote. Then the king's countenance was changed, and his knees smote one against another.

The king cried aloud to bring in the astrologers and

"And this is the writing"

soothsayers. But all the king's wise men could not read the writing, nor make known to the king the interpretation thereof.

The Interpretation. Then was Daniel called and brought in before the king. Daniel read the writing and made known unto the king the interpretation, saying, "O king, thou hast lifted up thyself against the Lord of heaven, and they have brought the vessels of His house before thee, and thou hast praised the gods which see not nor hear nor know; and the God in whose hand thy breath is and whose are all thy ways hast thou not glorified. Then was the part of the hand sent from Him and this writing.

"And this is the writing that was written: 'Mene, Mene, Tekel, Upharsin.' This is the interpretation of the thing: Mene, God hath numbered thy kingdom and finished it. Tekel, Thou art weighed in the balances and art found wanting. Peres, Thy kingdom is divided and given to the Medes and Persians."

In that night was Belshazzar, the king of the Chaldeans, slain. And Darius the Median took the kingdom.

Second Commandment.

Gal. 6, 7. Be not deceived; God is not mocked; for whatsoever a man soweth, that shall he also reap.

> But sinners, filled with guilty fears,
>   Behold His wrath prevailing,
> For they shall rise and find their tears
>   And sighs are unavailing;
> The day of grace is past and gone;
> They trembling stand before His throne,
>   All unprepared to meet Him. (604, 3.)

---

68. Daniel in the Lions' Den
Dan. 6

The King's Decree. It pleased Darius to set over the kingdom three presidents, of whom Daniel was first.[1] Then this Daniel was preferred above the presidents; and the king thought to set him over the whole realm.

Then the presidents and princes sought to find occasion against Daniel; but they could find no fault, forasmuch as he was faithful. Then said these men, "We shall not find any

---

[1] King Darius divided his empire into one hundred and twenty-seven provinces, or satrapies.

occasion against this Daniel except concerning the Law of his God."

Then these princes assembled together to the king and said, "King Darius, all the presidents and the princes have consulted together to establish a royal statute, that whosoever shall ask a petition of any God or man for thirty days save of thee, O king, he shall be cast into the den of lions." Wherefore King Darius signed the decree.

Daniel Steadfast. Now, when Daniel knew that the writing was signed, he went into his house; and his windows being open in his chamber toward Jerusalem, he kneeled upon his knees three times a day and prayed and gave thanks before his God as he did aforetime.

Then these men assembled and found Daniel praying and making supplication before his God. And they came before the king and said, "Daniel regardeth not thee nor the decree, but maketh his petition three times a day."

Then the king was sore displeased and set his heart on Daniel to deliver him. Then these men said unto the king, "Know, O king, that the law of the Medes and Persians is that no decree nor statute which the king establisheth may be changed."

In the Den of Lions. Then the king commanded, and they brought Daniel and cast him into the den of lions.

Now the king said unto Daniel, "Thy God, whom thou servest continually, He will deliver thee."

And a stone was brought and laid upon the mouth of the den; and the king sealed it with his own signet that the purpose might not be changed concerning Daniel. Then the king went to his palace and passed the night fasting; and his sleep went from him.

Daniel's Deliverance. Then the king arose very early in the morning and went in haste unto the den of lions and

DANIEL IN THE LIONS' DEN

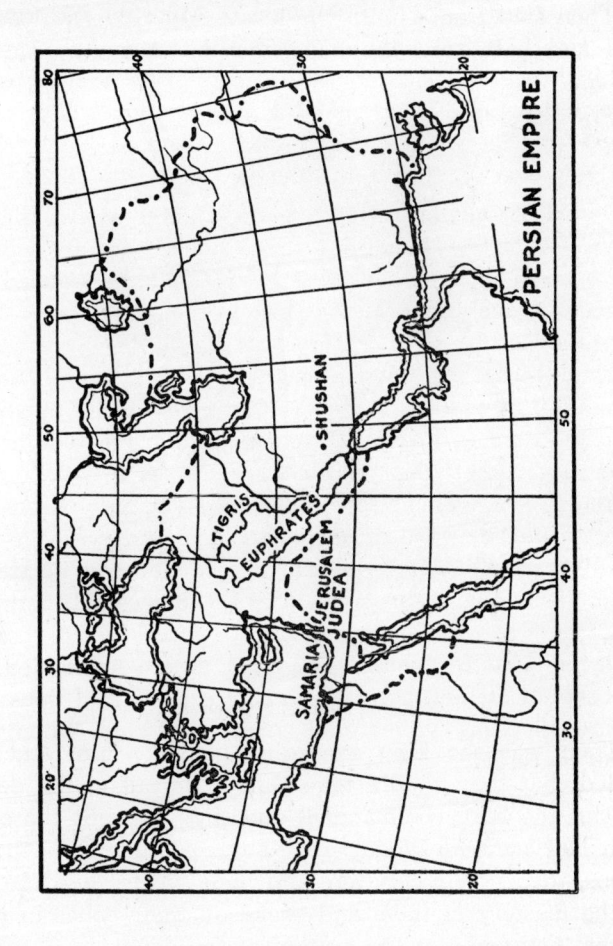

cried with a lamentable voice, "O Daniel, servant of the living God, is thy God able to deliver thee from the lions?"

Then said Daniel unto the king, "My God hath sent His angel and hath shut the lions' mouths that they have not hurt me."

"My God hath sent His angel"

Then was the king exceeding glad for him and commanded that they should take Daniel up out of the den.

And the king commanded, and they brought those men which had accused Daniel, and they cast them into the den of lions, them, their children, and their wives; and the lions had the mastery of them and brake all their bones in pieces or ever they came at the bottom of the den.[2]

---

2) "Or ever" = before ever.

BELSHAZZAR'S FEAST

Then King Darius wrote unto all people, "Peace be multiplied unto you. I make a decree, That in every dominion of my kingdom men tremble and fear before the God of Daniel; for He is the living God."

So Daniel prospered in the reign of Darius and in the reign of Cyrus the Persian.

First and Second Commandments.

Ps. 91, 11. 12. He shall give His angels charge over thee to keep thee in all thy ways. They shall bear thee up in their hands lest thou dash thy foot against a stone.

> Though destruction walk around us,
> Though the arrows past us fly,
> Angel guards from Thee surround us;
> We are safe if Thou art nigh. (565, 2.)

---

69. Esther *

Book of Esther

Esther Chosen Queen. Ahasuerus, which reigned from India even unto Ethiopia, made a feast unto all his princes and servants in Shushan and commanded to bring Vashti, the queen. But she refused to come. Therefore was the king very wroth and commanded that Vashti should come no more before him.

Then said the king's servants that ministered unto him, "Let there be fair young virgins sought for the king, and let the maiden which pleaseth the king be queen instead of Vashti."

Now, in Shushan, the palace, there was a Jew whose name was Mordecai. He had brought up Esther, his uncle's

---

* The story of Esther occurred after the seventy years of captivity.

Advanced Bible History.

daughter, fair and beautiful. And the king loved Esther and made her queen.

In those days two chamberlains sought to lay hand on the king. This was known to Mordecai, who told it unto Esther, and she told the king thereof in Mordecai's name. And when inquisition was made of the matter, it was found out; therefore they were both hanged on a tree; and it was written in the book of the chronicles.

Haman Seeks the Jews' Destruction. And King Ahasuerus promoted Haman, and all the king's servants bowed and reverenced Haman; but Mordecai bowed not.

Then was Haman full of wrath and sought to destroy all the Jews and said unto the king, "There is a people scattered in all thy provinces that keep not thy laws. If it please the king, let it be written that they be destroyed."

And the king said, "Do with them as it seemeth good to thee."

And letters were sent into all the provinces to kill all Jews, both young and old, little children and women, in one day. And there was great mourning among the Jews.

And Mordecai charged Esther that she should go in unto the king. And Esther said, "Whosoever cometh unto the king who is not called, the law is to put him to death, except the king hold out the scepter that he may live. But I will go in; and if I perish, I perish."

Esther before the King. And Esther put on her royal apparel and went into the court of the king's house. And when the king saw her, she obtained favor; and he held out to her the golden scepter. So she drew near and touched the top of the scepter.

Then said the king, "What is thy request? It shall be even given thee to the half of the kingdom."

Esther answered, "If it seem good unto the king, let the king and Haman come this day unto the banquet that I have prepared for him." So the king and Haman came to the banquet.

And the king said, "What is thy petition, Queen Esther? It shall be granted thee."

Esther

Then answered Esther, "Let the king and Haman come to the banquet that I shall prepare for them to-morrow."

Then went Haman forth with a glad heart; but when he saw Mordecai in the gate that he stood not up, he was full of anger.

And when he came home, he said, "The queen did let no man come in but myself; and to-morrow am I invited unto her also with the king."

Then said his wife and his friends unto him, "Let a gallows be made of fifty cubits high, and to-morrow speak thou unto the king that Mordecai may be hanged thereon." This pleased Haman; and he caused the gallows to be made.

The King Honors Mordecai. On that night could not the king sleep, and he commanded to bring the book of the chronicles. And it was found written that Mordecai had told of two of the chamberlains who sought to lay hand on the king. And the king said, "What honor and dignity hath been done to Mordecai for this?" They said, "There is nothing done for him."

And when Haman came in, the king said, "What shall be done unto the man whom the king delighteth to honor?"

Now Haman thought, "To whom would the king delight to do honor more than to myself?" And he said, "Let them array the man in the royal apparel which the king useth to wear, and let the crown royal be set upon his head, and set him upon the horse that the king rideth upon, and bring him through the city, and proclaim before him, 'Thus shall it be done to the man whom the king delighteth to honor.'"

Then said the king to Haman, "Make haste and do even so to Mordecai, the Jew." And Haman did so; and then he hasted to his house mourning and having his head covered.

Haman's Destruction. But the king's chamberlains came and hasted to bring Haman unto the banquet that Esther had prepared. And the king said unto Esther, "What is thy petition, Queen Esther?"

Then Esther said, "O king, let my life be given me at my petition and my people at my request; for we are sold to be slain and to perish."

Then the king said, "Who is he that durst presume in his heart to do so?"

And Esther said, "The enemy is this wicked Haman."

And the king arose in his wrath. And one of the chamberlains said, "Behold, the gallows which Haman made for Mordecai standeth in the house of Haman."

The king said, "Hang him thereon." So they hanged Haman on the gallows.

And the king took off his ring which he had taken from Haman and gave it unto Mordecai.

Third Petition: "When God breaks and hinders every evil counsel and will."

Gen. 50, 20. Ye thought evil against me, but God meant it unto good to bring to pass as it is this day, to save much people alive.

>Thine honor save, O Christ, our Lord!
>Hear Zion's cries and help afford;
>Destroy the wiles of mighty foes
>Who now Thy Word and truth oppose. (265, 1.)

70. The Return from the Captivity
(536 B. C.)
Ezra 1—6

The Proclamation of Cyrus. The LORD stirred up the spirit of Cyrus that he made a proclamation throughout all his kingdom: "The LORD God of heaven hath charged me to build Him a house at Jerusalem. Who is there among you of His people? Let him go up to Jerusalem and build the house of the LORD God of Israel. And whosoever remaineth in any place where he sojourneth, let the men of his place help him with silver, and gold, and goods, and with beasts, besides the free-will offering for the house of God that is in Jerusalem."

The Return. Then rose up the chief of the fathers of Judah and Benjamin, and the priests and the Levites, to go up to Jerusalem. And all they that were about them strengthened their hands with vessels of silver, with gold, goods, beasts, and precious things.

Also Cyrus, the king, brought forth the vessels of the house of the LORD which Nebuchadnezzar had brought forth out of Jerusalem and had put them in the house of his gods.

The whole congregation together was forty and two thousand three hundred and threescore persons, beside their servants and their maids, of whom there were seven thousand three hundred thirty and seven.

The Temple Foundation Laid. They gave money also unto the masons and to the carpenters; and meat and drink and oil unto them of Zidon and to them of Tyre to bring cedar-trees from Lebanon to the sea of Joppa, according to the grant that they had of Cyrus, king of Persia.

And some of the chief of the fathers, when they came to the house of the LORD which is at Jerusalem, offered freely for the house of God to set it up in his place. They gave after their ability unto the treasure of the work.

Then stood up Jeshua and his brethren, the priests, and Zerubbabel and his brethren and builded the altar of the God of Israel. And they offered burnt offerings thereon unto the LORD, even burnt offerings morning and evening. They kept also the Feast of Tabernacles.

And when the builders laid the foundation of the Temple of the LORD, they set the priests with trumpets and the Levites with cymbals to praise the LORD. And all the people shouted with a loud voice when they praised the LORD because the foundation of the house of the LORD was laid.

But many of the priests and Levites and of the fathers that had seen the first house, when the foundation of this house was laid before their eyes, wept with a loud voice, so that the people could not discern the noise of the shout of joy from the noise of the weeping of the people.

The Building Hindered. Now, when the adversaries [1] heard that the children of the captivity builded the Temple unto the Lord God of Israel, they came to Zerubbabel and to the chief of the fathers and said unto them, "Let us build with you; for we seek your God as ye do."

But they said unto them, "Ye have nothing to do with us to build an house unto our God; but we ourselves together

"The builders laid the foundation of the Temple"

will build unto the Lord, as King Cyrus, the king of Persia, hath commanded us."

Then the people of the land weakened the hands of the people of Judah and troubled them in building and hired counselors against them to frustrate their purpose, all the

---

[1] Inhabitants of the land, made up of remaining Israelites and others.

days of Cyrus, king of Persia, even until the reign of Darius, king of Persia.

The Temple Finished. Then the prophets Haggai and Zechariah prophesied unto the Jews that were in Judah and Jerusalem in the name of the God of Israel. Then rose up Zerubbabel and Jeshua and began to build the house of God which is at Jerusalem and finished it in the sixth year of Darius, the king. And the children of Israel kept the dedication of this house of God with joy.

Third Commandment.

Ps. 26, 8. Lord, I have loved the habitation of Thy house and the place where Thine honor dwelleth.

>Zions stands by hills surrounded,
>   Zion, kept by power divine;
>All her foes shall be confounded
>   Though the world in arms combine.
>   Happy Zion,
>What a favored lot is thine! (474, 1.)

NOTE. — The Jews returned under Zerubbabel, Ezra, and Nehemiah. It is estimated that not more than one in six of the exiles returned to Palestine, in all, 42,360, besides 7,337 servants.

Appendix

The Jews under Greek Rule. For about two hundred years after the return from the Babylonian Captivity the Jews led a quiet life under Persian rule. Then Alexander the Great overcame the Persians and founded the Greco-Macedonian Empire and also brought the Jews under his sway. The Greek language became the language of the world. At this time the Old Testament was translated from the Hebrew into the Greek language. This translation is known as the Septuagint and is still in existence.

The Jews under Syrian Rule. Antiochus, king of Syria, conquered Palestine about two hundred years before Christ. The Jews suffered terrible persecutions. Antiochus captured Jerusalem, killed 80,000 Jews, and sold a like number into slavery. He entered the Temple, took all the sacred vessels and treasures, sacrificed swine upon the altar of burnt offering, and sprinkled broth of swine-flesh all over the building, thus defiling it. No Jews entered the Temple thereafter; the daily sacrifices and services ceased altogether. Antiochus issued an edict declaring that all his subjects must worship the same gods. He forbade the keeping of the Sabbath, of festivals, and of other religious customs under pain of death; the sacred books of the Law and the Prophets were destroyed; the Temple was desecrated by heathen services, and a statue of Jupiter Olympus was erected on the altar of burnt offering. Eleazar, a God-fearing scribe, at the age of ninety years, was forced by the soldiers to eat swine-flesh. When he spit it out, he was tortured to death.

A mother and her seven sons were tortured because they refused to eat swine-flesh. The tongue of the eldest son was cut out, his fingers and toes cut off. Then he was cast into a large vessel and burned to death, while his mother and brothers were looking on, who comforted him and encouraged him to be faithful. When he was dead, the other brothers were asked whether they were ready to eat swine-flesh, and when they refused, one after the other was tortured and put to death. The mother, with undaunted firmness, admonished them to meet death bravely and to refuse all offers of wealth and honor. When she had seen her seven sons die, she, too, was tortured and slain.

The Maccabees. A God-fearing priest by the name of Mattathias, seeing a Jew sacrificing to the heathen gods, fell upon him and killed him and the king's servants who had set up the altar and destroyed the altar. Then he and his family, together with other like-minded Jews, fled into the mountains. Many of the Jews came to him, and when he had gathered a small army, they scoured the country and destroyed the heathen altars. After his death his son Judas Maccabeus succeeded him. Judas Maccabeus was bold and courageous, and his enemies feared him. After defeating Antiochus, he became governor of Palestine. The Temple was restored, purged, and rededicated, and the services of old were resumed. When the Syrians attacked Palestine again, Judas made a covenant with the Romans, who promised help, but failed to keep their promise. He was defeated by the Syrians and killed in battle. His brother Jonathan succeeded him, but he was treacherously murdered by the Syrians. Another brother, Simon, succeeded in capturing Zion, which the heathen had continued to hold. As long as he lived, the country had rest and peace.

The Jews under the Romans. The Maccabees ruled for nearly one hundred years. While two of the brothers were quarreling as to which of the two should be ruler, the Romans, led by Pompey, came to settle the quarrel. After a siege, which lasted three months, Jerusalem was taken, and a yearly tribute was imposed on Judea. About forty-eight years before the birth of Christ, Herod the Great, a descendant of Esau, was made governor of the land, and thirty-seven years before Christ the Romans made him king of Judea. He sought to fortify his throne by committing inhuman cruelties. He annihilated the Maccabees, put to death his wife Mariamne, daughter of the high priest and a descendant of the Maccabees; he slew her mother, father, and grandfather and drowned her brother in a bath. His sons Alexander and Aristobulus were strangled by his orders. He tried to appease the Jews by making improvements in his kingdom. He rebuilt Samaria. He built a magnificent palace on Zion for himself and the seaport of Caesarea. He rebuilt the Temple at Jerusalem, which, being now about five hundred years old, needed renovation.

During the latter part of his reign Jesus was born in Bethlehem. Soon after the slaughter of the children at Bethlehem a fearful disease put an end to this cruel ruler. After his death his kingdom was divided among his three sons, Archelaus, Herod Antipas, and Philip. Archelaus was banished to Gaul (France) for his cruelties by Augustus. Palestine now became a Roman province, ruled by Roman governors. The fifth of these governors was Pontius Pilate.

SUMMARY STUDY OF THE SEVENTH PERIOD

Name various proofs that faith in the true God was still evident in the captive Jews.

State the results of their testimony among the heathen on various occasions.

Describe Daniel's position in the civil government and in the Church of God.

What became of the ten tribes of Israel?

Tell why the house of Judah returned, who sent the people back, what they did upon their return, and relate something of their later history up to the beginning of the New Testament.

Discuss in class a number of the important lessons of this period for our personal faith and life.

"LIFT UP YOUR HEADS, O YE GATES; AND BE YE LIFT UP, YE EVERLASTING DOORS; AND THE KING OF GLORY SHALL COME IN." Ps. 24, 7.

THE NEW TESTAMENT

INTRODUCTION

"When the fulness of the time was come, God sent forth His Son, made of a woman, made under the Law, to redeem them that were under the Law, that we might receive the adoption of sons," Gal. 4, 4. 5.

The New Testament comprises the history of the life and work of Jesus Christ upon earth and of the early Christian Church. In the following stories we shall first learn of the childhood of Jesus. We shall see Him enter upon His public ministry at about thirty years of age and proving Himself the great Prophet promised by God. About three years later we see Him lay down His life for the sins of the world, rising in glory on the third day, and after forty days ascending into heaven to sit at the right hand of God the Father Almighty, from whence He shall come again to judge the quick and the dead. This was followed by the outpouring of the Holy Ghost on Pentecost and the establishment of the Christian Church.

The stories of the New Testament have been divided into the following sections, or periods: —

First Period: The Childhood of Jesus; 7 stories.
Second Period: The Public Ministry of Christ; 35 stories.
Third Period: The Passion of Our Lord Jesus Christ; 9 stories.
Fourth Period: The Glorified Lord; 6 stories.
Fifth Period: The Founding and Growth of the Christian Church; 13 stories.

FIRST PERIOD
THE CHILDHOOD OF JESUS

This period extends from the beginning of the New Testament to the time when Jesus entered upon His public ministry. The Word of God reveals but a few incidents from the childhood of the Savior, but they are of great importance. What could be of greater importance to us and to the world than the fact that the Son of God was born a human being, thereby assuming our flesh and blood and redeeming us from sin, death, and the devil? This period also tells of the birth of the forerunner of Christ, John the Baptist. It tells us of the circumcision of Jesus on the eighth day, His presentation to the Lord in the Temple on the fortieth day, the visit of the Wise Men from the East, the flight to Egypt, the return to Nazareth, and the twelve-year-old Jesus among the doctors in the Temple. The Bible is silent on the life of Jesus from the time that He was twelve years old until He began to appear in public.

1. Zacharias
Luke 1, 5—23

The Parents of John the Baptist. There was, in the days of Herod,[1)] the king of Judea, a priest named Zacharias, and his wife's name was Elisabeth.

They were both righteous before God, walking in all the commandments of the Lord, blameless.[2)] And they had no child, and they both were now well stricken in years.

The Message of Gabriel. And it came to pass that, while he executed the priest's office before God, his lot [3)] was to burn incense [4)] when he went into the Temple of the Lord. And the whole multitude of the people were praying without at the time of incense.

And there appeared unto him an angel of the Lord, standing on the right side of the altar of incense. And when Zacharias saw him, he was troubled.

But the angel said unto him, "Fear not, Zacharias; for thy prayer is heard, and thy wife Elisabeth shall bear thee a son, and thou shalt call his name John. He shall be great in the sight of the Lord, and he shall be filled with the Holy Ghost. And many of the children of Israel shall he turn to the Lord, their God.

"And he shall go before Him in the spirit and the power of Elias to turn the hearts of the fathers to the children and the disobedient to the wisdom of the just; to make ready a people prepared for the Lord."

Zacharias Stricken Dumb. And Zacharias said unto the angel, "Whereby shall I know this? For I am an old man, and my wife well stricken in years."

---

1) Herod the Great, son of Antipater, 37 to 4 B. C.
2) In the eyes of men.   3) His turn among other priests.
4) During the morning sacrifice and the period of prayer.

The angel, answering, said unto him, "I am Gabriel, that stand in the presence of God and am sent to show thee these glad tidings. And, behold, thou shalt be dumb and not able to speak until the day that these things shall be performed,

"Fear not, Zacharias"

because thou believest not my words, which shall be fulfilled in their season."

And the people waited for Zacharias and marveled that he tarried so long in the Temple. And when he came out, he could not speak unto them.

And they perceived that he had seen a vision in the Temple; for he beckoned unto them and remained speechless. And as soon as the days of his ministration were accomplished, he departed to his own house.

Second Petition.

Heb. 1, 14. Are they not all ministering spirits, sent forth to minister for them who shall be heirs of salvation?

> Let the earth now praise the Lord,
> Who hath truly kept His word
> And the sinners' Help and Friend
> Now at last to us doth send. (91, 1.)

---

2. The Annunciation
Luke 1, 25—56.   Matt. 1, 20—24

The Angel's Greeting. And in the sixth month the angel Gabriel was sent from God unto a city of Galilee,[1] named Nazareth,[2] to a virgin espoused [3] to a man whose name was Joseph, of the house of David; and the virgin's name was Mary.

And the angel came in unto her and said, "Hail,[4] thou that art highly favored! [5] The Lord is with thee; blessed art thou among women."

And when she saw him, she was troubled at his saying and cast in her mind [6] what manner of salutation this should be.

The Annunciation. And the angel said unto her, "Fear not, Mary; for thou hast found favor with God. And, behold, thou shalt conceive in thy womb and *bring forth a son and shalt call His name Jesus. He shall be great and shall be called the Son of the Highest; and the Lord God shall give unto Him the throne of His father David. And He shall reign*

---

1) Galilee was the northern province of Palestine at the time of Christ.   2) Nazareth was about 66 miles north of Jerusalem.
3) Engaged.   4) Be joyful; rejoice.
5) A great favor has been shown, or granted, to you.
6) Wondered.

THE ANNUNCIATION

over the house of Jacob forever; and of His kingdom there shall be no end."

Then said Mary unto the angel, "How shall this be, seeing I know not a man?"

And the angel answered and said unto her, "The Holy Ghost shall come upon thee, and the power of the Highest

"Hail, thou that art highly favored!"

shall overshadow thee; therefore also that Holy Thing which shall be born of thee shall be called the Son of God.

"And, behold, thy cousin Elisabeth, she hath also conceived a son in her old age; and this is the sixth month with her, who was called barren. For with God nothing shall be impossible."

And Mary said, "Behold the handmaid of the Lord; be it unto me according to thy word."

And the angel departed from her.

Mary with Elisabeth. And Mary arose in those days and entered into the house of Zacharias and saluted Elisabeth.

And Elisabeth was filled with the Holy Ghost; and she spake out with a loud voice and said, "Blessed art thou among women, and blessed is the fruit of thy womb. And whence is this to me that the mother of my Lord should come to me? Blessed is she that believed."

Mary's Song of Praise. (The Magnificat.*) And Mary said, *"My soul doth magnify the Lord, and my spirit hath rejoiced in God, my Savior. For He hath regarded the low estate of His handmaiden; for, behold, from henceforth all generations shall call me blessed. For He that is mighty hath done to me great things; and holy is His name.*

"And His mercy is on them that fear Him from generation to generation. He hath showed strength with His arm; He hath scattered the proud in the imagination of their hearts. He hath put down the mighty from their seats and exalted them of low degree.

"He hath filled the hungry with good things, and the rich He hath sent empty away. He hath holpen His servant Israel in remembrance of His mercy, as He spake to our fathers, to Abraham and to his seed forever."

And Mary abode with Elisabeth about three months and returned to her own house.

Joseph Takes unto Himself Mary, His Wife. But the angel of the Lord appeared unto Joseph in a dream, saying, "Joseph, thou son of David, fear not to take unto thee Mary, thy wife; for she shall bring forth a son, and thou shalt call His name Jesus; *for He shall save His people from their sins."*

Now, all this was done that it might be fulfilled which was spoken of the Lord by the prophet, saying, "Behold,

---

* So called because of the opening word in Latin *Magnificat,* "My soul doth *magnify* [make great, praise] the Lord."

a virgin shall be with child and shall bring forth a son, and they shall call His name Emmanuel, which, being interpreted, is, God with us."

Then Joseph did as the Lord had bidden him and took unto him his wife.

Second Article.

Is. 7, 14. Behold, a virgin shall conceive and bear a son and shall call His name Immanuel.

> Let us all with gladsome voice
> Praise the God of heaven,
> Who, to bid our hearts rejoice,
> His own Son hath given. (97, 1.)

---

3. The Birth of John the Baptist
Luke 1, 57—80

John Named. Elisabeth brought forth a son. And her neighbors and her cousins heard how the Lord had showed great **mercy** upon her, and they rejoiced with her.

And on the eighth day they came to circumcise the child; and they called him Zacharias, after the name of his father. And his mother answered and said, "Not so; but he shall be called John."

And they said unto her, "There is none of thy kindred that is called by this name." And they made signs to his father how he would have him called.

And he asked for a writing-table and wrote, saying, "His name is John." And they marveled all. And his mouth was opened immediately and his tongue loosed, and he spake and praised God.

And fear came on all that dwelt round about them; and all these sayings were noised abroad throughout all the hill country of Judea. And all that heard them laid them up in their hearts,¹⁾ saying, "What manner of child shall this be!"

And the hand of the Lord was with him.

Zacharias's Song of Praise. (The Benedictus.*) And his father Zacharias was filled with the Holy Ghost and prophesied, saying, *"Blessed be the Lord God of Israel; for He hath*

"And they rejoiced with her"

visited and redeemed His people. And thou, child, shalt be called the prophet of the Highest; for thou shalt go before the face of the Lord to prepare His ways, to give knowledge of salvation unto His people by the remission of their sins."

John's Childhood. And the child grew and waxed strong

---

1) Pondered over these sayings.

* So called because of the opening word in Latin, *Benedictus,* "Blessed be [the Lord]."

THE BIRTH OF CHRIST

in spirit. And John was in the deserts till the day of his showing unto Israel.

Conclusion of the Lord's Prayer.

Mal. 3, 1. Behold, I will send My messenger, and he shall prepare the way before Me; and the Lord, whom ye seek, shall suddenly come to His Temple, even the Messenger of the Covenant, whom ye delight in.

Welcome, O my Savior, now!	Here, too, in my heart, I pray,
Hail! My Portion, Lord, art Thou.	Oh, prepare Thyself a way!

(91, 4.)

4. The Birth of Jesus Christ
Luke 2, 1—20

The Decree of Caesar. And it came to pass in those days that there went out a decree from Caesar Augustus [1] that all the world [2] should be taxed.[3] This taxing was first made when Cyrenius was governor of Syria.

And all went to be taxed, every one into his own city.[4]

And Joseph also went up from Galilee, out of the city of Nazareth, into Judea, unto the city of David, which is called Bethlehem,[5] because he was of the house and lineage of David, to be taxed with Mary, his espoused wife, being great with child.

Jesus Born in Bethlehem. And so it was that, while they were there, the days were accomplished that she should be delivered. And she brought forth her first-born son and wrapped him in swaddling-clothes [6] and laid him in a manger, because there was no room for them in the inn.

---

1) First Roman Emperor, 31 B. C. to 14 A. D.
2) The Roman Empire.
3) A census to be taken, with the listing of property for taxation.
4) The city of his ancestors, where the family records were kept.
5) Bethlehem is a town about six miles south of Jerusalem.
6) Strips of cloth three or four inches wide and several feet long, wound around the child.

The Announcement to the Shepherds. And there were in the same country shepherds abiding in the field, keeping watch over their flock by night.

And, lo, the angel of the Lord came upon them, and the

"She laid Him in a manger"

glory of the Lord shone round about them; and they were sore afraid.

And the angel said unto them, *"Fear not; for, behold, I bring you good tidings of great joy, which shall be to all people. For unto you is born this day, in the city of David, a Savior, which is Christ the Lord. And this shall be a sign unto you: Ye shall find the Babe wrapped in swaddling-clothes, lying in a manger."*

And suddenly there was with the angel a multitude of the heavenly host, praising God and saying,

> "Glory to God in the highest
> And on earth peace,
> Good will toward men."

The Shepherd's Adoration. And it came to pass, as the

"I bring you good tidings of great joy"

angels were gone away from them into heaven, the shepherds said one to another, "Let us now go even unto Bethlehem and see this thing which is come to pass, which the Lord hath made known unto us."

And they came with haste and found Mary and Joseph and the Babe lying in a manger.

And when they had seen it, they made known abroad the saying which was told them concerning this Child.

And all they that heard it wondered at those things which were told them by the shepherds.

But Mary kept all these things and pondered them in her heart.

And the shepherds returned, glorifying and praising God for all the things that they had heard and seen, as it was told unto them.

Second Article.

Is. 9, 6. For unto us a Child is born, unto us a Son is given; and the government shall be upon His shoulder; and His name shall be called Wonderful, Counselor, The Mighty God, The Everlasting Father, The Prince of Peace.

John 3, 16. God so loved the world that He gave His only-begotten Son, that whosoever believeth in Him should not perish, but have everlasting life.

From heav'n above to earth I come
To bear good news to ev'ry home;
Glad tidings of great joy I bring,
Whereof I now will say and sing.

To you this night is born a child
Of Mary, chosen virgin mild;
This little child, of lowly birth,
Shall be the joy of all the earth.
(85, 1. 2.)

5. The Circumcision and the Presentation
Luke 2, 21—40

THE CIRCUMCISION

And when eight days were accomplished for the circumcising of the Child, His name was called Jesus, which was so named of the angel before He was conceived in the womb.

THE PRESENTATION

And when the days of her purification according to the Law of Moses were accomplished,[1] they brought Him to Jerusalem to present Him to the Lord [2] and to offer a sacri-

---

[1] Lev. 12, 1—8.
[2] The presentation of the Christ-child took place on the fortieth day after His birth. According to the Law (Ex. 13, 2) all the first-born, both of man and of beasts, were the Lord's and were to be sanctified unto Him; but some animals as well as the first-born of man were to be redeemed by an offering (Ex. 13, 12. 13).

THE CIRCUMCISION AND THE PRESENTATION 265

fice according to that which is said in the Law of the Lord, A pair of turtle-doves or two young pigeons.

Simeon. And, behold, there was a man in Jerusalem whose name was Simeon; and the same man was just and devout, waiting for the Consolation of Israel;[3] and the Holy

"Lord, now lettest Thou Thy servant depart in peace"

Ghost was upon him. It was revealed unto him by the Holy Ghost that he should not see death before he had seen the Lord's Christ.[4]

And he came by the Spirit into the Temple; and when the parents brought in the Child Jesus to do for Him after the custom of the Law, then took he Him up in his arms

---

3) The Savior.   4) The Lord's Anointed; the Messiah.

and blessed God and said, *"Lord, now lettest Thou Thy servant depart in peace according to Thy word; for mine eyes have seen Thy Salvation, which Thou hast prepared before the face of all people, a Light to lighten the Gentiles, and the Glory of Thy people Israel."*

And Joseph and His mother marveled at those things which were spoken of Him.

And Simeon blessed them and said unto Mary, His mother, "Behold, this Child is set for the fall and rising again of many in Israel [5] and for a sign which shall be spoken against; [6] yea, a sword shall pierce through thy own soul also [7] that the thoughts of many hearts may be revealed." [8]

Anna. There was a prophetess, Anna, who was of a great age and a widow of about fourscore and four years, who departed not from the Temple, but served God with fastings and prayers night and day.

And she, coming in that instant, gave thanks likewise unto the Lord and spake of Him to all them that looked for redemption in Jerusalem.

Third Commandment.

Mark 10, 14. Suffer the little children to come unto Me and forbid them not; for of such is the kingdom of God.

>Ah, dearest Jesus, holy Child,
>Make Thee a bed, soft, undefiled,
>Within my heart, that it may be
>A quiet chamber kept for Thee.   (85, 13.)

---

5) Many will take offense, and many will believe.

6) Jesus was to become a sign of God's grace to mankind, against which many would speak or rebel.

7) The suffering and death of Jesus would cause her severe grief.

8) In accepting or in rejecting the God-given Savior. "He that believeth," etc.

6. The Wise Men from the East. The Flight to Egypt
a. Matt. 2, 1—12.   b. Matt. 2,13—23

THE WISE MEN

The Appearance of the Star. Now, when Jesus was born in Bethlehem of Judea, in the days of Herod the king, behold, there came wise men from the East [1] to Jerusalem, saying, "Where is He that is born King of the Jews? For we have seen His star in the East and are come to worship Him."

When Herod the king had heard these things, he was troubled and all Jerusalem with him.

And when he had gathered all the chief priests and scribes of the people together, he demanded of them where Christ should be born.

And they said unto him, "In Bethlehem of Judea; for thus it is written by the prophet, 'And thou Bethlehem, in the land of Juda, art not the least among the princes of Juda; for out of thee shall come a Governor, that shall rule My people Israel.' "

Then Herod, when he had privily called the wise men, inquired of them diligently what time the star appeared.

And he sent them to Bethlehem and said, "Go and search diligently for the young Child; and when ye have found Him, bring me word again that I may come and worship Him also."

The Adoration of the Wise Men. When they had heard the king, they departed; and, lo, the star which they saw in the East went before them, till it came and stood over where the young Child was.

When they saw the star, they rejoiced with exceeding great joy.

And when they were come into the house, they saw the

---

[1] A country east of Jerusalem; whether Babylonia or some other country we do not know.

young Child with Mary, His mother, and fell down and worshiped Him; and when they had opened their treasures, they presented unto Him gifts: gold and frankincense [2] and myrrh.[3]

And being warned of God in a dream that they should

"They fell down and worshiped Him"

not return to Herod, they departed into their own country another way.

THE FLIGHT TO EGYPT

Joseph Told to Flee. And when they were departed, behold, the angel of the Lord appeareth to Joseph in a dream,

---

[2] Frankincense is a substance obtained from a tree which grows in the East. It is of a white or yellowish color and bitter to the taste. It has an exceedingly pleasant odor when burned.

[3] Myrrh, a gum, the thickened sap of a low, thorny tree.

saying, "Arise and take the young Child and His mother and flee into Egypt and be thou there until I bring thee word; for Herod will seek the young Child to destroy Him."

When he arose, he took the young Child and His mother by night and departed into Egypt and was there until the

"He departed into Egypt"

death of Herod, that it might be fulfilled which was spoken of the Lord by the prophet, saying, "Out of Egypt have I called My Son."

The Children of Bethlehem Slain. Then Herod, when he saw that he was mocked of the wise men, was exceeding wroth and sent forth and slew all the children that were in Bethlehem and in all the coasts thereof,[4] from two years

---

4) Surrounding country.

old and under, according to the time which he had diligently inquired of the wise men.

Then was fulfilled that which was spoken by Jeremy, the prophet, saying, "In Rama was there a voice heard, lamentation, and weeping, and great mourning, Rachel weeping for her children, and would not be comforted because they are not."

The Return to Nazareth. But when Herod was dead,[5] behold, an angel of the Lord appeareth in a dream to Joseph in Egypt, saying, "Arise and take the young Child and His mother and go into the land of Israel; for they are dead which sought the young Child's life."

And he arose and took the young Child and His mother and came into the land of Israel.

But when he heard that Archelaus did reign in Judea in the room of [6] his father Herod, he was afraid to go thither; notwithstanding, being warned of God in a dream, he turned aside into the parts of Galilee; and he came and dwelt in a city called Nazareth, that it might be fulfilled which was spoken by the prophets, "He shall be called a Nazarene."

Fifth Commandment. — Second Petition.

Is. 60, 1. Arise, shine; for thy light is come, and the glory of the Lord is risen upon thee.

> As with gladness men of old
> Did the guiding star behold;
> As with joy they hailed its light,
> Leading onward, beaming bright:
> So, most gracious Lord, may we
> Evermore be led by Thee. (127, 1)

---

[5] Probably not more than two years after the flight to Egypt.
[6] In place of.

7. The Child Jesus in the Temple
Luke 2, 41—52

Missed by His Parents. Now, His parents went to Jerusalem every year at the feast of the Passover. And when He was twelve years old,[1)] they went up to Jerusalem after the custom of the feast.

And when they had fulfilled the days, as they returned,

"In the midst of the doctors"

the Child Jesus tarried behind in Jerusalem; and Joseph and His mother knew not of it. But they, supposing Him to have been in the company, went a day's journey; and they sought Him among their kinsfolk and acquaintance.

---

1) Of an age to assume all rights and duties of the local synagog and privileged to study the Holy Scriptures Himself and to take part in the celebration of the three great festivals at Jerusalem; corresponding in a way to our confirmation age.

And when they found Him not, they turned back again to Jerusalem, seeking Him.

Found in the Temple. And it came to pass that after three days they found Him in the Temple, sitting in the midst of the doctors, both hearing them and asking them questions. And all that heard Him were astonished at His understanding and answers.

And when they saw Him, they were amazed; and His mother said unto Him, "Son, why hast Thou thus dealt with us? Behold, Thy father and I have sought Thee sorrowing."

And He said unto them, "How is it that ye sought Me? Wist ye not that I must be about My Father's business?"

And they understood not the saying which He spake unto them.

The Return. And He went down with them and came to Nazareth and was subject unto them; but His mother kept all these sayings in her heart.

And Jesus increased in wisdom [2] and stature [3] and in favor with God and man. [4]

Third and Fourth Commandments.

Col. 3, 20. Children, obey your parents in all things; for this is well pleasing unto the Lord.

>Lord, open Thou my heart to hear
>And through Thy Word to me draw near;
>Let me Thy Word e'er pure retain,
>Let me Thy child and heir remain. **(5, 1.)**

SUMMARY STUDY OF THE FIRST PERIOD

1. Restate in connected story form the main events of this period of Bible History.

2. Mention various evidences that John the Baptist was truly the forerunner of Christ.

---

2) Knowledge and understanding.   3) Bodily growth.
4) God and man were pleased with Him. He led a perfect life.

3. State prophecies concerning Christ that were fulfilled in this period.

4. Give several reasons why the birth of Christ is the greatest event in all history.

5. Picture your own hopeless condition and that of fallen mankind if Jesus had not been born; on the other hand, describe the chief benefits of His birth to you and all the world.

6. Name several ways in which Jesus in His childhood a) fulfilled the Law, b) suffered for our sakes, and c) set a good example to children.

7. Point out various lessons that we should draw from the stories in this period for our personal faith and life.

"WHEN THE FULNESS OF THE TIME WAS COME, GOD SENT FORTH HIS SON, MADE OF A WOMAN, MADE UNDER THE LAW, TO REDEEM THEM THAT WERE UNDER THE LAW, THAT WE MIGHT RECEIVE THE ADOPTION OF SONS." Gal. 4, 4. 5.

SECOND PERIOD

THE PUBLIC MINISTRY OF CHRIST

Beginning with the preaching of John the Baptist, this period embraces the entire public ministry of Christ and extends over three years. Here we see the Savior, now about thirty years old (Luke 3, 23), manifest Himself publicly as the Son of God and the Redeemer of the world.

As the great Prophet, long foretold by Moses, He preached and taught both publicly and privately. "God, who at sundry times and in divers manners spake in time past unto the fathers by the prophets, hath in these last days spoken unto us by His Son," Heb. 1, 1. 2. "He taught as one having authority [with great power and effect] and not as the scribes," Matt. 7, 29. He exhorted all people to repent and invited those who labored and were heavy laden to come to Him for rest. He fearlessly condemned the religious leaders of His day because of their self-righteousness, formalism, and hypocrisy and warned the people against these sins. He associated much with the common people, even with publicans and sinners, endeavoring always to bring them to true faith and to lead them into the paths of righteousness. He went about doing good, healing the sick, casting out devils, and raising the dead, thus confirming His preaching and teaching with the most marvelous works of service to stricken mankind. He called unto Himself twelve disciples, who were to be eye-witnesses of His life and ministry and the great teachers of the Church for all ages.

As the true High Priest He led a holy life, perfectly fulfilled the Law, forgave sins, and interceded with the Father for all mankind and especially for the believers. As King He exercised His power over nature, sickness, death, and the devil and built up His Kingdom of Grace.

In short, this is a period in which Jesus reveals Himself as the long-awaited Savior from sin.

8. John the Baptist

Matt. 3, 1—12. Mark 1, 1—8. Luke 3, 1—18. John 1, 19—28

John Preaching Repentance. In the fifteenth year of the reign of Tiberius Caesar, Pontius Pilate being governor of

Judea, the word of God came unto John the Baptist in the wilderness of Judea.[1]

And he came into all the country about Jordan, preaching the baptism of repentance for the remission of sins, saying, "Repent ye; for the kingdom of heaven is at hand."

And John was clothed with camel's hair and with

"Repent ye"

a leathern girdle about his loins; and he did eat locusts and wild honey.

Then went out to him Jerusalem and all Judea and all the region round about Jordan, and were baptized of him in Jordan, confessing their sins.

Warning the Pharisees and Sadducees. But when he saw many of the Pharisees and Sadducees come to his baptism, he said unto them, "O generation of vipers, who hath warned you to flee from the wrath to come? Bring forth therefore fruits meet for repentance.

---

1) The "wilderness" where John the Baptist preached was in the region of Jordan, north of the Dead Sea.

"Think not to say within yourselves, 'We have Abraham to our father'; for I say unto you, God is able of these stones to raise up children unto Abraham. And now also the ax is laid unto the root of the trees; therefore every tree which bringeth not forth good fruit is hewn down and cast into the fire."

The Effect of John's Preaching. And the people asked him, saying, "What shall we do, then?"

He answereth and saith unto them, "He that hath two coats, let him impart to him that hath none; and he that hath meat, let him do likewise."

Then came also publicans to be baptized and said, "Master, what shall we do?"

And he said unto them, "Exact no more than that which is appointed you."

And the soldiers likewise demanded of him, saying, "And what shall we do?"

And he said unto them, "Do violence to no man, neither accuse any falsely, and be content with your wages."

John's Testimony of Christ. And as the people were in expectation and all men mused in their hearts of John whether he were the Christ or not, the Jews sent priests and Levites from Jerusalem to ask him, "Who art thou?"

And he confessed and denied not, but confessed, "I am not the Christ."

And they asked him, "What then? Art thou Elias?"

And he saith, "I am not."

"Art thou that Prophet?"

And he answered, "No."

Then said they unto him, "Who art thou? What sayest thou of thyself?"

He said, "I am the voice of one crying in the wilderness:

'Make straight the way of the Lord,' as said the prophet Esaias."

And they which were sent were of the Pharisees. And they asked him and said unto him, "Why baptizest thou then if thou be not Christ nor Elias, neither that Prophet?"

John answered them, saying, "I indeed baptize you with water; but there standeth one among you whom ye know not. He it is who, coming after me, is mightier than I, whose shoe's latchet I am not worthy to unloose. He shall baptize you with the Holy Ghost and with fire; whose fan is in His hand, and He will throughly purge His floor [2] and gather the wheat into His garner; [3] but the chaff He will burn with fire unquenchable."

These things were done in Bethabara, beyond Jordan, where John was baptizing.

Confession. — Baptism.

Acts 2, 38. Repent and be baptized, every one of you, in the name of Jesus Christ for the remission of sins, and ye shall receive the gift of the Holy Ghost.

> Yea, as I live, Jehovah saith,
> I would not have the sinner's death,
> But that he turn from error's ways,
> Repent, and live through endless days. (331, 1.)

---

2) **Threshing-floor.**   3) **Granary.**

9. The Baptism of Jesus and His Temptation
a. Matt. 3, 13—17. Mark 1, 1—11. Luke 3, 21—23
b. Matt. 4, 1—11. Mark 1, 12. 13. Luke 4, 1—13

THE BAPTISM

Fulfilling All Righteousness. Now, when all the people were baptized, it came to pass that Jesus came from Galilee to Jordan unto John to be baptized of him.[1]

"This is My beloved Son"

But John forbade Him, saying, "I have need to be baptized of Thee, and comest Thou to me?"

And Jesus said unto him, "Suffer it to be so now; for thus it becometh us to fulfil all righteousness."

Then he suffered Him.

---

[1] Jesus came to John to be baptized about six months after John had begun to preach.

Revealed as the Son of God. And Jesus, when He was baptized, went up straightway out of the water; and, lo, the heavens were opened unto Him, and he saw the Spirit of God descending like a dove and lighting upon Him; and, lo, a voice from heaven, saying, "This is My beloved Son, in whom I am well pleased."

And Jesus began to be about thirty years of age.

THE TEMPTATION

First Temptation. And Jesus, being full of the Holy Ghost, returned from Jordan, and immediately the Spirit driveth Him into the wilderness to be tempted of the devil.

And when He had fasted forty days and forty nights, He was afterward an hungered.

And when the Tempter came to Him, he said, "If Thou be the Son of God, command that these stones be made bread."

But He answered and said, "It is written, 'Man shall not live by bread alone, but by every word that proceedeth out of the mouth of God.'"

Second Temptation. Then the devil taketh Him up into the Holy City and setteth Him on a pinnacle [2] of the Temple and saith unto Him, "If Thou be the Son of God, cast Thyself down; for it is written, 'He shall give His angels charge concerning thee, and in their hands they shall bear thee up, lest at any time thou dash thy foot against a stone.'"

And Jesus said unto him, "It is written again, 'Thou shalt not tempt the Lord, thy God.'"

Third Temptation. Again, the devil taketh Him up into an exceeding high mountain and showeth Him all the kingdoms of the world and the glory of them and saith unto Him,

---

[2] "Probably the elevation over the roof of Solomon's Porch, to which there was a passage by stairs and which had a perpendicular depth of 600 or 700 feet into the valley below."

"All these things will I give Thee if Thou wilt fall down and worship me."

Then saith Jesus unto him, "Get thee hence, Satan; for it is written, *Thou shalt worship the Lord, thy God, and Him only shalt thou serve.*'"

Then the devil leaveth Him, and, behold, angels came and ministered unto Him.

Baptism. — *Sixth Petition.* — *First Article:* The Triune God; Evil Angels.

1 Pet. 5, 8. 9. Be sober, be vigilant, because your adversary, the devil, as a roaring lion, walketh about, seeking whom he may devour; whom resist steadfast in the faith.

John 3, 5. Verily, verily, I say unto thee, Except a man be born of water and of the Spirit, he cannot enter into the kingdom of God.

> He that believes and is baptized
> Shall see the Lord's salvation;
> Baptized into the death of Christ,
> He is a new creation.
> Through Christ's redemption he shall stand
> Among the glorious heav'nly band
> Of every tribe and nation.   (301, 1.)

10. The First Disciples
John 1, 29—51

John Testifies to His Disciples of Jesus. And John seeth Jesus coming unto him and saith, *"Behold the Lamb of God, which taketh away the sin of the world.* This is He of whom I said, 'After me cometh a Man which is preferred before me; for He was before me. This is the Son of God.'"

The next day after, John stood and two of his disciples; and looking upon Jesus as He walked, he saith, "Behold the Lamb of God!"

THE FIRST DISCIPLES 281

John, Andrew, and Peter. And the two disciples heard him speak, and they followed Jesus. Then Jesus turned and saw them following and saith unto them, "What seek ye?"

They said unto Him, "Rabbi" (which is Master), "where dwellest Thou?"

"Rabbi, where dwellest Thou?"

He saith unto them, "Come and see."

They came and saw where He dwelt and abode with Him that day.

One of the two,[1] which heard John speak and followed Him was Andrew, Simon Peter's brother. He first findeth his

---

1) The other was John, who became one of the apostles.

own brother Simon and saith unto him, "We have found the Messias [Christ]." And he brought him to Jesus.

And when Jesus beheld him, He said, "Thou art Simon, the son of Jona; thou shalt be called Cephas [Stone]."

Philip and Nathanael. The day following, Jesus findeth Philip and saith unto him, "Follow Me."

Philip findeth Nathanael and saith unto him, "We have found Him of whom Moses in the Law, and the prophets, did write, Jesus of Nazareth, the son of Joseph."

And Nathanael said unto him, "Can there any good thing come out of Nazareth?"

Philip saith unto him, "Come and see."

Jesus saw Nathanael coming to Him and saith of him, "Behold an Israelite indeed, in whom is no guile."

Nathanael saith unto him, "Whence knowest Thou me?"

Jesus answered and said unto him, "Before that Philip called thee, when thou wast under the fig-tree, I saw thee."

Nathanael answered and saith unto Him, "Rabbi, Thou art the Son of God; Thou art the King of Israel."

Jesus answered and said unto him, "Because I said unto thee, 'I saw thee under the fig-tree,' believest thou? Thou shalt see greater things than these. Verily, verily, I say unto you, Hereafter ye shall see heaven open and the angels of God ascending and descending upon the Son of Man."

Second Petition.

Matt. 9, 37. 38. The harvest, truly, is plenteous, but the laborers are few; pray ye therefore the Lord of the harvest that He will send forth laborers into His harvest.

> Come, follow Me, the Savior spake,
>   All in My way abiding;
> Deny yourselves, the world forsake,
>   Obey My call and guiding.
> Oh, bear the cross, whate'er betide;
> Take My example for your guide. (421, 1.)

11. The Marriage in Cana
John 2, 1—11

Jesus at the Marriage. And the third day there was a marriage in Cana of Galilee;[1] and the mother of Jesus was

"Fill the water-pots with water"

there; and both Jesus was called, and His disciples, to the marriage.

And when they wanted wine, the mother of Jesus saith unto Him, "They have no wine."

Jesus saith unto her, "Woman, what have I to do with thee? Mine hour is not yet come."

---

1) Cana was a village near Nazareth.

His mother saith unto the servants, "Whatsoever He saith unto you, do it."

The First Miracle. And there were set there six water-pots of stone, after the manner of the purifying of the Jews, containing two or three firkins apiece.[2]

Jesus saith unto them, "Fill the water-pots with water." And they filled them up to the brim.

And He saith unto them, "Draw out now and bear unto the governor of the feast." And they bare it.

When the ruler of the feast had tasted the water that was made wine and knew not whence it was (but the servants which drew the water knew), the governor of the feast called the bridegroom and saith unto him, "Every man at the beginning doth set forth good wine, and when men have well drunk, then that which is worse; but thou hast kept the good wine until now."

This beginning of miracles did Jesus in Cana of Galilee and manifested forth His glory; and His disciples believed on Him.

Second Article: Rays of hidden glory.

John 1, 14. And the Word was made flesh and dwelt among us; and we beheld His glory, the glory as of the Only-begotten of the Father, full of grace and truth.

>   Oh, blest the house, whate'er befall,
>   Where Jesus Christ is all in all!
>   Yea, if He were not dwelling there,
>   How dark and poor and void it were! (625, 1.)

---

[2] The six water-pots held from ninety to one hundred twenty gallons. A firkin equals seven and a half gallons.

12. Nicodemus
John 2, 13. 23; 3, 1—17

Nicodemus is Instructed. And the Jews' Passover was at hand, and Jesus went up to Jerusalem.[1)] Now, when He was in Jerusalem, many believed in His name when they saw the miracles which He did.

There was a man of the Pharisees named Nicodemus, a ruler of the Jews. The same came to Jesus by night and said unto Him, "Rabbi, we know that Thou art a teacher come from God; for no man can do these miracles that Thou doest except God be with him."

Jesus said unto him, "Verily, verily, I say unto thee: *'Except a man be born again, he cannot see the kingdom of God.'*"

Nicodemus saith unto Him, "How can a man be born when he is old?"

Jesus answered, *"Except a man be born of water and of the Spirit, he cannot enter into the kingdom of God.* That which is born of the flesh is flesh, and that which is born of the Spirit is spirit.

"Marvel not that I said unto thee, 'Ye must be born again.' The wind bloweth where it listeth, and thou hearest the sound thereof, but canst not tell whence it cometh and whither it goeth. So is every one that is born of the Spirit."

Urged to Accept the Messiah. Nicodemus answered and said unto Him, "How can these things be?"

Jesus answered and said unto him, "Art thou a master of Israel and knowest not these things? Verily, verily, I say unto thee, We speak that we do know and testify that we

---

1) At this time the first cleansing of the Temple took place, John 2, 14—17. Jesus cleansed the Temple a second time, after His last entry into Jerusalem, Matt. 21, 12. 13.

have seen; and ye receive not our witness. If I have told you earthly things and ye believe not, how shall ye believe if I tell you of heavenly things?

"And as Moses lifted up the serpent in the wilderness,

"So must the Son of Man be lifted up"

even so must the Son of Man be lifted up that whosoever believeth in Him should not perish, but have eternal life.

"God so loved the world that He gave His only-begotten Son, that whosoever believeth in Him should not perish, but have everlasting life.

"For God sent not His Son into the world to condemn the world, but that the world through Him might be saved."

Baptism: Regeneration.

Eph. 4, 24. Put on the new man, which after God is created in righteousness and true holiness.

> My loving Father, Thou dost take me
> To be henceforth Thy child and heir;
> My faithful Savior, Thou dost make me
> The fruit of all Thy sorrows share;
> Thou, Holy Ghost, wilt comfort me
> When darkest clouds around I see. (298, 2.)

---

13. Jesus and the Samaritans
John 4, 1—43

At Jacob's Well. And Jesus left Judea and departed again into Galilee. And He must needs go through Samaria.

Then cometh He to a city of Samaria which is called Sychar.[1)] Now, Jacob's Well was there. Jesus therefore, being wearied with His journey, sat thus at the well.

There cometh a woman of Samaria to draw water. Jesus saith unto her, "Give Me to drink." (For His disciples were gone away unto the city to buy meat.)

Then saith the woman of Samaria unto Him, "How is it that Thou, being a Jew, askest drink of me, which am a woman of Samaria?" (For the Jews have no dealings with the Samaritans.)

Christ the Living Water. Jesus answered, "If thou knewest the gift of God and who it is that saith to thee, 'Give Me to drink,' thou wouldest have asked of Him, and He would have given thee living water."

The woman saith unto Him, "Sir, Thou hast nothing to draw with, and the well is deep; from whence, then, hast

---

[1)] Sychar, near Shechem, is situated between Mount Gerizim and Mount Ebal in Samaria.

Thou that living water? Art Thou greater than our father Jacob, which gave us the well and drank thereof himself and his children and his cattle?"

Jesus answered, "Whosoever drinketh of this water shall

"If thou knewest the gift of God"

thirst again; but whosoever drinketh of the water that I shall give him shall never thirst."

The woman saith unto Him, "Sir, give me this water that I thirst not, neither come hither to draw."

Jesus saith unto her, "Go, call thy husband and come hither."

The woman answered and said, "I have no husband."

Jesus said unto her, "Thou hast well said, I have no husband; for thou hast had five husbands; and he whom thou now hast is not thy husband."

The woman saith unto Him, "Sir, I perceive that Thou art a prophet.

"Our Fathers worshiped in this mountain;[2] and ye say that in Jerusalem is the place where men ought to worship."

True Worship. Jesus saith unto her, "Woman, believe Me, the hour cometh when ye shall neither in this mountain nor yet at Jerusalem worship the Father. Ye worship ye know not what; we know what we worship; for salvation is of the Jews.

"But the hour cometh, and now is, when the true worshipers shall worship the Father in spirit and in truth; for the Father seeketh such to worship Him. *God is a spirit; and they that worship Him must worship Him in spirit and in truth.*"

The woman saith unto Him, "I know that Messias cometh, which is called Christ; when He is come, He will tell us all things."

Jesus saith unto her, "I that speak unto thee am He."

The Samaritans Believe. The woman then left her waterpot and went her way into the city and saith to the men, "Come, see a man which told me all the things that ever I did; is not this the Christ?"

Then they went out of the city and came unto Him and besought Him that He would tarry with them; and He abode there two days.

And many more believed because of His own word and

---

[2] The religion of the Samaritans was a mixture of Judaism and heathenism. Their temple was on Mount Gerizim. Intense hatred existed between Jews and Samaritans.

Advanced Bible History.

said unto the woman, "Now we believe, not because of thy saying; for we have heard Him ourselves and know that this is indeed the Christ, the Savior of the world."

Now, after two days He departed thence and went into Galilee.

Third and Sixth Commandments. — Of Prayer in General: How and where should we pray?

Rom. 10, 17. So, then, faith cometh by hearing and hearing by the Word of God.

> I heard the voice of Jesus say,
> "Behold, I freely give
> The living water; thirsty one,
> Stoop down and drink and live!"
> I came to Jesus, and I drank
> Of that life-giving stream;
> My thirst was quenched, my soul revived,
> And now I live in Him. (277, 2.)

14. Bethesda. The Withered Hand
a. John 5, 1—16. b. Matt. 12, 10—13

BETHESDA

The Pool of Bethesda. Now, there is at Jerusalem by the sheep-market a pool, which is called in the Hebrew tongue Bethesda, having five porches.

In these lay a great multitude of impotent folk, of blind, halt, withered, waiting for the moving of the water. For an angel went down at a certain season into the pool and troubled the water; whosoever then first, after the troubling of the water, stepped in was made whole of whatsoever disease he had.

The Sick Man. And a certain man was there which had an infirmity thirty and eight years.

When Jesus saw him lie and knew that he had been now

a long time in that case, He saith unto him, "Wilt thou be made whole?"

The impotent man answered him, "Sir, I have no man, when the water is troubled, to put me into the pool; but while I am coming, another steppeth down before me."

"Rise, take up thy bed"

Jesus saith unto him, "Rise, take up thy bed, and walk." And immediately the man was made whole and took up his bed and walked; and on the same day was the Sabbath.

The Anger of the Jews. The Jews, therefore, said unto

him that was cured, "It is the Sabbath-day; it is not lawful for thee to carry thy bed."

He answered them, "He that made me whole, the same said unto me, 'Take up thy bed and walk.'"

Then asked they him, "What man is that which said unto thee, 'Take up thy bed and walk'?"

And he that was healed wist not who it was; for Jesus had conveyed Himself away, a multitude being in that place.

Afterward Jesus findeth him in the Temple and said unto him, "Behold, thou art made whole; sin no more, lest a worse thing come unto thee."

The man departed and told the Jews that it was Jesus which had made him whole.

And therefore did the Jews persecute Jesus and sought to slay Him, because He had done these things on the Sabbath-day.

THE WITHERED HAND *

"Is It Lawful to Heal on the Sabbath-Days?" At that time Jesus went on the Sabbath-day into their synagog. And, behold, there was a man which had his hand withered.

And they asked him, saying, "Is it lawful to heal on the Sabbath-days?" that they might accuse Him.

And He said unto them, "What man shall there be among you that shall have one sheep, and if it fall into a pit on the Sabbath-day, will he not lay hold on it and lift it out? How much, then, is a man better than a sheep! Wherefore it is lawful to do well on the Sabbath-days."

Then saith He to the man, "Stretch forth thine hand."

And he stretched it forth; and it was restored whole like as the other.

---

* This miracle occurred much later; in point of time it belongs after Story 24.

Third Commandment: Sabbath.
Matt. 12, 8. For the Son of Man is Lord even of the Sabbath-day.

> Be patient and await His leisure
>   In cheerful hope, with heart content,
> To take whate'er thy Father's pleasure
>   And His discerning love hath sent
> Nor doubt our inmost wants are known
> To Him who chose us for His own. (518, 3.)

---

15. Peter's Draught of Fishes. The Twelve Apostles
a. Luke 5, 1—11. b. Matt. 10, 1—10

THE DRAUGHT OF FISHES

The Sermon. And it came to pass that, as the people pressed upon Him to hear the Word of God, He stood by the Lake of Gennesaret [1)] and saw two ships standing by the lake; but the fishermen were gone out of them and were washing their nets.

And He entered into one of the ships, which was Simon's, and prayed him that he would thrust out a little from the land. And He sat down and taught the people out of the ship.

The Miracle. Now, when He had left speaking, He said unto Simon, "Launch out into the deep and let down your nets for a draught."

And Simon, answering, said unto Him "Master, we have toiled all the night and have taken nothing; nevertheless, at Thy word I will let down the nets."

And when they had this done, they inclosed a great multitude of fishes; and their net brake.

---

1) The Lake of Gennesaret, also called Sea of Tiberias or Sea of Galilee, is thirteen miles long and about seven miles wide. Now, as in the time of this story, it abounds with fish. Among the cities which stood on its shore were Capernaum, Bethsaida, and Tiberias.

And they beckoned unto their partners, which were in the other ship, that they should come and help them. And they came and filled both ships, so that they began to sink.

When Simon Peter saw it, he fell down at Jesus' knees, saying, "Depart from me; for I am a sinful man, O Lord."

"And they filled both ships"

For he was astonished, and all that were with him, at the draught of the fishes which they had taken; and so was also James and John, the sons of Zebedee, which were partners with Simon.

The Call. And Jesus said unto Simon, "Fear not; from henceforth thou shalt catch men."

And when they had brought their ships to land, they forsook all and followed Him.

THE TWELVE APOSTLES *

And Jesus called unto Him His twelve disciples and gave them power against unclean spirits, to cast them out, and to heal all manner of sickness and all manner of disease.

Now, the names of the twelve apostles are these: The first, *Simon,* who is called *Peter,* and *Andrew,* his brother; *James,* the son of Zebedee, and *John,* his brother; *Philip* and *Bartholomew; Thomas* and *Matthew,* the publican; *James,* the son of Alphaeus, and *Lebbaeus,* whose surname was Thaddaeus; *Simon,* the Canaanite, and *Judas Iscariot,* who also betrayed Him.

These twelve Jesus sent forth and commanded them, saying, "Go, preach, saying, 'The kingdom of heaven is at hand.' Heal the sick, cleanse the lepers, raise the dead, cast out devils. Freely ye have received, freely give."

Third Commandment. — Fourth Petition.

Ps. 127, 2. It is vain for you to rise up early, to sit up late, to eat the bread of sorrows; for so He giveth His beloved sleep.

>And gently grant Thy blessing
>That we may do Thy will,
>No more Thy ways transgressing,
>Our proper task fulfill,
>With Peter's full assurance
>Let down our nets again.
>Success will crown endurance
>If faithful we remain. (544, 5.)

---

* In point of time this account follows the raising of Jairus's daughter. Jesus also sent out seventy disciples, which occurred after the raising of the young man of Nain, Luke 10, 1—20.

16. The Stilling of the Tempest. The Gergesenes The Man Sick of the Palsy

a. Matt. 8, 23—27. Luke 8, 22—25. Mark 4, 35—41
b. Matt. 8, 28—34. Luke 8, 26—40. Mark 5, 1—21
c. Matt. 9, 1—8. Mark 2, 1—12

THE TEMPEST

And when He was entered into a ship, His disciples followed Him.

And, behold, there arose a great tempest in the sea, insomuch that the ship was covered with the waves; but He was asleep.

And His disciples came to Him and awoke Him, saying, "Lord, save us; we perish."

And He saith unto them, "Why are ye fearful, O ye of little faith?"

Then He arose and rebuked the winds and the sea; and there was a great calm.

But the men marveled, saying, "What manner of man is this that even the winds and the sea obey Him!"

THE GERGESENES

Men Possessed with Devils. And when He was come to the other side, into the country of the Gergesenes, there met Him two possessed with devils, coming out of the tombs, exceeding fierce, so that no man might pass by that way.

And, behold, they cried out, saying, "What have we to do with Thee, Jesus, Thou Son of God? Art Thou come hither to torment us before the time?"

One of them had been often bound with fetters and chains, and the chains had been plucked asunder by him and the fetters broken in pieces; neither could any man tame him.

And Christ asked him, "What is thy name?"

And he answered, saying, "My name is Legion;[1] for we are many."

Jesus Casts Out the Devils. And there was a good way off from them an herd of many swine feeding. So the devils besought Him, saying, "If Thou cast us out, suffer us to go away into the herd of swine."

"Then He rebuked the winds"

And He said unto them, "Go."

And when they were come out, they went into the herd of swine; and, behold, the whole herd of swine ran violently down a steep place into the sea and perished in the waters.

And they that kept them fled and went their ways into the city and told everything and what was befallen to the possessed of the devils.

---

[1] A legion was an army of from 5,000 to 6,000 soldiers.

And, behold, the whole city came out to meet Jesus; and when they saw Him, they besought Him that He would depart out of their coasts.

THE MAN SICK OF THE PALSY

Faith in Jesus. And He passed over and came into His own city.[2] And, behold, they brought to Him a man sick of the palsy, lying on a bed, which was borne of four.

"Son, be of good cheer"

And when they could not come nigh unto Him for the press, they uncovered the roof where He was and let down the bed wherein the sick of the palsy lay.

And Jesus, seeing their faith, said unto the sick of the palsy, "Son, be of good cheer; thy sins be forgiven thee."

Jesus Proves His Divinity. And, behold, the scribes [3] and

---

2) Capernaum.
3) The copyists of the Law, who also taught the Law to the people.

the Pharisees began to reason in their hearts, saying, "This man blasphemeth. Who can forgive sins but God only?"

And Jesus, knowing their thoughts, said, "Wherefore think ye evil in your hearts? For whether is easier to say, 'Thy sins be forgiven thee,' or to say, 'Arise and take up thy bed and walk'?

"But that ye may know that the Son of Man hath power on earth to forgive sins," (then saith He to the sick of the palsy,) "Arise, take up thy bed, and go thy way into thine house."

And immediately he arose, took up the bed, and departed to his own house.

But when the multitude saw it, they marveled and glorified God, which had given such power unto men.

Matt. 28, 18. All power is given unto Me in heaven and in earth.

First Article: Evil Angels. Faith. — *Second Article:* Jesus true God and true man.

Mark 5, 36. Be not afraid, only believe.

Jas. 2, 19. Thou believest that there is one God; thou doest well; the devils also believe and tremble.

> Though devils all the world should fill,
>   All eager to devour us,
> We tremble not, we fear no ill,
>   They shall not overpower us.
> This world's prince may still
> Scowl fierce as he will,
> He can harm us none,
> He's judged; the deed is done;
>   One little word can fell him. (262, 3.)

17. The Daughter of Jairus. The Young Man of Nain

a. Matt. 9, 18—26; Mark 5, 22—43; Luke 8, 41—56. b. Luke 7, 11—17

THE DAUGHTER OF JAIRUS

Jairus Pleads for Help. And, behold, there came a man named Jairus, a ruler of the synagog, and he fell down at

"I say unto thee, Arise"

Jesus' feet and besought Him that He would come into his house; for he had one only daughter, about twelve years of age, and she lay a-dying.

But as He went, there cometh one from the ruler of the synagog's house, saying to him, "Thy daughter is dead; trouble not the Master."

But when Jesus heard it, He answered him, saying, "Fear not, only believe, and she shall be made whole."

The Maiden Raised. And when Jesus came into the ruler's house and saw the minstrels and the people making a noise, He said unto them, "Give place; for the maid is not dead, but sleepeth."

And they laughed Him to scorn.

But when the people were put forth, He went in and took her by the hand and said unto her, "Talitha, cumi," which is, being interpreted, "Damsel, I say unto thee, Arise."

And straightway the damsel arose and walked; and He commanded to give her meat.

And the fame hereof went abroad into all that land.

THE YOUNG MAN OF NAIN *

Death Enters Nain. And it came to pass the day after that He went into a city called Nain;[1)] and many of His disciples went with Him and much people.

Now, when He came nigh to the gate of the city,[2)] behold, there was a dead man carried out, the only son of his mother, and she was a widow; and much people of the city was with her.

The Son Restored to His Mother. And when the Lord saw her, He had compassion on her and said unto her, "Weep not."

And He came and touched the bier; and they that bare him stood still.

And He said, "Young man, I say unto thee, Arise."

---

* This miracle occurred later than that of the raising of Jairus's daughter; in point of time it would belong after the account of the centurion of Capernaum.

1) Nain ("beauty"), a considerable town six miles southeast of Nazareth.

2) Even many smaller towns were surrounded by walls, and the entrances to them were secured by gates of either wood, iron, or brass.

And he that was dead sat up and began to speak.
And He delivered him to his mother.

And there came a fear on all; and they glorified God, saying, "That a great prophet is risen up among us"; and, "That God hath visited His people."

"And He delivered him to his mother"

And this rumor of Him went forth throughout all Judea and throughout all the region round about.

Third Article: "I believe in the resurrection of the body."

John 5, 28. 29. The hour is coming in the which all that are in the graves shall hear His voice, and shall come forth: they that have done good, unto the resurrection of life; and they that have done evil, unto the resurrection of damnation.

    Jesus, my Redeemer, lives!
     I, too, unto life shall waken;
    Endless joy my Savior gives;
     Shall my courage, then, be shaken?
    Shall I fear, or could the Head
    Rise and leave His members dead? (206, 2.)

18. The Sower

Matt. 13, 1—23.   Mark 4, 1—20.   Luke 8, 4—15

The Parable.   And when much people were gathered together and were come to Him out of every city, He spake by a parable: "A sower went out to sow his seed; and as he sowed, some fell by the wayside; and it was trodden down, and the fowls of the air devoured it.

"And some fell upon a rock; and as soon as it was sprung up, it withered away because it lacked moisture.

"A sower went out to sow his seed"

"And some fell among thorns, and the thorns sprang up with it and choked it.

"And others fell on good ground and sprang up and bare fruit, some an hundredfold, some sixtyfold, some thirtyfold."

And when He had said these things, He cried, "He that hath ears to hear, let him hear."

The Explanation.   And His disciples asked Him, saying, "What might this parable be?"

And He said, "The seed is the Word of God.

"Those by the wayside are they that hear; then cometh

the devil and taketh away the Word out of their hearts lest they should believe and be saved.

"They on the rock are they which, when they hear, receive the Word with joy; and these have no root, which for a while believe and in time of temptation fall away.

"And that which fell among the thorns are they which, when they have heard, go forth and are choked with cares of this world and the deceitfulness of riches and pleasures of this life and bring no fruit to perfection.

"But that on the good ground are they which in an honest and good heart, having heard the Word, keep it and bring forth fruit with patience."

Second Petition.
Luke 11, 28. Blessed are they that hear the Word of God and keep it

> Lord, open Thou my heart to hear
> And through Thy Word to me draw near.
> Let me Thy Word e'er pure retain;
> Let me Thy child and heir remain. (5, 1.)

---

19. The Tares among the Wheat. The Draw-Net
a. Matt. 13, 24—30. 36—43. b. Matt. 13, 47—50

THE TARES AMONG THE WHEAT

The Parable. Another parable put He forth unto them, saying, "The kingdom of heaven is likened unto a man which sowed good seed in his field; but while men slept, his enemy came and sowed tares among the wheat and went his way.

"But when the blade was sprung up and brought forth fruit, then appeared the tares also.

"So the servants of the householder came and said unto him, 'Sir, didst not thou sow good seed in thy field? From whence, then, hath it tares?'

"He said unto them, 'An enemy hath done this.'

"The servants said unto him, 'Wilt thou, then, that we go and gather them up?'

"But he said, 'Nay; lest, while ye gather up the tares, ye root up also the wheat with them. Let both grow together until the harvest; and in the time of harvest I will say to the reapers, "Gather ye together first the tares and bind them

"Gather ye together first the tares"

in bundles to burn them; but gather the wheat into my barn."'"

The Explanation. Then Jesus sent the multitude away and went into the house.

And His disciples came unto Him, saying, "Declare unto us the parable of the Tares of the Field."

He answered and said unto them, "He that soweth the good seed is the Son of Man; the field is the world; the good seed are the children of the Kingdom; but the tares are the children of the Wicked One; the enemy that sowed them is the devil; the harvest is the end of the world; and the reapers are the angels.

"As therefore the tares are gathered and burned in the fire, so shall it be in the end of this world.

"The Son of Man shall send forth His angels, and they shall gather out of His kingdom all things that offend and them which do iniquity and shall cast them into a furnace of fire; there shall be wailing and gnashing of teeth.

"Then shall the righteous shine forth as the sun in the kingdom of their Father.

"Who hath ears to hear, let him hear."

THE DRAW-NET

"Again, the kingdom of heaven is like unto a net that was cast into the sea and gathered of every kind; which, when it was full, they drew to shore and sat down and gathered the good into vessels, but cast the bad away.

"So shall it be at the end of the world. The angels shall come forth and sever the wicked from among the just and shall cast them into the furnace of fire; there shall be wailing and gnashing of teeth."

Third Article: The Church.

2 Cor. 13, 5. Examine yourselves whether ye be in the faith; prove your own selves.

> For the Lord, our God, shall come
> And shall take His harvest home;
> From His field shall in that day
> All offenses purge away;
> Give His angels charge at last
> In the fire the tares to cast,
> But the fruitful ears to store
> In His garner evermore: (574, 3.)

20. The Sermon on the Mount
Matt. 5—7

The Beatitudes. And Jesus, seeing the multitudes, went up into a mountain; and when He was set, His disciples came unto Him, and He taught them, saying,

"Blessed are the poor in spirit; for theirs is the kingdom of heaven.

"Blessed are they that mourn; for they shall be comforted.

"And He taught them"

"Blessed are the meek; for they shall inherit the earth.

"Blessed are they which do hunger and thirst after righteousness; for they shall be filled.

"Blessed are the merciful; for they shall obtain mercy.

"Blessed are the pure in heart; for they shall see God.

"Blessed are the peacemakers; for they shall be called the children of God.

"Blessed are they which are persecuted for righteousness' sake; for theirs is the kingdom of heaven.

"Blessed are ye when men shall revile you and persecute you and shall say all manner of evil against you falsely for My sake.

"Rejoice and be exceeding glad; for **great** is your reward in heaven; for so persecuted they the **prop**hets which were before you."

Love of Enemies. "Love your enemies, bless them that curse you, do good to them that hate you, and pray for them which despitefully use you and persecute you, that ye may be the children of your Father which is in heaven; for He maketh His sun to rise on the evil and on the good and sendeth rain on the just and on the unjust.

"Be ye therefore perfect, even as your Father which is in heaven is perfect.

"When thou doest alms, let not thy left hand know what thy right hand doeth."

Prayer. "When thou prayest, thou shalt not be as the hypocrites are; for they love to pray standing in the synagogs and in the corners of the streets that they may be seen of men. Verily I say unto you, They have their reward.

"But thou, when thou prayest, enter into thy closet, and when thou hast shut thy door, pray to thy Father, which is in secret; and thy Father, which seeth in secret, shall reward thee openly.

"But when ye pray, use not vain repetitions, as the heathen do; for they think that they shall be heard for their much speaking. Be not ye therefore like unto them."

The Lord's Prayer. "After this manner therefore pray ye: *"Our Father who art in heaven; Hallowed be thy name; Thy kingdom come; Thy will be done on earth as it is in heaven; Give us this day our daily bread; And forgive us* *our trespasses, as we forgive those who trespass against us; And lead us not into temptation; But deliver us from evil; For Thine is the kingdom and the power and the glory forever and ever. Amen.*

"For if ye forgive men their trespasses, your heavenly Father will also forgive you; but if ye forgive not men their trespasses, neither will your Father forgive your trespasses."

Care. "Take no thought for your life what ye shall eat or what ye shall drink; nor yet for your body what ye shall put on. Is not the life more than meat and the body than raiment?

"Behold the fowls of the air; for they sow not, neither do they reap nor gather into barns; yet your heavenly Father feedeth them. Are ye not much better than they?

"Consider the lilies of the field how they grow; they toil not, neither do they spin; and yet I say unto you, That even Solomon in all his glory was not arrayed like one of these.

"Wherefore, if God so clothe the grass of the field which to-day is and to-morrow is cast into the oven, shall He not much more clothe you, O ye of little faith?

"Therefore take no thought, saying, 'What shall we eat?' or, 'What shall we drink?' or, 'Wherewithal shall we be clothed?' (for after all these things do the Gentiles seek). For your heavenly Father knoweth that ye have need of all these things.

"But seek ye first the kingdom of God and His righteousness, and all these things shall be added unto you."

First and Third Chief Parts.

Matt. 7, 29. He taught them as one having authority and not as the scribes.

        Almighty God, Thy Word is cast
        Like seed into the ground;
        Now let the dew of heaven descend
        And righteous fruits abound. (49, 1.)

21. The Leper. The Centurion of Capernaum
a. Matt. 8, 1—4.   b. Matt. 8, 5—13

THE LEPER

When Jesus was come down from the mountain, great multitudes followed Him.

And, behold, there came a leper [1] and worshiped Him, saying, "Lord, if Thou wilt, Thou canst make me clean."

And Jesus put forth His hand and touched him, saying, "I will; be thou clean."

And immediately his leprosy was cleansed.

And Jesus saith unto him, "See thou tell no man; but go thy way, show thyself to the priest, and offer the gift that Moses commanded, for a testimony unto them."

THE CENTURION

The Gentile's Great Faith. And when Jesus was entered into Capernaum, there came unto Him a centurion,[2] beseeching Him and saying, "Lord, my servant [3] lieth at home sick of the palsy,[4] grievously tormented."

And Jesus saith unto him, "I will come and heal him."

The centurion answered and said, "Lord, I am not worthy that Thou shouldest come under my roof; but speak the word only, and my servant shall be healed. For I am a man under authority, having soldiers under me; and I say to this man, 'Go,' and he goeth; and to another, 'Come,' and he cometh; and to my servant, 'Do this,' and he doeth it."

A Warning to the Jews. When Jesus heard it, He mar-

---

1) Leprosy is a dreadful disease, still found in the East.

2) Centurion was the title of a Roman officer, captain of a company of one hundred soldiers.

3) A servant in those days was a slave.

4) Palsy is a disease which deprives the part affected of sensation or the power of motion or of both.

veled and said to them that followed, "Verily I say unto you, I have not found so great faith, no, not in Israel. And I say unto you, That many shall come from the East and West and shall sit down with Abraham and Isaac and Jacob in the kingdom of heaven; but the children of the kingdom shall

"I will come and heal him"

be cast out into outer darkness; there shall be weeping and gnashing of teeth."

And Jesus said unto the centurion, "Go thy way; and as thou hast believed, so be it done unto thee."

And his servant was healed in the selfsame hour.

First Article: Faith.

Heb. 11, 1. Faith is the substance of things hoped for, the evidence of things not seen.

John 20, 29. Blessed are they that have not seen and yet have believed.

When in the hour of utmost need
We know not where to look for aid;
When days and nights of anxious thought
Nor help nor counsel yet have brought,

Then this our comfort is alone,
That we may meet before Thy throne
And cry, O faithful God, to Thee
For rescue from our misery. (522, 1. 2.)

22. Death of John the Baptist
Matt. 11, 2—6; 14, 1—12. Mark 6, 14—29

Herod Imprisons John. At that time Herod the Tetrarch heard of the fame of Jesus and said unto his servants, "This is John the Baptist; he is risen from the dead, and therefore mighty works do show forth themselves in Him."

For Herod had laid hold on John and bound him and put him in prison for Herodias' sake, his brother Philip's wife. For John said unto him, "It is not lawful for thee to have her."

And when he would have put him to death, he feared the multitude, because they counted him as a prophet.

John's Message to Jesus. Now, when John had heard in the prison the works of Christ, he sent two of his disciples and said unto Him, "Art Thou He that should come, or do we look for another?"

Jesus answered and said unto them, "Go and show John again those things which ye do hear and see: The blind receive their sight, and the lame walk, the lepers are cleansed, and the deaf hear, the dead are raised up, and the poor have the Gospel preached to them. And blessed is he whosoever shall not be offended in Me."

Herod's Birthday. But when Herod's birthday was kept, the daughter of Herodias danced before them, and pleased Herod.

And the king said unto the damsel, "Ask of me whatsoever thou wilt, and I will give it thee."

And he sware unto her, "Whatsoever thou shalt ask of me, I will give it thee, unto the half of my kingdom."

And she went forth and said unto her mother, "What shall I ask?"

And she said, "The head of John the Baptist."

"Herod had put him in prison"

And she came in straightway with haste unto the king and asked, saying, "I will that thou give me the head of John the Baptist."

John Beheaded. And the king was exceeding sorry; yet for his oath's sake and for their sakes which sat with him he would not reject her.

And he sent an executioner and commanded his head to be brought; and he went, and beheaded him in the prison, and brought his head in a charger, and gave it to the damsel; and the damsel gave it to her mother.

And when his disciples heard of it, they came and took up his corpse and laid it in a tomb.

Second Commandment: Oaths in Uncertain Things. — *Fifth Commandment.* — *Sixth Commandment.*

Rev. 2, 10. Be thou faithful unto death, and I will give thee a crown of life.

> And take they our life,
> Goods, fame, child, and wife:
> Let these all be gone,
> They yet have nothing won;
> The Kingdom ours remaineth. (262, 4 b.)

23. Feeding of the Five Thousand

Matt. 14, 13—21. Mark 6, 30—44. Luke 9, 10—17. John 6, 1—15

Seeking Rest. And the apostles, when they were returned,[1] told Jesus all that they had done. And He said unto them, "Come ye yourselves apart into a desert place and rest a while"; for there were many coming and going, and they had no leisure so much as to eat.

And they departed into a desert place by ship privately.[2] And the people saw them departing, and many knew Him, and ran afoot thither out of all cities, and outwent them, and came together unto Him. And the Passover was nigh.

Jesus Preaches and Heals. And Jesus, when He came out, saw much people and was moved with compassion toward them because they were as sheep not having a shepherd. And He received them and spake unto them of the kingdom of God and healed them that had need of healing.

---

1) From their first trip of preaching and miracle-working.
2) To the northeastern shore of the Sea of Galilee, near Bethsaida.

Philip Tested. And Jesus went up into a mountain, and there He sat with His disciples.

When Jesus then lifted up His eyes and saw a great company come unto Him,[3] He saith unto Philip, "Whence shall we buy bread that these may eat?" And this He said to prove him; for He Himself knew what He would do.

But Philip answered Him, "Two hundred pennyworth[4] of bread is not sufficient for them that every one of them may take a little."

The Disciples Tested. And when the day was now far spent, His disciples came unto Him and said, "This is a desert place, and now the time is far passed; send them away that they may go into the country round about and into the villages and buy themselves bread; for they have nothing to eat."

But Jesus said unto them, "They need not depart; give ye them to eat."

One of His disciples, Andrew, Simon Peter's brother, said unto Him, "There is a lad here which hath five barley loaves and two small fishes. But what are they among so many?"

Jesus Feeds the Multitude. And He commanded them to make all sit down by companies upon the green grass; and they sat down in ranks by hundreds and by fifties. So the men sat down, in number about five thousand, beside women and children.

And when He had taken the five loaves and the two fishes, He looked up to heaven, and blessed, and brake the loaves, and gave them to His disciples and the disciples to them that were set down; and likewise of the fishes, as much as they would.

---

[3] Both people from His first audience and additional people that had arrived.

[4] About $32. (Penny = denarius, a Roman silver coin, worth about 16 cents.)

When they were filled, He said unto His disciples, "Gather up the fragments that remain, that nothing be lost." Therefore they gathered them together and filled twelve baskets with the fragments of the five barley loaves and of the fishes.

The Attempt to Make Jesus King. Then those men, when they had seen the miracle that Jesus did, said, "This is of

"He blessed and brake the loaves"

a truth that Prophet that should come into the world." When Jesus therefore perceived that they would come and take Him by force to make Him a king, He departed into a mountain to pray, Himself alone.

Fourth Petition.

Matt. 6, 33. Seek ye first the kingdom of God and His righteousness, and all these things shall be added unto you.

> Thou feedest us from year to year
> And constant dost abide;
> With ready help in time of fear
> Thou standest at our side. (569, 8.)

24. Jesus Walks on the Sea
Matt. 14, 22—34.   Mark 6, 45—53.   John 6, 16—21

The Multitudes Sent Away. And straightway Jesus constrained His disciples to get into a ship and to go before Him unto the other side while He sent the multitudes away.[1)]

The Fear of the Disciples. And when even was now come, His disciples went down unto the sea and entered into

"It is I; be not afraid"

a ship and went over the sea toward Capernaum. And it was now dark, and Jesus was not come to them.

But the ship was now in the midst of the sea, tossed with waves; for the wind was contrary.

And in the fourth watch of the night [2)] Jesus went unto them, walking on the sea.

---

1) After the feeding of the five thousand.
2) The night was divided into four watches: 6 to 9 P.M.; 9 to 12 P.M.; 12 P.M. to 3 A.M.; 3 to 6 A.M. Jesus came to His disciples between 3 and 6 A.M.

And when the disciples saw Him walking on the sea, they were troubled, saying, "It is a spirit"; and they cried out for fear.

But straightway Jesus spake unto them, saying, "Be of good cheer; it is I; be not afraid."

Peter's Faith. And Peter answered Him and said, "Lord, if it be Thou, bid me come unto Thee on the water." And He said, "Come."

And when Peter was come down out of the ship, he walked on the water to go to Jesus. But when he saw the wind boisterous, he was afraid; and beginning to sink, he cried, saying, "Lord, save me!"

And immediately Jesus stretched forth His hand and caught him and said unto him, "O thou of little faith, wherefore didst thou doubt?"

And when they were come into the ship, the wind ceased. Then they that were in the ship came and worshiped Him, saying, "Of a truth Thou art the Son of God."

And when they were gone over, they came into the land of Gennesaret.[3]

First Article: Faith. *Second Article:* Son of God.

Mark 5, 36. Be not afraid, only believe.

> Faint not nor fear, His arms are near;
> He changeth not, and thou art dear;
> Only believe, and thou shalt see
> That Christ is all in all to thee. (447, 4.)

---

3) A small strip of country on the northwest side of the Sea of Galilee, a plain shut in by hills; only a few miles from Capernaum.

25. The Woman of Canaan. The Deaf-and-Dumb The Ten Lepers

a. Matt. 15, 21—28.   Mark 7, 24—30.   b. Mark 7, 31—37
c. Luke 17, 11—19

THE WOMAN OF CANAAN

A Mother's Intercession. Then Jesus went thence and departed into the coasts of Tyre and Sidon.[1] And, behold, a woman of Canaan, a Greek, came out of the same coasts

"O woman, great is thy faith!"

and cried unto Him, saying, "Have mercy on me, O Lord, Thou Son of David! My daughter is grievously vexed with a devil."

---

[1] Tyre and Sidon were two famous trading-centers in Phenicia, north of Palestine, on the coast of the Mediterranean. Because the Romans had joined the province of Phenicia to Syria, it was also called Syrophenicia.

Her Great Faith Tried. But Jesus answered her not a word.

And His disciples came and besought Him, saying, "Send her away; for she crieth after us."

But He answered and said, "I am not sent but unto the lost sheep of the house of Israel."

Then came she and worshiped Him, saying, "Lord, help me!"

But He answered and said, "It is not meet to take the children's bread and to cast it to the dogs."

And she said, "Truth, Lord; yet the dogs eat of the crumbs which fall from their masters' table."

Then Jesus answered and said unto her, "O woman, great is thy faith! Be it unto thee even as thou wilt."

And her daughter was made whole from that very hour.

THE DEAF-AND-DUMB

And again, departing from the coasts of Tyre and Sidon, Jesus came unto the Sea of Galilee. And they bring unto Him one that was deaf and had an impediment in his speech; and they beseech Him to put His hand upon him.

And He took him aside from the multitude and put His fingers into his ears; and He spit and touched his tongue; and looking up to heaven, He sighed and saith unto him, "Ephphatha," that is, "Be open."

And straightway his ears were opened, and the string of his tongue was loosed, and he spake plain.

And He charged them that they should tell no man; but the more He charged them, so much the more a great deal they published it; and were beyond measure astonished, saying, "He hath done all things well; He maketh both the deaf to hear and the dumb to speak."

THE TRANSFIGURATION

THE TEN LEPERS *

And it came to pass, as Jesus went to Jerusalem, that He passed through the midst of Samaria and Galilee.

And as He entered into a certain village, there met Him ten men that were lepers, which stood afar off; and they lifted up their voices and said, "Jesus, Master, have mercy on us."

And when He saw them, He said unto them, "Go, show yourselves unto the priests."

And it came to pass that, as they went, they were cleansed.

And one of them, when he saw that he was healed, turned back and with a loud voice glorified God and fell down on his face at His feet, giving Him thanks; and he was a Samaritan.

And Jesus, answering, said, "Were there not ten cleansed? But where are the nine? There are not found that returned to give glory to God save this stranger."

And He said unto him, "Arise, go thy way; thy faith hath made thee whole."

First Article: Faith. — *Prayer.* — *Seventh Petition.* — *Second Commandment.*

Ps. 103, 1. Bless the Lord, O my soul; and all that is within me, bless His holy name.

> O bless the Lord, my soul!
> Let all within me join
> And aid my tongue to bless His name
> Whose favors are divine. (27, 1.)

---

* This incident occurred after the Transfiguration (No. 26).

26. Peter's Confession. Christ's Transfiguration
a. Matt. 16, 13—21.   b. Matt. 17, 1—9

THE CONFESSION

The Important Question. When Jesus came into the coasts of Caesarea Philippi, He asked His disciples, saying, "Whom do men say that I, the Son of Man, am?"

And they said, "Some say that Thou art John the Baptist; some, Elias; and others, Jeremias or one of the prophets."

He saith unto them, "But whom say ye that I am?"

Peter's Answer. And Simon Peter answered and said, *"Thou art the Christ, the Son of the living God."*

And Jesus answered and said unto him, "Blessed art thou, Simon Bar-jona; for flesh and blood hath not revealed it unto thee, but My Father which is in heaven."

Jesus Predicts His Passion. From that time forth began Jesus to show unto His disciples how that He must go unto Jerusalem, and suffer many things of the elders and chief priests and scribes, and be killed, and be raised again the third day.

THE TRANSFIGURATION

Christ Shows His Divine Majesty. And after six days Jesus taketh Peter, James, and John, his brother, and bringeth them up into an high mountain apart and was transfigured before them; and His face did shine as the sun, and His raiment was white as the light. And, behold, there appeared unto them Moses and Elias, talking with Him.

Then Peter said unto Jesus, "Lord, it is good for us to be here; if Thou wilt, let us make here three tabernacles; one for Thee and one for Moses and one for Elias."

Christ Acknowledged by the Father. While he yet spake, behold, a bright cloud overshadowed them; and, behold, a voice out of the cloud, which said, *"This is My beloved Son, in whom I am well pleased; hear ye Him."*

PETER'S CONFESSION. CHRIST'S TRANSFIGURATION 323

And when the disciples heard it, they fell on their face and were sore afraid.

And Jesus came and touched them and said, "Arise and be not afraid."

And when they had lifted up their eyes, they saw no

"Moses and Elias talking with Him"

man save Jesus only. And as they came down from the mountain, Jesus charged them, saying, "Tell the vision to no man until the Son of Man be risen again from the dead."

Second Article: "And in Jesus Christ, His only Son."

1 John 4, 15. Whosoever shall confess that Jesus is the Son of God, God dwelleth in him and he in God.

>Jesus, the very thought of Thee
>   With sweetness fills the breast;
>But sweeter far Thy face to see
>   And in Thy presence rest. (350, 1.)

27. The Unmerciful Servant
Matt. 18, 21—35

Peter's Question. And Peter came to Jesus and said, "Lord, how oft shall my brother sin against me and I forgive him? Till seven times?"

"Lord, have patience with me"

Jesus saith unto him, "I say not unto thee, Until seven times, but, Until seventy times seven."

The Forgiving Master. "Therefore is the kingdom of heaven likened unto a certain king which would take account of his servants.

"And when he had begun to reckon, one was brought unto him which owed him ten thousand talents.[1] But forasmuch as he had not to pay, his lord commanded him to be sold, and his wife, and children, and all that he had, and payment to be made.

"The servant therefore fell down and worshiped him, saying, 'Lord, have patience with me, and I will pay thee all.'

"Then the lord of that servant was moved with compassion and loosed him and forgave him the debt."

The Unforgiving Servant. "But the same servant went out and found one of his fellow-servants which owed him an hundred pence;[2] and he laid hands on him and took him by the throat, saying, 'Pay me that thou owest.'

"And his fellow-servant fell down at his feet and besought him, saying, 'Have patience with me, and I will pay thee all.'

"And he would not, but went and cast him into prison till he should pay the debt.

"So, when his fellow-servants saw what was done, they were very sorry and came and told unto their lord all that was done."

The Sin of Not Forgiving. "Then his lord, after that he had called him, said unto him, 'O thou wicked servant! I forgave thee all that debt because thou desiredst me; shouldest thou not also have had compassion on thy fellow-servant even as I had pity on thee?'

"And his lord was wroth and delivered him to the tormentors till he should pay all that was due unto him.

"So, likewise, shall My heavenly Father do also unto you if ye from your hearts forgive not every one his brother their trespasses."

---

1) A talent of silver is $1,000; of gold, $30,000.
2) $16.

Fifth Petition.

Matt. 5, 25. 26. Agree with thine adversary quickly, whiles thou art in the way with him lest at any time the adversary deliver thee to the Judge and the Judge deliver thee to the officer and thou be cast into prison. Verily, I say unto thee, Thou shalt by no means come out thence till thou hast paid the uttermost farthing.

> Forgive our sins, Lord, we implore,
> Remove from us their burden sore,
> As we their trespasses forgive
> Who by offenses us do grieve.
> Thus let us dwell in charity
> And serve our brother willingly. (458, 6.)

---

28. The Good Samaritan
Luke 10, 25—37

The Sum of the Law. And, behold, a certain lawyer stood up and tempted Him, saying, "Master, what shall I do to inherit eternal life?"

He said unto him, "What is written in the Law? How readest thou?"

And he, answering, said, "Thou shalt love the Lord, thy God, with all thy heart, and with all thy soul, and with all thy strength, and with all thy mind; and thy neighbor as thyself."

And He said unto him, "Thou hast answered right; this do, and thou shalt live."

But he, willing to justify himself, said unto Jesus, "And who is my neighbor?"

The Man Fallen among Thieves. And Jesus, answering, said, "A certain man went down from Jerusalem to Jericho and fell among thieves, which stripped him of his raiment and wounded him and departed, leaving him half dead.

"And by chance there came down a certain priest that way; and when he saw him, he passed by on the other side.

"And likewise a Levite, when he was at the place, came and looked on him and passed by on the other side."

The True Neighbor. "But a certain Samaritan, as he

"He had compassion on him"

journeyed, came where he was; and when he saw him, he had compassion on him, and went to him, and bound up his wounds, pouring in oil and wine, and set him on his own beast, and brought him to an inn, and took care of him.

"And on the morrow, when he departed, he took out two pence and gave them to the host and said unto him,

'Take care of him; and whatsoever thou spendest more, when I come again, I will repay thee.'

"Which, now, of these three, thinkest thou, was neighbor unto him that fell among the thieves?"

And he said, "He that showed mercy on him."

Then said Jesus unto him, "Go, and do thou likewise."

The Sum of the Second Table. — Fifth Commandment.

Matt. 7, 12. All things whatsoever ye would that men should do to you, do ye even so to them; for this is the Law and the prophets.

Matt. 5, 7. Blessed are the merciful; for they shall obtain mercy.

> O gentle Dew, from heaven now fall
> With power upon the hearts of all,
>   Thy tender love instilling,
> That heart to heart more closely bound,
> In kindly deeds be fruitful found,
>   The law of love fulfilling. (235, 7 a.)

29. Mary and Martha. Jesus and the Child Jesus Blessing Little Children

a. Luke 10, 38—42.   b. Matt. 18, 1—14.   c. Mark 10, 13—16
Luke 18, 15—17

MARY AND MARTHA

Now, it came to pass, as they went, that He entered into a certain village,[1] and a certain woman named Martha received Him into her house. And she had a sister called Mary, which also sat at Jesus' feet and heard His Word.

But Martha was cumbered about much serving and came to Him and said, "Lord, dost Thou not care that my sister hath left me to serve alone? Bid her therefore that she help me."

---

[1] Bethany, on the eastern slope of Mount Olivet, about two miles east of Jerusalem.

And Jesus answered and said unto her, "Martha, Martha, thou art careful and troubled about many things; *but one thing is needful; and Mary hath chosen that good part, which shall not be taken away from her.*"

"Martha, Martha, . . . one thing is needful"

JESUS AND THE CHILD

"Who Is the Greatest?" And the disciples came unto Jesus, saying, "Who is the greatest in the kingdom of heaven?"

And Jesus called a little child unto Him and set him in the midst of them and said, "Verily I say unto you, Except ye be converted and become as little children, ye shall not enter into the kingdom of heaven.

"Whosoever, therefore, shall humble himself as this little child, the same is greatest in the kingdom of heaven."

Children Not to be Offended or Despised. "And whoso shall receive one such little child in My name receiveth Me.

"But whoso shall offend one of these little ones which believe in Me, it were better for him that a millstone were

"And He took them up in His arms"

hanged about his neck and that he were drowned in the depth of the sea.

"Take heed that ye despise not one of these little ones; for I say unto you, That in heaven their angels do always behold the face of My Father which is in heaven.

"For the Son of Man is come to save that which was lost.

"Even so it is not the will of your Father which is in heaven that one of these little ones should perish."

JESUS BLESSING LITTLE CHILDREN

And they brought young children to Jesus that He should touch them; and His disciples rebuked those that brought them.

But when Jesus saw it, He was much displeased and said unto them, *"Suffer the little children to come unto Me and forbid them not; for of such is the kingdom of God. Verily I say unto you, Whosoever shall not receive the kingdom of God as a little child, he shall not enter therein."*

And He took them up in His arms, put His hands upon them, and blessed them.

Third Commandment. — Baptism. — First Commandment.

Matt. 6, 33. Seek ye first the kingdom of God and His righteousness; and all these things shall be added unto you.

Eph. 6, 4. Ye fathers, provoke not your children to wrath, but bring them up in the nurture and admonition of the Lord.

John 21, 15. Feed My lambs.

> How were Mary's thoughts devoted
>   Her eternal joy to find,
> As intent each word she noted,
>   At her Savior's feet reclined!
> How kindled her heart, how devout was its feeling,
> While hearing the lessons that Christ was revealing!
>
> (366, 3 a.)

30. The Rich Young Ruler. The Foolish Rich Man
a. Matt. 19, 16—22. Mark 10, 17—22. Luke 18, 18—23
b. Luke 12, 16—21

THE RICH YOUNG RULER

"What Shall I Do?" A certain ruler asked Jesus, saying, "Good Master, what shall I do to inherit eternal life?"

And Jesus said unto him, "Why callest thou Me good?

"Sell, and give to the poor"

None is good save One, that is, God. Thou knowest the commandments, 'Do not commit adultery, Do not kill, Do not steal, Do not bear false witness, Honor thy father and thy mother.'"

And he said, "All these have I kept from my youth up."

The Test. Then Jesus, beholding him, loved him and said unto him, "One thing thou lackest: go thy way, sell whatsoever thou hast, and give to the poor, and thou shalt have treasure in heaven; and come, take up the cross, and follow Me."

But when the young man heard that saying, he went away sorrowful; for he had great possessions.

Then said Jesus unto His disciples, "Verily I say unto you, That a rich man shall hardly enter into the kingdom of heaven."

THE FOOLISH RICH MAN

And He spake a parable unto them, saying, "The ground of a certain rich man brought forth plentifully.

"And he thought within himself, saying, 'What shall I do because I have no room where to bestow my fruits?'

"And he said, 'This will I do: I will pull down my barns and build greater; and there will I bestow all my fruits and my goods. And I will say to my soul, "Soul, thou hast much goods laid up for many years; take thine ease, eat, drink, and be merry."'

"But God said unto him, 'Thou fool! This night thy soul shall be required of thee; then whose shall those things be which thou hast provided?'

"So is he that layeth up treasure for himself and is not rich toward God."

First Commandment: Fine Idolatry.—*Fourth Petition.*

Eph. 5, 5. For this ye know, that no whoremonger nor unclean person nor covetous man, who is an idolater, hath any inheritance in the kingdom of Christ and God.

>   The world abideth not;
>   Lo, like a flash 'twill vanish;
>   With all its gorgeous pomp
>   Pale death it cannot banish;
>   Its riches pass away,
>   And all its joys must flee.
>   But Jesus doth abide,—
>   What is the world to me! (430, 7.)

31. The Great Supper. The Lost Sheep
a. Luke 14, 16—24.   b. Luke 15, 1—7.   Matt. 18, 12—14

THE GREAT SUPPER

The Invitation. Then said Jesus, "A certain man made a great supper and bade many; and sent his servant at supper-

"I have found My sheep"

time to say to them that were bidden, 'Come; for all things are now ready.'"

The Excuses. "And they all with one consent began to make excuse. The first said unto him, 'I have bought a piece of ground, and I must needs go and see it; I pray thee have me excused.'

"And another said, 'I have bought five yoke of oxen, and I go to prove them; I pray thee have me excused.'

"And another said, 'I have married a wife, and therefore I cannot come.'

"So that servant came and showed his lord these things."

The Invitation to Others. "Then the master of the house, being angry, said to his servant, 'Go out quickly into the streets and lanes of the city and bring in hither the poor, and the maimed, and the halt, and the blind.'

"And the servant said, 'Lord, it is done as thou hast commanded, and yet there is room.'

"And the lord said unto the servant, 'Go out into the highways and hedges and compel them to come in that my house may be filled. For I say unto you, That none of those men which were bidden shall taste of my supper.'"

THE LOST SHEEP

Then drew near unto Him all the publicans [1] and sinners for to hear Him.

And the Pharisees and scribes murmured, saying, "This man receiveth sinners and eateth with them."

And He spake this parable unto them, saying, "What man of you, having an hundred sheep, if he lose one of them, doth not leave the ninety and nine in the wilderness and go after that which is lost until he find it?

"And when he hath found it, he layeth it on his shoulders, rejoicing. And when he cometh home, he calleth together his friends and neighbors, saying unto them, 'Rejoice with me; for I have found my sheep which was lost.'

"I say unto you that likewise joy shall be in heaven over

---

[1] Collectors of the Roman tribute-money (taxes). The publicans were generally despised because they were agents of the hated Roman government and because they usually compelled people to pay more than was required. They were often rich men, but regarded as public grafters and thieves.

one sinner that repenteth, more than over ninety and nine just persons which need no repentance."

Third Commandment. — *Third Article:* "He has called me by the Gospel." — *Second Article:* "Redeemed me, a lost and condemned creature."

Matt. 28, 19. Go ye therefore and teach all nations, baptizing them in the name of the Father and of the Son and of the Holy Ghost.

Matt. 18, 11. The Son of Man is come to save that which was lost.

I am Jesus' little lamb, Ever glad at heart I am;
For my Shepherd gently guides me, Knows my need, and
    well provides me,
Loves me ev'ry day the same, Even calls me by my name. (648, 1.)

32. The Prodigal Son
Luke 15, 11—32

The Erring Sinner. And Jesus said, "A certain man had two sons. And the younger of them said to his father, 'Father, give me the portion of goods that falleth to me.' And he divided unto them his living.

"And not many days after the younger son gathered all together and took his journey into a far country and there wasted his substance with riotous living."

The Penitent Sinner. "And when he had spent all, there arose a mighty famine in that land; and he began to be in want.

"And he went and joined himself to a citizen of that country; and he sent him into his fields to feed swine. And he would fain have filled his belly with the husks that the swine did eat; and no man gave unto him.

"And when he came to himself, he said, 'How many hired servants of my father's have bread enough and to spare, and I perish with hunger! I will arise and go to my father and will say unto him, "Father, I have sinned against Heaven and before thee and am no more worthy to be called thy son; make me as one of thy hired servants."'"

The Forgiving Father. "And he arose and came to his father. But when he was yet a great way off, his father saw

"And he came to his father"

him, and had compassion, and ran, and fell on his neck, and kissed him.

"And the son said unto him, *'Father, I have sinned against Heaven and in thy sight and am no more worthy to be called thy son.'*

"But the father said to his servants, 'Bring forth the best robe and put it on him; and put a ring on his hand and shoes on his feet; and bring hither the fatted calf and kill it;

and let us eat and be merry. For this my son was dead and is alive again; he was lost and is found.'

"And they began to be merry."

The Self-Righteous Brother. "Now, his elder son was in the field; and as he came and drew nigh to the house, he heard music and dancing. And he called one of the servants and asked what these things meant.

"And he said unto him, 'Thy brother is come, and thy father hath killed the fatted calf because he hath received him safe and sound.'

"And he was angry and would not go in. Therefore came his father out and entreated him.

"And he, answering, said to his father, 'Lo, these many years do I serve thee, neither transgressed I at any time thy commandment; and yet thou never gavest me a kid that I might make merry with my friends; but as soon as this thy son was come, which hath devoured thy living with harlots, thou hast killed for him the fatted calf.'

"And he said unto him, 'Son, thou art ever with me, and all that I have is thine. It was meet that we should make merry and be glad; for this thy brother was dead and is alive again and was lost and is found.'"

Confession and Absolution.—Third Article: Justification.—*Fifth Petition.*

Ps. 51, 17. The sacrifices of God are a broken spirit; a broken and a contrite heart, O God, Thou wilt not despise.

"Jesus sinners doth receive!"
  Oh, may all this saying ponder
Who in sin's delusions live
  And from God and heaven wander!
Here is hope for all who grieve —
"Jesus sinners doth receive!" (324, 1.)

33. The Rich Man and Poor Lazarus
Luke 16, 19—31

Their Life on Earth. "There was a certain rich man which was clothed in purple and fine linen and fared sumptuously every day.

"And there was a certain beggar, named Lazarus, which

"Lazarus at his gate"

was laid at his gate, full of sores, and desiring to be fed with the crumbs which fell from the rich man's table; moreover, the dogs came and licked his sores."

Their Lot in Eternity. "And it came to pass that the beggar died and was carried by the angels into Abraham's bosom.

"The rich man also died and was buried.

"And in hell he lifted up his eyes, being in torments, and seeth Abraham afar off and Lazarus in his bosom.

"And he cried and said, 'Father Abraham, have mercy on me and send Lazarus that he may dip the tip of his finger in water and cool my tongue; for I am tormented in this flame.'

"But Abraham said, 'Son, remember that thou in thy lifetime receivedst thy good things and likewise Lazarus evil things; but now he is comforted, and thou art tormented. And beside all this, between us and you there is a great gulf fixed, so that they which would pass from hence to you cannot, neither can they pass to us that would come from thence.'

"Then he said, 'I pray thee therefore, Father, that thou wouldst send him to my father's house, for I have five brethren, that he may testify unto them lest they also come into this place of torment.'"

God's Word the Only Power unto Salvation. "Abraham saith unto him, 'They have Moses and the prophets; let them hear them.'

"And he said, 'Nay, Father Abraham; but if one went unto them from the dead, they will repent.'

"And he said unto him, 'If they hear not Moses and the prophets, neither will they be persuaded though one rose from the dead.'"

Third Article: Eternal Life and Eternal Damnation.

Matt. 7, 13. Enter ye in at the strait gate; for wide is the gate, and broad is the way that leadeth to destruction, and many there be which go in thereat.

> Then woe to those who scorned the Lord
>   And sought but carnal pleasures,
> Who here despised His precious Word
>   And loved their earthly treasures!
> With shame and trembling they will stand
>   And at the Judge's stern command
>   To Satan be delivered. (611, 4.)

34. The Pharisee and the Publican
Luke 18, 9—14

Self-Righteousness. Jesus spake this parable unto certain which trusted in themselves that they were righteous and despised others: "Two men went up into the Temple to pray; the one a Pharisee and the other a publican.

"The Pharisee stood and prayed thus with himself, 'God,

"God, I thank Thee that I am not as other men are"

I thank Thee that I am not as other men are, extortioners, unjust, adulterers, or even as this publican. I fast twice in the week; I give tithes of all that I possess.'"

Penitence. "And the publican, standing afar off, would not lift up so much as his eyes unto heaven, but smote upon his breast, saying, '*God be merciful to me, a sinner.*'

"I tell you, this man went down to his house justified

rather than the other; for every one that exalteth himself shall be abased; and he that humbleth himself shall be exalted."

Confession. — Justification. — Of Prayer in General.

Rom. 3, 28. Therefore we conclude that a man is justified by faith, without the deeds of the Law.

> I smite upon my troubled breast,
> With deep and conscious guilt opprest;
> Christ and His Cross my only plea, —
> O God, be merciful to me! (323, 2.)

---

35. The Raising of Lazarus
John 11

Sickness and Death of Lazarus. Now, a certain man was sick, named Lazarus, of Bethany. Therefore his sisters Mary and Martha sent unto Jesus, saying, "Lord, behold, he whom Thou lovest is sick."

When Jesus heard that, He said, "This sickness is not unto death, but for the glory of God, that the Son of God might be glorified thereby."

And He abode two days still in the same place where He was.

After that He saith unto His disciples, "Our friend Lazarus sleepeth; but I go that I may awake him out of sleep."

They thought that He had spoken of taking of rest in sleep.

Then said Jesus unto them plainly, "Lazarus is dead. And I am glad for your sakes that I was not there, to the intent ye may believe; nevertheless let us go unto him."

Mary and Martha. Then, when Jesus came, He found that he had lain in the grave four days already.

And many of the Jews came to Martha and Mary to comfort them concerning their brother.

Then Martha, as soon as she heard that Jesus was coming, went and met Him; but Mary sat still in the house.

Then said Martha unto Jesus, "Lord, if Thou hadst been here, my brother had not died. But I know that even now, whatsoever Thou wilt ask of God, God will give it Thee."

Jesus saith unto her, "Thy brother shall rise again."

Martha saith unto Him, "I know that he shall rise again in the resurrection at the Last Day."

Jesus said unto her, *"I am the Resurrection and the Life. He that believeth in Me, though he were dead, yet shall he live; and whosoever liveth and believeth in Me shall never die. Believest thou this?"*

She saith unto Him, "Yea, Lord; I believe that Thou art the Christ, the Son of God, which should come into the world."

And when she had so said, she went and called Mary, her sister, saying, "The Master is come and calleth for thee."

And she arose quickly and came unto Him.

The Jews then which were with her in the house followed her, saying, "She goeth unto the grave to weep there."

Jesus' Grief. Then, when Mary was come where Jesus was and saw Him, she fell down at His feet, saying unto Him, "Lord, if Thou hadst been here, my brother had not died."

When Jesus therefore saw her weeping and the Jews also weeping which came with her, He groaned in the spirit and was troubled and said, "Where have ye laid him?"

They say unto Him, "Lord, come and see."

Jesus wept.

Then said the Jews, "Behold, how He loved him!"

And some of them said, "Could not this man which opened the eyes of the blind have caused that even this man should not have died?"

Lazarus Raised. Jesus cometh to the grave. It was a cave, and a stone lay upon it.

Jesus said, "Take ye away the stone."

Martha saith unto Him, "Lord, by this time he stinketh; for he hath been dead four days."

Jesus saith unto her, "Said I not unto thee that, if thou wouldest believe, thou shouldest see the glory of God?"

"And he that was dead came forth"

Then they took away the stone from the place where the dead was laid.

And Jesus lifted up His eyes and said, "Father, I thank Thee that Thou hast heard Me. And I knew that Thou hearest Me always; but because of the people which stand by I said it that they may believe that Thou hast sent Me."

And He cried with a loud voice, "Lazarus, come forth!"

And he that was dead came forth, bound hand and foot

with grave-clothes; and his face was bound about with a napkin.

Jesus saith unto them, "Loose him and let him go."

The Effect on the Jews. Then many of the Jews which had seen the things which Jesus did, believed on Him. But some of them went their ways to the Pharisees and told them what things Jesus had done.

Then the chief priests and the Pharisees from that day forth took counsel together for to put Him to death.

Third Article: "I believe in the resurrection of the body."

Job 19, 25. 26. I know that my Redeemer liveth and that He shall stand at the Latter Day upon the earth; and though after my skin worms destroy this body, yet in my flesh shall I see God.

> I am flesh and must return
> Unto dust, whence I am taken;
> But by faith I now discern
> That from death I shall awaken
> With my Savior to abide
> In His glory, at His side. (206, 4.)

36. The Blind Man. Zacchaeus
a. Luke 18, 35—43. Mark 10, 46—52. Matt. 20, 29—34
b. Luke 19, 1—10

THE BLIND MAN

A Plea for Help. And as Jesus was come nigh unto Jericho, a certain blind man sat by the wayside, begging; and hearing the multitude pass by, he asked what it meant.

And they told him that Jesus of Nazareth passeth by.

And he cried, saying, "Jesus, Thou Son of David, have mercy on me."

And they which went before rebuked him that he should hold his peace; but he cried so much the more, "Thou Son of David, have mercy on me."

Sight Restored. And Jesus stood and commanded him to be brought unto Him.

And when he was come near, He asked him, saying, "What wilt thou that I shall do unto thee?"

And he said, "Lord, that I may receive my sight."

"Make haste and come down"

And Jesus said unto him, "Receive thy sight; thy faith hath saved thee."

And immediately he received his sight and followed Him, glorifying God; and all the people, when they saw it, gave praise unto God.

ZACCHAEUS

Eager to See Jesus. Jesus passed through Jericho. And, behold, there was a man named Zacchaeus, which was the chief among the publicans, and he was rich.

And he sought to see Jesus who He was and could not for the press, because he was little of stature. And he ran before and climbed up into a sycamore-tree [1] to see Him.

Jesus at the House of Zacchaeus. And when Jesus came to the place, he looked up and saw him and said unto him, "Zacchaeus, make haste and come down; for to-day I must abide at thy house."

And he made haste and came down and received Him joyfully.

And when they saw it, they all murmured, saying, That He was gone to be guest with a man that is a sinner.

And Zacchaeus said unto the Lord, "Behold, Lord, the half of my goods I give to the poor; and if I have taken anything from any man by false accusation,[2] I restore him fourfold."

And Jesus said unto him, *"This day is salvation come to this house, forsomuch as he also is a son of Abraham. For the Son of Man is come to seek and to save that which was lost."*

Second Article: "That I may be His own," etc.

1 Tim. 1, 15. This is a faithful saying, and worthy of all acceptation, that Christ Jesus came into the world to save sinners.

Come, ye sinners, one and all,
   Come, accept His invitation;
Come, obey His gracious call,
   Come and take His free salvation!
Firmly in these words believe:
Jesus sinners doth receive. (324, 4.)

---

1) A sort of fig-tree.

2) By falsely accusing him of making understatements regarding his property and income for the purpose of tax evasion and consequently demanding penality payment of him.

37. Jesus Enters Jerusalem

Matt. 21, 1—16.   Mark 11, 1—11.   Luke 19, 28—48
John 12, 12—15

The Preparation. And it came to pass, when He was come nigh to Bethphage and Bethany, at the mount called the Mount of Olives, He sent two of His disciples, saying, "Go ye into the village over against you, in the which, at your entering, ye shall find a colt tied whereon yet never man sat; loose him and bring him hither. And if any man ask you, 'Why do ye loose him?' thus shall ye say unto him, 'Because the Lord hath need of him.'"

All this was done that it might be fulfilled which was spoken by the prophet, saying, "Tell ye the daughter of Zion, 'Behold, thy King cometh unto thee.'"

The Reception. And they that were sent went their way and found even as He had said unto them.

And they brought the colt to Jesus; and they cast their garments upon the colt, and they set Jesus thereon.

And a very great multitude spread their garments in the way; others cut down branches from the trees and strewed them in the way.

And the multitudes that went before and that followed, cried, saying, "Hosanna to the Son of David! Blessed is He that cometh in the name of the Lord; hosanna in the highest!"

And when He was come nigh, the whole multitude of the disciples began to rejoice and praise God with a loud voice for all the mighty works they had seen.

And some of the Pharisees said unto Him, "Master, rebuke Thy disciples."

And He answered and said unto them, "I tell you that, if these should hold their peace, the stones would immediately cry out."

The Destruction of Jerusalem Foretold. And when He was come near, He beheld the city and wept over it, saying, "If thou hadst known, even thou, at least in this thy day, the things which belong unto thy peace! But now they are hid from thine eyes.

"For the days shall come upon thee that thine enemies

"Hosanna to the Son of David!"

shall cast a trench about thee, and compass thee round, and keep thee in on every side, and shall lay thee even with the ground and thy children within thee; and they shall not leave in thee one stone upon another because thou knewest not the time of thy visitation."

Jerusalem Stirred. And when He was come into Jerusalem, all the city was moved, saying, "Who is this?" And the multitude said, "This is Jesus, the Prophet of Nazareth, of Galilee."

Cleansing of the Temple.* And Jesus went into the Temple of God and cast out all them that sold and bought in the Temple and overthrew the tables of the money-changers and the seats of them that sold doves and said unto them, "It is written, 'My house shall be called the house of prayer; but ye have made it a den of thieves.'"

The Praise of Children. And the blind and the lame came to Him in the Temple, and He healed them.

And when the chief priests and scribes saw the wonderful things that He did and the children crying in the Temple and saying, "Hosanna to the Son of David!" they were sore displeased and said unto Him, "Hearest Thou what these say?"

And Jesus saith unto them, "Yea, have ye never read: 'Out of the mouths of babes and sucklings Thou hast perfected praise'?"

Second Petition. — Second Article: Christ Our King. — *Third Commandment.*

Ps. 24, 7. Lift up your heads, O ye gates; and be ye lift up, ye everlasting doors; and the King of Glory shall come in.

> Hail, hosanna, David's Son!
> Help, Lord, hear our supplication!
> Let Thy kingdom, scepter, crown,
> Bring us blessing and salvation
> That forever we may sing:
> Hail, hosanna! to our King. **(55, 4.)**

* Concerning the first cleansing of the Temple see the story of Nicodemus (No. 12).

38. Jesus' Last Discourses *

a-b. Matt. 22, 15 ff.   Mark 12, 13 ff.   Luke 20, 21 ff.
c. Mark 12, 41—44.   Luke 21, 1—4

TRIBUTE TO CAESAR

Then went the Pharisees and took counsel how they might entangle Jesus in His talk.

And they sent out to Him their disciples with the Herodians, saying, "Master, we know that Thou art true and teachest the way of God in truth. Neither carest Thou for any man; for Thou regardest not the person of men. Tell us therefore, what thinkest Thou? Is it lawful to give tribute unto Caesar or not?"

But Jesus perceived their wickedness and said, "Why tempt ye Me, ye hypocrites? Show me the tribute-money."

And they brought unto Him a penny.

And He saith unto them, "Whose is this image and superscription?"

They say unto Him, "Caesar's."

Then saith He unto them, "Render therefore unto Caesar the things which are Caesar's and unto God the things that are God's."

When they had heard these words, they marveled and left Him and went their way.

"WHAT THINK YE OF CHRIST?"

While the Pharisees were gathered together, Jesus asked them, saying, *"What think ye of Christ? Whose son is He?"*

They say unto Him, "The son of David."

He saith unto them, "How, then, doth David in spirit call Him Lord, saying, 'The Lord said unto My Lord, "Sit

---

* This is only the beginning of the last discourses; they extend over Stories 38—41.

Thou on My right hand till I make Thine enemies Thy footstool" '? If David, then, call Him Lord, how is He his son?"

And no man was able to answer Him a word, neither durst any man from that day forth ask Him any more questions.

THE WIDOW'S MITES

And Jesus sat over against the treasury and beheld how the people cast money into the treasury.

"And she threw in two mites"

And many that were rich cast in much.

And there came a certain poor widow, and she threw in two mites,¹⁾ which make a farthing.

And He called unto Him His disciples and saith unto

---

1) A mite is about ⅛ cent.

them, "Verily I say unto you, That this poor widow hath cast more in than all they which have cast into the treasury.

"For all they did cast in of their abundance unto the offerings of God; but she of her want did cast in all that she had, even all her living."

Table of Duties: Cf Subjects. — *Second Article:* Who Is Christ? — *Third Article:* Good Works.

Rom. 13, 7. Render therefore to all their dues: tribute to whom tribute is due; custom, to whom custom; fear, to whom fear; honor, to whom honor.

> We give Thee but Thine own,
> Whate'er the gift may be;
> All that we have is Thine alone,
> A trust, O Lord, from Thee. (441, 1.)

---

39. The Ten Virgins
Matt. 25, 1—13

The Wise and the Foolish. "Then shall the kingdom of heaven be likened unto ten virgins, which took their lamps and went forth to meet the bridegroom.

"And five of them were wise, and five were foolish.

"They that were foolish took their lamps and took no oil with them.

"But the wise took oil in their vessels with their lamps.

"While the bridegroom tarried, they all slumbered and slept.

"And at midnight there was a cry made, 'Behold, the bridegroom cometh; go ye out to meet him.'

"Then all those virgins arose and trimmed their lamps.

"And the foolish said unto the wise, 'Give us of your oil; for our lamps are gone out.'

"But the wise answered, saying, 'Not so, lest there be not

enough for us and you. But go ye rather to them that sell and buy for yourselves.'

"And while they went to buy, the bridegroom came; and they that were ready went in with him to the marriage; and the door was shut."

The Fate of the Foolish Virgins. "Afterward came also the other virgins, saying, 'Lord, lord, open to us!'

"They that were ready went in"

"But he answered and said, 'Verily I say unto you, I know you not.'

"Watch therefore; for ye know neither the day nor the hour wherein the Son of Man cometh."

First Article: No one can be saved by another's faith.

Mark 13, 32. But of that day and that hour knoweth no man, no, not the angels which are in heaven, neither the Son, but the Father.

With my lamp well trimmed and burning,
   Swift to hear and slow to roam,
Watching for Thy glad returning
   To restore me to Thy home.
Come, my Savior, Come, my Savior,
O my Savior, quickly come. (606, 4.)

---

40. The Signs of Christ's Coming
Luke 21, 25—36

Signs Pointing to the End. "And there shall be signs in the sun and in the moon and in the stars; and upon the earth distress of nations with perplexity; the sea and the waves roaring; men's hearts failing them for fear and for looking after those things which are coming on the earth; for the powers of heaven shall be shaken.

"And then shall they see the Son of Man coming in a cloud with power and great glory.

"And when these things begin to come to pass, then look up and lift up your heads; for your redemption draweth nigh."

The End Near. And He spake to them a parable: "Behold the fig-tree and all the trees; when they now shoot forth, ye see and know of your own selves that summer is now nigh at hand.

"So likewise ye, when ye see these things come to pass, know ye that the kingdom of God is nigh at hand.

"Verily I say unto you, This generation shall not pass away till all be fulfilled. Heaven and earth shall pass away, but My words shall not pass away."

Watch and Pray. "And take heed to yourselves lest at any time your hearts be overcharged with surfeiting and drunkenness and cares of this life and so that day come upon you unawares.

"For as a snare shall it come on all them that dwell on the face of the whole earth.

"Watch ye therefore and pray always that ye may be accounted worthy to escape all these things that shall come to pass and to stand before the Son of Man."

Second Article: The Last Judgment.

2 Pet. 3, 10. But the Day of the Lord will come as a thief in the night, in the which the heavens shall pass away with a great noise and the elements shall melt with fervent heat; the earth also and the works that are therein shall be burned up.

>That day of wrath, that dreadful day,
>When heaven and earth shall pass away!
>What power shall be the sinner's stay?
>How shall he meet that dreadful day? (612, 1.)

---

41. The Day of Judgment
Matt. 25, 31—46

Christ the Judge. "When the Son of Man shall come in His glory and all the holy angels with Him, then shall He sit upon the throne of His glory; and before Him shall be gathered all nations.

"And He shall separate them one from another as a shepherd divideth his sheep from the goats.

"And He shall set the sheep on His right hand, but the goats on the left."

The Blessed. "Then shall the King say unto them on His right hand, 'Come, ye blessed of My Father, inherit the kingdom prepared for you from the foundation of the world. For I was an hungred, and ye gave Me meat; I was thirsty, and ye gave Me drink; I was a stranger, and ye took Me in; naked, and ye clothed Me; I was sick, and ye visited Me; I was in prison, and ye came unto Me.'

"Then shall the righteous answer Him, saying, 'Lord, when saw we Thee an hungred and fed Thee? or thirsty, and gave Thee drink? When saw we Thee a stranger and took Thee in? or naked, and clothed Thee? Or when saw we Thee sick or in prison and came unto Thee?'

"And the King shall answer and say unto them, 'Verily I say unto you, Inasmuch as ye have done it unto one of the least of these My brethren, ye have done it unto Me.'"

"And He shall separate them"

The Rejected. "Then shall He say also unto them on the left hand, 'Depart from Me, ye cursed, into everlasting fire, prepared for the devil and his angels. For I was an hungred, and ye gave Me no meat; I was thirsty, and ye gave Me no drink; I was a stranger, and ye took Me not in; naked, and ye clothed Me not; sick and in prison, and ye visited Me not.'

"Then shall they also answer Him, saying, 'Lord, when saw we Thee an hungred, or athirst, or a stranger, or naked, or sick, or in prison and did not minister unto Thee?'

"Then shall He answer them, saying, 'Verily I say unto you, Inasmuch as ye did it not to one of the least of these, ye did it not to Me.' And these shall go away into everlasting punishment, but the righteous into life eternal."

Second Article: The Last Judgment.

2 Cor. 5, 10. We must all appear before the judgment-seat of Christ that every one may receive the things done in his body, according to that he hath done, whether it be good or bad.

> The day is surely drawing near
> When God's Son, the Anointed,
> Shall with great majesty appear
> As Judge of all appointed.
> All mirth and laughter then shall cease
> When flames on flames will still increase,
> As Scripture truly teacheth. (611, 1.)

42. The Lord's Supper

Matt. 26, 1—5. 17—29.   Mark 14, 1. 2. 10—25.   Luke 22, 1—30
John 13, 1—30.   1 Cor. 11, 23—25

Judas Bargains to Betray Jesus. Now, the Feast of Unleavened Bread drew nigh, which is called the Passover.

Then assembled together the chief priests and the scribes and the elders of the people unto the palace of the high priest, who was called Caiaphas, and consulted that they might take Jesus by subtilty [1] and kill Him.

But they said, "Not on the feast-day lest there be an uproar among the people."

Then entered Satan into Judas, surnamed Iscariot, being of the number of the Twelve. And he went unto the chief priests and said, "What will ye give me, and I will deliver Him unto you?"

And when they heard it, they were glad, and they covenanted with him for thirty pieces of silver.[2]

---

1) Subtlety, cunning, guile.
2) Thirty pieces of silver = $18.75, the price generally paid for a slave.

And from that time he sought opportunity to betray Him unto them in the absence of the multitude.

Preparing the Passover. And Jesus sent Peter and John, saying, "Go and prepare us the passover that we may eat."

And they said unto Him, "Where wilt Thou that we prepare?"

And He said unto them, "Behold, when ye are entered into the city, there shall a man meet you bearing a pitcher of water; follow him into the house where he entereth in. And ye shall say unto the goodman of the house, 'The Master saith unto thee, "Where is the guest-chamber where I shall eat the passover with My disciples?"' And he shall show you a large upper room, furnished; there make ready."

And they went and found as He had said unto them. And they made ready the passover.

And in the evening He sat down and the twelve apostles with Him. And He said unto them, "With desire I have desired to eat this passover with you before I suffer."

The Institution of the Sacrament of the Altar. And as they were eating, Jesus took bread; and when He had given thanks, He brake it and gave it to His disciples and said, *"Take, eat; this is My body, which is given for you. This do in remembrance of Me."*

After the same manner also He took the cup, when He had supped, gave thanks, and gave it to them, saying, *"Take, drink ye all of it; this cup is the new testament in My blood, which is shed for you for the remission of sins. This do ye, as oft as ye drink it, in remembrance of Me."*

The Traitor Exposed. When Jesus had thus said, He was troubled in spirit and testified and said, "Verily, verily, I say unto you that one of you shall betray Me."

Then the disciples looked one on another, doubting of whom He spake.

Now, there was leaning on Jesus' bosom one of His disciples, whom Jesus loved. Simon Peter therefore beckoned to him that he should ask who it should be of whom He spake.

He then, lying on Jesus' breast, saith unto Him, "Lord, who is it?"

Jesus answered, "He it is to whom I shall give a sop when I have dipped it."

And when He had dipped the sop, He gave it to Judas Iscariot. And after the sop Satan entered into him.

"Master, is it I?"

Then Judas, which betrayed Him, answered and said, "Master, is it I?"

He said unto him, "Thou hast said. That thou doest, do quickly."

He then, having received the sop, went immediately out; and it was night.

Sacrament of the Altar.

1 Cor. 11, 26. For as often as ye eat of this bread and drink of this **cup,** ye do show the Lord's death till He come.

> Thy table I approach;
> Dear Savior, hear my prayer.
> Oh, let no unrepented sin
> Prove hurtful to me there! (310, 1.)

SUMMARY STUDY OF THE SECOND PERIOD

1. Classify the activities of the public ministry of Christ during this period under several headings, such as preaching and teaching, performing miracles, fulfilling the Law, and the like.

2. Discuss the general effects, or results, of Christ's public ministry upon a) His disciples, b) the people in general, c) the Gentiles, and d) the enemies.

3. How would you prove by the accounts in this period that Jesus is a) true God, b) true man, and c) the only Savior?

4. What are parables?

5. Classify the parables of Christ according to the lessons they were to teach.

6. What was the purpose of Christ's miracles?

7. Classify the miracles of Christ according to the divine power which He manifested over a) nature, b) sickness, c) devil, d) death.

8. As a class exercise let pupils recall some of the chief lessons taught by Christ during this period.

"THE SON OF MAN IS COME TO SEEK AND TO SAVE THAT WHICH WAS LOST." Matt. 18, 11.

Christ

John
Peter
Judas
Andrew
James the Less
Barthanel

Tomas
James the elder
Phillip
Mattew
Lebbaeous
Simom

THIRD PERIOD

THE PASSION OF OUR LORD JESUS CHRIST

The nine stories of this section cover a period of less than twenty-four hours, from Thursday night to Friday evening. We have here the account of the suffering, death, and burial of the Redeemer. As all men are sinners and hence are subject to temporal and eternal death, they were all redeemed by the suffering and death of the Son of God. "He was wounded for our transgressions, He was bruised for our iniquities," Is. 53, 5.

Though Jesus here again manifests Himself as Prophet and King, we see Him chiefly as our High Priest, fulfilling the Law and paying its penalty — death; sacrificing Himself as the Lamb of God to atone for the sins of the world; thus redeeming sinful mankind and purchasing for it full justification and righteousness before God. "Such an High Priest became us who is holy, harmless, undefiled, separate from sinners, and made higher than the heavens; who needeth not daily as those high priests to offer up sacrifice first for His own sins and then for the people's; for this He did once, when He offered up Himself," Heb. 7, 26. 27.

43. Jesus in Gethsemane

Matt. 26, 30—46.   Mark 14, 26—42.   Luke 22, 29—46
John 18, 1. 2

Jesus Going to Gethsemane. And when they had sung a hymn, they went over the brook Kidron into the Mount of Olives.

Then saith Jesus unto them, "All ye shall be offended because of Me this night; for it is written, 'I will smite the Shepherd, and the sheep of the flock shall be scattered abroad.' But after I am risen again, I will go before you into Galilee."

Peter answered and said unto Him, "Though all men shall be offended because of Thee, yet will I never be offended."

Jesus said unto him, "Verily I say unto thee, That this night, before the cock crow twice, thou shalt deny Me thrice."

JESUS IN GETHSEMANE

Peter said unto Him, "Though I should die with Thee, yet I will not deny Thee."

Likewise also said all the disciples.

Jesus' Agony in the Garden. Then cometh Jesus with them unto a place called Gethsemane [1] and saith unto the disciples, "Sit ye here while I go and pray yonder."

"O My Father, if it be possible —"

And He took with Him Peter and James and John and began to be sorrowful and very heavy.

Then saith He unto them, "My soul is exceeding sorrowful, even unto death; tarry ye here and watch with Me."

---

1) Gethsemane ("oil-press") was a place at the foot of the Mount of Olives. A garden, or orchard, was attached to it.

And He went a little further and fell on His face and prayed, saying, "O My Father, if it be possible, let this cup pass from Me; nevertheless, not as I will, but as Thou wilt."

Jesus Finds His Disciples Sleeping. And He cometh unto the disciples and findeth them asleep and saith unto Peter, "Simon, sleepest thou? Could ye not watch with Me one hour? Watch and pray that ye enter not into temptation; the spirit indeed is willing, but the flesh is weak."

He went away again the second time and prayed, saying, "O My Father, if this cup may not pass away from Me except I drink it, Thy will be done." And He came and found them asleep again.

And He went and prayed the third time, saying the same words.

And there appeared an angel unto Him from heaven, strengthening Him.

And being in an agony, He prayed more earnestly; and His sweat was as it were great drops of blood falling down to the ground.

Then cometh He to His disciples and saith unto them, "Sleep on now and take your rest; behold, the hour is at hand, and the Son of Man is betrayed into the hands of sinners. Rise, let us be going; behold, he is at hand that doth betray Me."

Second Article: Christ's Suffering. — *Third Petition:* "Thy will be done."

1 John 5, 14. This is the confidence that we have in Him, that, if we ask anything according to His will, He heareth us.

Heb. 5, 8. Though He were a Son, yet learned He obedience by the things which He suffered.

> Go to dark Gethsemane,
>   Ye that feel the Tempter's power;
> Your Redeemer's conflict see,
>   Watch with Him one bitter hour;
> Turn not from His griefs away,
> Learn of Jesus Christ to pray. (159, 1.)

44. Jesus Taken Captive

Matt. 26, 47—56. Mark 14, 42—52. Luke 22, 47—53. John 18, 3—12

The Betrayal of Jesus. While He yet spake, lo, Judas came and with him a great multitude, with swords and staves, from the chief priests and elders of the people.

Jesus therefore, knowing all things that should come upon Him, went forth and said unto them, "Whom seek ye?"

"Judas, betrayest thou the Son of Man with a kiss?"

They answered Him, "Jesus of Nazareth."

Jesus saith unto them, "I am He."

As soon as He had said this unto them, they went backward and fell to the ground.

Then asked He them again, "Whom seek ye?"

And they said, "Jesus of Nazareth."

Jesus answered, "I have told you that I am He; if, therefore, ye seek Me, let these go their way."

Now, he that betrayed Him gave them a sign, saying, "Whomsoever I shall kiss, that same is He; hold Him fast."

And he came to Jesus and said, "Hail, Master," and kissed Him.

And Jesus said unto him, "Friend, wherefore art thou come? Judas, betrayest thou the Son of Man with a kiss?"

Then came they and laid hands on Jesus and took Him.

Peter Reproved. When they which were about Him saw what would follow, they said unto Him, "Lord, shall we smite with the sword?"

Then Peter drew his sword and struck a servant of the high priest and cut off his right ear. The servant's name was Malchus.

Then said Jesus unto him, "Put up thy sword into the sheath; for all they that take the sword shall perish with the sword. The cup which My Father hath given Me, shall I not drink it? Thinkest thou that I cannot now pray to My Father and He shall presently give Me more than twelve legions of angels? But how, then, shall the Scriptures be fulfilled that thus it must be?"

And He touched the servant's ear and healed him.

The Disciples Offended. And Jesus said to the multitudes, "Are ye come out, as against a thief, with swords and staves for to take Me? I sat daily with you teaching in the Temple, and ye laid no hold on Me; but this is your hour and the power of darkness."

Then all the disciples forsook Him and fled.

Eighth Commandment. — Fifth Commandment.

Gen. 9, 6. Whoso sheddeth man's blood, by man shall his blood be shed; for in the image of God made He man.

> Oh, what a marvelous offering!
> Behold, the Master spares
> His servants, and their suffering
> And grief for them He bears.
> God stoopeth from His throne on high;
> For me, His guilty creature,
> He deigns as man to die. (152, 2.)

45. Jesus before the High Priest
Matt. 26, 57—68. Mark 14, 53—65. Luke 22, 54. 63—71.
John 18, 13. 14. 19—27.

Before Annas. Then the band bound Jesus and led Him away to Annas first; for he was father-in-law to Caiaphas, which was the high priest that same year.

Now, Caiaphas was he which gave counsel to the Jews that it was expedient that one man should die for the people.

The high priest [1] then asked Jesus of His disciples and of His doctrine.

Jesus answered him, "I spake openly to the world; I ever taught in the synagog and in the Temple, whither the Jews always resort; and in secret have I said nothing. Why askest thou Me? Ask them which heard Me what I have said unto them; behold, they know what I said."

And when He had thus spoken, one of the officers which stood by struck Jesus with the palm of his hand, saying, "Answerest Thou the high priest so?"

Jesus answered him, "If I have spoken evil, bear witness of the evil; but if well, why smitest thou Me?"

Before Caiaphas. Now Annas sent Him bound unto Caiaphas, the high priest, and with him were assembled all the chief priests and the elders and the scribes.

Now, the chief priest and elders and all the council sought false witness against Jesus to put Him to death, but found none; yea, though many false witnesses came, yet found they none, for their witness agreed not together.

At the last came two false witnesses and said, "This fellow said, 'I am able to destroy the Temple of God and to build it in three days.'"

And the high priest arose and stood in the midst and

---

[1] Annas.

said unto Him, "Answerest Thou nothing? What is it which these witness against Thee?"

But Jesus held His peace.

And the high priest said unto Him, "I adjure Thee by the living God that Thou tell us whether Thou be the Christ, the Son of God."

And Jesus said, "I am. Nevertheless I say unto you,

"What further need have we of witnesses?"

Hereafter shall ye see the Son of Man sitting on the right hand of power and coming in the clouds of heaven."

Then the high priest rent his clothes, saying, "He hath spoken blasphemy; what further need have we of witnesses? Behold, now ye have heard His blasphemy; what think ye?"

They answered and said, "He is guilty of death."

The Savior Mocked. And the men that held Jesus mocked Him and smote Him.

And when they had blindfolded Him, they struck Him on the face and asked Him, saying, "Prophesy unto us, Thou Christ, Who is he that smote Thee?"

And many other things blasphemously spake they against Him.

Eighth Commandment: False Witness.

Prov. 19, 5. A false witness shall not be unpunished, and he that speaketh lies shall not escape.

>Thou, ah! Thou, hast taken on Thee
>   Bonds and stripes, a cruel rod;
>Pain and scorn were heaped upon Thee,
>   O Thou sinless Son of God!
>Thus didst Thou my soul deliver
>From the bonds of sin forever.
>Thousand, thousand thanks shall be,
>Dearest Jesus, unto Thee. (151, 2.)

46. Peter's Denial and the Death of Judas

a. Matt. 26, 58. 69—75.   Mark 14, 54. 66—72.   Luke 22, 54—62
John 18, 15—18. 25—27.   b. Matt. 27, 3—10

PETER'S DENIAL

Peter Follows Christ. And Simon Peter followed Jesus, and so did another disciple; that disciple was known unto the high priest and went in with Jesus into the palace of the high priest.

But Peter stood at the door without.

Then that other disciple went out and spake unto her that kept the door and brought in Peter.

And the servants and officers had made a fire of coals, for it was cold; and they warmed themselves.

And Peter sat down among them to see the end.

The Denial. And when one of the maids of the high priest that kept the door saw Peter by the fire warming himself, she earnestly looked upon him and said, "Art thou not also one of this Man's disciples?"

But he denied before them all, saying, "I am not."

And he went out into the porch; and the cock crew.

And as he went out another maid saw him and said

"Surely thou art one of them"

unto them that were there, "This fellow was also with Jesus of Nazareth."

And again he denied, with an oath, "I do not know the Man."

And after a while another of them that stood by confidently affirmed and said to Peter, "Surely thou also art one of them; for thou art a Galilean, and thy speech betrayeth thee."

One of the servants of the high priest, being his kinsman whose ear Peter cut off, saith, "Did I not see thee in the garden with Him?"

But he began to curse and to swear, saying, "I know not this Man of whom ye speak."

And immediately, while he yet spake, the cock crew the second time.

Peter's Repentance. And the Lord turned and looked upon Peter.

And Peter remembered the word of Jesus, which said unto him, "Before the cock crow twice, thou shalt deny Me thrice."

And Peter went out and wept bitterly.

THE DEATH OF JUDAS

The Remorse of Judas. When the morning was come, all the chief priests and elders of the people took counsel against Jesus; and when they had bound Him, they led Him away and delivered Him to Pontius Pilate, the governor.

Then Judas, which had betrayed Him, when he saw that He was condemned to death, repented himself and brought again the thirty pieces of silver to the chief priests and elders, saying, "I have sinned in that I have betrayed the innocent blood."

And they said, "What is that to us? See thou to that."

Judas Despairs. And he cast down the pieces of silver in the Temple and departed and went and hanged himself; and he burst asunder in the midst, and all his bowels gushed out.

The Potter's Field. And the chief priests took the silver pieces and said, "It is not lawful for to put them into the treasury, because it is the price of blood."

And they bought with them the potter's field [1] to bury

---

1) A clay pit used by potters.

strangers [2] in. Wherefore that field was called The Field of Blood unto this day.

Then was fulfilled that which was spoken by Jeremy, the prophet, saying, "And they took the thirty pieces of silver, the price of Him that was valued, whom they of the children of Israel did value; and gave them for the potter's field, as the Lord appointed me."

Second Commandment. — Eighth Commandment. — Sixth Petition. — Repentance.

1 Cor. 10, 12. Let him that thinketh he standeth take heed lest he fall.

In the hour of trial,	When Thou see'st me waver,
Jesus, plead for me	With a look recall
Lest by base denial	Nor from fear or favor
I depart from Thee;	Suffer me to fall. (516, 1.)

47. Christ before Pilate
Matt. 27, 1. 2. 11—14. Mark 15, 1—5. Luke 23, 1—12. John 18, 28—38

The Accusations. And the whole multitude arose, and bound Jesus, and led Him from Caiaphas unto the hall of judgment, and delivered Him to Pontius Pilate; [1] and it was early.

And they themselves went not into the judgment-hall lest they should be defiled, but that they might eat the passover.

Pilate then went out unto them and said, "What accusation bring ye against this man?"

---

[2] Jews from other countries who died at Jerusalem.

[1] Pilate had been governor of Judea for six years. A few years after the crucifixion of Jesus he was deposed from office on account of cruelty and banished to Gaul (France).

They answered and said unto him, "If He were not a malefactor, we would not have delivered Him up unto thee."

Then said Pilate unto them, "Take ye Him and judge Him according to your law."

The Jews therefore said unto Him, "It is not lawful for us to put any man to death (that the saying of Jesus

"They delivered Him to Pontius Pilate"

might be fulfilled which He spake, signifying what death He should die)."

And they began to accuse Him, saying, "We found this fellow perverting the nation and forbidding to give tribute to Caesar, saying that He Himself is Christ, a king."

Questioned Concerning His Kingdom. Then Pilate entered into the judgment-hall again and called Jesus and said unto Him, "Art Thou the King of the Jews?"

Jesus answered him, "Sayest thou this thing of thyself, or did others tell it thee of Me?"

Pilate answered, "Am I a Jew? Thine own nation and

the chief priests have delivered Thee unto me; what hast Thou done?"

Jesus answered, "My kingdom is not of this world; if My kingdom were of this world, then would My servants fight that I should not be delivered to the Jews; but now is My kingdom not from hence."

Pilate therefore said unto Him, "Art Thou a king, then?"

Jesus answered, "Thou sayest I am a king. To this end was I born, and for this cause came I into the world that I should bear witness unto the truth. Every one that is of the truth heareth My voice."

Pilate saith unto Him, "What is truth!"

And when he had said this, he went out again unto the Jews and saith unto them, "I find in Him no fault at all."

And when He was accused of the chief priests and elders, He answered nothing.

Then saith Pilate unto Him, "Hearest Thou not how many things they witness against Thee?"

And He answered him to never a word, insomuch that the governor marveled greatly.

Sent to Herod. And they were the more fierce, saying, "He stirreth up the people, teaching throughout all Jewry, beginning from Galilee to this place."

When Pilate heard of Galilee, he asked whether the man were a Galilean. And as soon as he knew that He belonged unto Herod's jurisdiction, he sent Him to Herod, who himself also was at Jerusalem at that time.

And when Herod saw Jesus, he was exceeding glad; for he was desirous to see Him of a long season because he had heard many things of Him; and he hoped to have seen some miracle done by Him.

Then he questioned with Him in many words; but He answered him nothing.

And the chief priests and scribes stood and vehemently accused Him.

And Herod with his men of war set Him at naught, and mocked Him, and arrayed Him in a gorgeous robe, and sent Him again to Pilate.

And the same day Pilate and Herod were made friends together; for before they were at enmity between themselves.

Second Article: "Suffered under Pontius Pilate."

2 Cor. 5, 21. He hath made Him to be sin for us who knew no sin that we might be made the righteousness of God in Him.

My burden in Thy Passion,
  Lord, Thou hast borne for me,
For it was my transgression
  Which brought this woe on Thee.
	I cast me down before Thee,
	  Wrath were my rightful lot;
	Have mercy, I implore Thee,
	  Redeemer, spurn me not!
	(172, 4.)

48. The Savior Condemned
Matt. 27, 15—30. Mark 15, 6—20. Luke 23, 13—25
John 18, 31—40; 19, 1—16

Not Guilty. And Pilate, when he had called together the chief priests and the rulers and the people, said unto them, "Ye have brought this man unto me as one that perverteth the people; and, behold, I, having examined Him before you, have found no fault in this man touching those things whereof ye accuse Him; no, nor yet Herod; for I sent you to him; and, lo, nothing worthy of death is done unto Him. I will therefore chastise Him and release Him."

Barabbas. Now, at that feast the governor was wont to release unto the people a prisoner, whomsoever they desired.

And they had then a notable prisoner, called Barabbas, who for a certain sedition made in the city and for murder was cast into prison. Therefore, when they were gathered together, Pilate said, "Ye have a custom that I should release unto you one at the Passover; whom will ye that I release unto you, Barabbas or Jesus, which is called Christ?" For he knew that for envy they had delivered Him.

Pilate's Wife. When Pilate was set down on the judgment-seat, his wife sent unto him, saying, "Have thou nothing to do with that just man; for I have suffered many things this day in a dream because of Him."

But the chief priests and elders persuaded the multitude that they should ask Barabbas and destroy Jesus.

The governor answered and said unto them, "Whether of the twain will ye that I release unto you?"

The Choice. Then cried they out all at once, saying, "Away with this man and release unto us Barabbas!"

Pilate therefore, willing to release Jesus, spake again to them, "What shall I do, then, with Jesus, which is called Christ?"

They cried, saying, "Crucify Him, crucify Him!"

And he said unto them the third time, "Why? What evil hath He done? I have found no cause of death in Him. I will therefore chastise Him and let Him go."

And they were instant with loud voices, requiring that He might be crucified.

And the voices of them and of the chief priests prevailed.

The Scourging. Then Pilate took Jesus and scourged Him.[1] And the soldiers took Jesus into the common hall and gathered unto Him the whole band of soldiers.

And they stripped Him, and put on Him a scarlet robe, and platted a crown of thorns, and put it upon His head and

---

1) The scourge was formed of three lashes made of leather or small cords, thirteen strokes of which were equal to thirty-nine lashes, and not more than forty could be given under the Law. Sometimes sharp iron points were fastened to the end of the thongs to render the suffering still more intense.

a reed in His right hand; and they bowed the knee before Him and mocked Him, saying, "Hail, King of the Jews!"

And they smote Him with their hands, and spit upon Him, and took the reed, and smote Him on the head.

Pilate therefore went forth again and saith unto them, "Behold, I bring Him forth to you that ye may know that I find no fault in Him."

"Behold the Man!"

Then came Jesus forth, wearing the crown of thorns and the purple robe.

And Pilate saith unto them, "Behold the Man!"

Christ's Death Demanded. When the chief priests therefore and officers saw Him, they cried out, saying, "Crucify Him, crucify Him!"

Pilate saith unto them, "Take ye Him and crucify Him; for I find no fault in Him."

The Jews answered him, "We have a law, and by our

law He ought to die, because He made Himself the Son of God."

When Pilate therefore heard that saying, he was the more afraid and went again into the judgment-hall and saith unto Jesus, "Whence art Thou?"

But Jesus gave him no answer.

Then saith Pilate unto Him, "Speakest Thou not unto me? Knowest Thou not that I have power to crucify Thee and have power to release Thee?"

Jesus answered, "Thou couldest have no power at all against Me except it were given thee from above; therefore he that delivered Me unto thee hath the greater sin."

And from thenceforth Pilate sought to release Him; but the Jews cried out, saying, "If thou let this man go, thou art not Caesar's friend; whosoever maketh himself a king speaketh against Caesar."

The Sentence. When Pilate therefore heard that saying and saw that he could prevail nothing, but that rather a tumult was made, he took water and washed his hands before the multitude, saying, "I am innocent of the blood of this just person; see ye to it."

Then answered all the people and said, "His blood be on us and on our children."

Then released he Barabbas unto them; but he delivered Jesus to their will to be crucified.

Second Article: "Not with gold or silver," etc.

1 Pet. 1, 18. 19. Forasmuch as ye know that ye were not redeemed with corruptible things, as silver and gold, from your vain conversation received by tradition from your fathers, but with the precious blood of Christ, as the Lamb without blemish and without spot.

O sacred Head, now wounded,
   With grief and shame weighed down,
Now scornfully surrounded
   With thorns, Thine only crown.
	O sacred Head, what glory,
	   What bliss, till now was Thine!
	Yet, though despised and gory,
	   I joy to call Thee mine.
	(172, 1.)

49. The Crucifixion
(Part I)

Matt. 27, 31—43. Mark 15, 21—32. Luke 23, 26—38
John 19, 17—24

The Way to Calvary. And they took off the purple robe from Him and put His own clothes on Him and led Him out to crucify Him.

And He, bearing His cross, went forth into a place called

"They led Him out to crucify Him"

the place of a skull, which is called in the Hebrew Golgotha. And as they led Him away, they found a man of Cyrene,[1] Simon by name, coming out of the country; him they compelled to bear the cross after Jesus.

---

1) A city in Northern Africa.

And there followed Him a great company of people and of women, which also bewailed and lamented Him.

But Jesus, turning unto them, said, "Daughters of Jerusalem, weep not for Me, but weep for yourselves and for your children. For, behold, the days are coming in the which they shall begin to say to the mountains, 'Fall on us,' and to the hills, 'Cover us.' For if they do these things in a green tree, what shall be done in the dry?"

And there were also two others, malefactors, led with Him to be put to death.

And when they were come to the place which is called Calvary, they gave Him vinegar to drink, mingled with gall; and when He had tasted thereof, He would not drink.

The Crucifixion. And they crucified Him [2] and the malefactors with Him, one on the right hand and the other on the left.

And the scripture was fulfilled which saith, "And He was numbered with the transgressors."

And it was the third hour.

Then said Jesus, *"Father, forgive them; for they know not what they do."*

The Superscription. And Pilate wrote a title in letters of Greek and Latin and Hebrew and put it on the cross. And the writing was "JESUS OF NAZARETH, THE KING OF THE JEWS."

Then said the chief priests of the Jews to Pilate, "Write not 'The King of the Jews,' but that He said, 'I am King of the Jews.'"

And Pilate answered, "What I have written I have written."

---

2) Crucifixion, a most disgraceful and extremely painful means of putting a man to death, was used by the Romans, as a rule, only for slaves and great criminals.

The Parting of Jesus' Garments. Then the soldiers, when they had crucified Jesus, took His garments and made four parts, to every soldier a part; and also His coat. Now, the coat was without seam, woven from the top throughout.

They said therefore among themselves, "Let us not rend it, but cast lots for it whose it shall be," that the scripture might be fulfilled which saith, "They parted My raiment among them, and for My vesture they did cast lots."

And sitting down, they watched Him there.

These things the soldiers did, and the people stood beholding.

Blasphemy. And they that passed by reviled Him, wagging their heads and saying, "Ah, Thou that destroyest the Temple and buildest it in three days, save Thyself. If Thou be the Son of God, come down from the cross."

Likewise also the chief priests, mocking Him, with the scribes and elders, said, "He saved others; Himself He cannot save. If He be the King of Israel, let Him now come down from the cross that we may see and believe. He trusted in God; let Him deliver Him now if He will have Him; for He said, 'I am the Son of God.'"

And the soldiers also mocked Him, coming to Him and offering Him vinegar and saying, "If Thou be the King of the Jews, save Thyself."

Second Article: Crucifixion of Christ.

Gal. 3, 13. Christ hath redeemed us from the curse of the Law, being made a curse for us; for it is written, Cursed is every one that hangeth on a tree.

> Stricken, smitten, and afflicted,
>   See Him dying on the tree!
> 'Tis the Christ by man rejected;
>   Yes, my soul, 'tis He! 'tis He!
> 'Tis the long-expected Prophet,
>   David's Son, yet David's Lord;
> Proofs I see sufficient of it:
>   'Tis the true and faithful Word.   (153, 1.)

50. The Crucifixion
(PART II)

Matt. 27, 44—55.   Mark 15, 33—41.   Luke 23, 39—49
John 19, 25—30

The Dying Thief. And one of the malefactors which were hanged railed on Him, saying, "If Thou be Christ, save Thyself and us."

But the other, answering, rebuked him, saying, "Dost not thou fear God, seeing thou art in the same condemnation? And we indeed justly; for we receive the due reward of our deeds; but this Man hath done nothing amiss."

And he said unto Jesus, "Lord, remember me when Thou comest into Thy kingdom."

And Jesus said unto him, *"Verily I say unto thee, To-day shalt thou be with Me in paradise."*

John and Mary. Now, there stood by the cross of Jesus His mother and His mother's sister, Mary, the wife of Cleophas, and Mary Magdalene.

When Jesus therefore saw His mother and the disciple standing by whom He loved, He saith unto His mother, *"Woman, behold thy son!"*

Then saith He to the disciple, *"Behold thy mother!"*

And from that hour that disciple took her unto his own home.

The Darkness. And it was about the sixth hour, and there was a darkness over all the earth unto the ninth hour.

And the sun was darkened.

And at the ninth hour Jesus cried with a loud voice, saying, "Eli, Eli, lama sabachthani," that is to say, *"My God, My God, why hast Thou forsaken Me?"*

Some of them that stood there, when they heard that, said, "This man calleth for Elias."

And straightway one of them ran, and took a sponge, and filled it with vinegar, and put it on a reed, and gave Him to drink.

The rest said, "Let be; let us see whether Elias will come to save Him."

Intense Suffering. After this, Jesus, knowing that all

"My God, My God, why hast Thou forsaken Me?"

things were now accomplished, that the Scripture might be fulfilled, saith, *"I thirst."*

Now, there was set a vessel full of vinegar; and they filled a sponge with vinegar, and put it upon hyssop, and put it to His mouth, and gave Him to drink.

Death. When Jesus therefore had received the vinegar, He said, *"It is finished."*

And when He had cried with a loud voice, He said,

"*Father, into Thy hands I commend My spirit*"; and having said thus, He bowed His head and gave up the ghost.

Miracles Attending Jesus' Death. And, behold, the veil of the Temple [1] was rent in twain from the top to the bottom; and the earth did quake, and the rocks rent; and the graves were opened; and many bodies of the saints which slept, arose, and came out of the graves after His resurrection, and went into the Holy City, and appeared unto many.

Now, when the centurion and they that were with him watching Jesus saw the earthquake and those things that were done, they feared greatly; and the centurion glorified God, saying, "Certainly, this was a righteous man; this was the Son of God."

And all the people that came together to see that sight, beholding the things which were done, smote their breasts and returned.

Second Article: "Was crucified, dead, and buried."

John 1, 29. Behold the Lamb of God, which taketh away the sin of the world.

> Lamb of God, pure and holy,
>   Who on the cross didst suffer,
> Ever patient and lowly,
>   Thyself to scorn didst offer.
> All sins Thou borest for us,
> Else had despair reigned o'er us:
> Have mercy on us, O Jesus! (146, 1.)

---

[1] Before the entrance to the Holy of Holies hung a veil, or curtain, about three inches thick.

51. The Burial of Jesus
Matt. 27, 56—66. Mark 15, 42—47. Luke 23, 50—56
John 19, 31—42

Jesus' Side is Pierced. The Jews therefore, because it was the Preparation, that the bodies should not remain upon the cross on the Sabbath-day, (for that Sabbath-day was an high day,) besought Pilate that their legs might be broken and they might be taken away.

Then came the soldiers and brake the legs of the first and of the other which was crucified with Him; but when they came to Jesus and saw that He was dead already, they brake not His legs, but one of the soldiers with a spear pierced His side, and forthwith came there out blood and water.

These things were done that the scripture should be fulfilled "A bone of Him shall not be broken." And again another scripture saith, "They shall look on Him whom they pierced."

Jesus Removed from the Cross. And when the even was come, there came Joseph of Arimathea, an honorable counselor, a good man and a just, (the same had not consented to the counsel and deed of them,) who also himself waited for the kingdom of God, being a disciple of Jesus, but secretly, for fear of the Jews; this man went in boldly unto Pilate and begged the body of Jesus.

And Pilate marveled if He were already dead; and calling unto him the centurion, he asked him whether He had been any while dead.

And when he knew it of the centurion, he gave the body to Joseph. And he bought fine linen and took Him down.

And there came also Nicodemus, which at the first came to Jesus by night, and brought a mixture of myrrh and aloes, about a hundred pound weight.[1)]

[1)] About seventy-five pounds avoirdupois.

Then took they the body of Jesus and wound it in linen clothes with the spices,[2] as the manner of the Jews is to bury.

The Sepulcher. Now, in the place where He was crucified there was a garden and in the garden Joseph's own new tomb, hewn in stone, wherein never man before was laid. There laid they Jesus therefore because of the Jews' Preparation

"There laid they Jesus"

Day (for the sepulcher was nigh at hand) and rolled a great stone unto the door of the sepulcher and departed.

And the women also which came with Him from Galilee followed after and beheld the sepulcher and how His body was laid.

And they returned and prepared spices and ointments and rested the Sabbath-day according to the commandment.

The Bad Conscience of the High Priests. Now, the next

---

2) Aromatic substances used in embalming.

day the chief priests and Pharisees came together unto Pilate, saying, "Sir, we remember that that deceiver said while He was yet alive, 'After three days I will rise again.' Command therefore that the sepulcher be made sure until the third day lest His disciples come by night and steal Him away and say unto the people, 'He is risen from the dead'; so the last error shall be worse than the first."

Pilate said unto them, "Ye have a watch; go your way; make it as sure as ye can." So they went and made the sepulcher sure, sealing the stone and setting a watch.

Second Article: "Was crucified, dead, and buried."

Ps. 16, 10. Thou wilt not suffer Thine Holy One to see corruption.

> O darkest woe!
> Ye tears, forth flow!
> Has earth so sad a wonder?
> God the Father's only Son
> Now is buried yonder. (167, 1.)

SUMMARY STUDY OF THE THIRD PERIOD

1. List or name all the events which occurred within the twenty-four hours of Christ's Passion.

2. Discuss this period in the light of the prophecy concerning the Woman's Seed.

3. Make a list of the prophecies that were fulfilled during this period.

4. Show from various particulars a) that Jesus was able to redeem us because He is true God; b) that He was true man; c) that He suffered in His soul as well as in His body; d) that He suffered and died willingly; e) that He suffered and died for *our* sakes.

5. Explain how Jesus manifested Himself in the foregoing stories a) as the true High Priest, b) as Prophet, c) as King.

6. Discuss in class a number of the personal lessons we should derive from this period.

"THANKS BE TO GOD, WHICH GIVETH US THE VICTORY THROUGH OUR LORD JESUS CHRIST." 1 Cor. 15, 57.

FOURTH PERIOD
THE GLORIFIED LORD

Christ had declared on the cross, "It is finished." His suffering in our stead had come to an end. He had laid down His life and was buried. The Law of God was fulfilled and its penalty paid. However, Scripture had prophesied — and Jesus had repeatedly foretold — not only His death, but also His resurrection and ascension into heaven. The resurrection of Christ is an all-important part in God's plan of salvation, as Christ Himself testifies, Luke 24, 26: "Ought not Christ to have suffered these things and to enter into His glory?" If Christ had not risen, His suffering and death could not have saved us from sin and death. St. Paul states very definitely, 1 Cor. 15, 17. 18: "If Christ be not raised, your faith is vain; ye are yet in your sins. Then they also which are fallen asleep in Christ are perished." His resurrection proved beyond a doubt that He was indeed the Son of God, that His doctrine is God's own truth, that He had conquered all His enemies, and that all mankind is now reconciled to God by the all-sufficient sacrifice of Christ, 2 Cor. 5, 17.

In this period we behold the glorified Lord: rising from the dead, proving His resurrection by appearing to His disciples, and departing visibly from the earth to sit at the right hand of God the Father Almighty and rule over His Church on earth until He shall again come visibly to judge the quick and the dead and lead His Church to eternal glory.

52. The Resurrection

Matt. 28, 1—8.   Mark 16, 1—8.   Luke 24, 1—12.   John 20, 1—10

The Women Go to the Sepulcher. And when the Sabbath was past, Mary Magdalene and Mary, the mother of James, and Salome had bought sweet spices that they might come and anoint Him.

And very early in the morning, the first day of the week, they came unto the sepulcher at the rising of the sun, bringing the spices which they had prepared. And they said among themselves, "Who shall roll us away the stone from the door of the sepulcher?"

The Empty Sepulcher. And, behold, there was a great earthquake; for the angel of the Lord descended from heaven and came and rolled back the stone from the door and sat upon it.

His countenance was like lightning and his raiment white as snow; and for fear of him the keepers did shake and became as dead men.

And when the women looked, they saw that the stone was rolled away; for it was very great.

"He is risen"

And they entered in and found not the body of the Lord Jesus.

The Easter-Message. And it came to pass as they were much perplexed thereabout, behold, they saw a young man sitting on the right side clothed in a long white garment; and they were affrighted.

And he saith unto the women, "Be not affrighted; *ye seek Jesus of Nazareth, which was crucified. He is risen; He is not here. Behold the place where they laid Him.* But go your way, tell His disciples and Peter that He goeth before you into Galilee; there shall ye see Him, as He said unto you."

And they remembered His words and went out quickly and fled from the sepulcher, for they trembled and were amazed; and told all these things unto the Eleven and to all the rest.

And their words seemed to them as idle tales, and they believed them not.

Then Mary Magdalene runneth and cometh to Simon Peter and to the other disciple, whom Jesus loved, and saith unto them, "They have taken away the Lord out of the sepulcher, and we know not where they have laid Him."

Peter and John at the Sepulcher. Then arose Peter and ran unto the sepulcher and that other disciple.

So they ran both together; and the other disciple did outrun Peter and came first to the sepulcher.

And he, stooping down and looking in, saw the linen clothes lying; yet went he not in.

Then cometh Simon Peter and went into the sepulcher and seeth the linen clothes lie and the napkin that was about His head, not lying with the linen clothes, but wrapped together in a place by itself.

Then went in also that other disciple, which came first to the sepulcher; and he saw and believed. For as yet they knew not the scripture that He must rise again from the dead.

Then the disciples went away again unto their own home.

Second Article: "The third day He arose again from the dead."

Rom. 1, 4. He was declared to be the Son of God with power, according to the Spirit of Holiness, by the resurrection from the dead.

The Foe in triumph shouted
   When Christ lay in the tomb
But lo, he now is routed,
   His boast is turned to gloom.
For Christ again is free;
In glorious victory
He who is strong to save
Has triumphed o'er the grave.
(192, 2.)

53. The First Appearances of the Risen Lord
Matt. 28, 9—15. John 20, 11—18

Mary Magdalene. But Mary Magdalene stood without at the sepulcher weeping; and as she wept, she stooped down and looked into the sepulcher and seeth two angels in white, sitting, the one at the head and the other at the feet where the body of Jesus had lain.

And they say unto her, "Woman, why weepest thou?"

"They have taken away my Lord"

She saith unto them, "Because they have taken away my Lord, and I know not where they have laid Him."

And when she had thus said, she turned herself back, and saw Jesus standing and knew not that it was Jesus.

Jesus saith unto her, "Woman, why weepest thou? Whom seekest thou?"

She, supposing Him to be the gardener, saith unto Him,

"Sir, if thou have borne Him hence, tell me where thou hast laid Him, and I will take Him away."

Jesus saith unto her, "Mary!"

She turned herself and saith unto Him, "Rabboni," which is to say, "Master."

Jesus saith unto her, "Touch Me not; for I am not yet ascended to My Father. But go to My brethren and say unto them, 'I ascend unto My Father and your Father, and to My God and your God.'"

The Other Women. And as the other women went to tell His disciples, behold, Jesus met them, saying, "All hail!"

And they came and held Him by the feet and worshiped Him.

Then said Jesus unto them, "Be not afraid; go, tell My brethren that they go into Galilee, and there shall they see Me."

The Guards Bribed. Now, some of the watch came into the city and showed unto the chief priests all the things that were done.

And when they were assembled with the elders and had taken counsel, they gave large money unto the soldiers, saying, "Say ye, 'His disciples came by night and stole Him away while we slept.' And if this come to the governor's ears, we will persuade him and secure you."

So they took the money and did as they were taught; and this saying is commonly reported among the Jews until this day.

Second Article: "Even as He is risen from the dead, lives and reigns to all eternity."

1 Cor. 15, 17. If Christ be not raised, your faith is vain; ye are yet in your sins.

> Vain the stone, the watch, the seal;
> Christ has burst the gates of hell.
> Death in vain forbids His rise;
> Christ has opened Paradise. (193, 3.)

54. Jesus Appears on the Way to Emmaus
Luke 24, 13—25. Mark 16, 12. 13

The Two Disciples. And, behold, two of them went that same day to a village called Emmaus, which was from Jerusalem about sixty furlongs.[1]

And they talked together of all these things which had happened.

The Stranger. And it came to pass that, while they communed together and reasoned, Jesus Himself drew near and went with them.

But their eyes were holden that they should not know Him.

And He said unto them, "What manner of communications are these that ye have one to another as ye walk and are sad?"

And the one of them, whose name was Cleopas, answering, said unto Him, "Art Thou only a stranger in Jerusalem and hast not known the things which are come to pass there in these days?"

And He said unto them, "What things?"

And they said unto Him, "Concerning Jesus of Nazareth, which was a prophet mighty in deed and word before God and all the people; and how the chief priests and our rulers delivered Him to be condemned to death and have crucified Him.

"But we trusted that it had been He which should have redeemed Israel. And besides all this, to-day is the third day since these things were done.

"Yea, and certain women also of our company made us astonished, which were early at the sepulcher; and when they found not His body, they came, saying that they had also seen a vision of angels, which said that He was alive.

---

1) About seven and a half miles.

"And certain of them which were with us went to the sepulcher and found it even so as the women had said; but Him they saw not."

Jesus Expounds the Scripture. Then He said unto them, "O fools and slow of heart to believe all that the prophets

"Ought not Christ to have suffered these things?"

have spoken! *Ought not Christ to have suffered these things and to enter into His glory?*"

And beginning at Moses and all the prophets, He expounded unto them in all the Scriptures the things concerning Himself.

And they drew nigh unto the village whither they went; and He made as though He would have gone further.

But they constrained Him, saying, "Abide with us; for it is toward evening, and the day is far spent."

And He went in to tarry with them.

Jesus Makes Himself Known. And it came to pass, as He sat at meat with them, He took bread, and blessed it, and brake, and gave to them.

And their eyes were opened, and they knew Him; and He vanished out of their sight.

And they said one to another, "Did not our heart burn within us while He talked with us by the way and while He opened to us the Scriptures?"

And they rose up the same hour and returned to Jerusalem and found the Eleven gathered together and them that were with them, saying, "The Lord is risen indeed and hath appeared to Simon."

And they told what things were done in the way and how He was known of them in breaking of bread.

Second Petition.

Is. 42, 3. A bruised reed shall He not break, and the smoking flax shall He not quench.

>Lord Jesus Christ, with us abide,
>For round us falls the eventide;
>Nor let Thy Word, that heavenly light,
>For us be ever veiled in night. (202, 1.)

55. Christ Appears to the Disciples
Mark 16, 14.   Luke 24, 36—48.   John 20, 19—31

The Easter-Greeting. Then the same day, at evening, being the first day of the week, when the doors were shut where the disciples were assembled for fear of the Jews, came Jesus and stood in the midst and saith unto them, "Peace be unto you." But they were terrified and affrighted and supposed that they had seen a spirit.

And He said unto them, "Why are ye troubled, and why do thoughts arise in your hearts? Behold My hands and My feet that it is I Myself; handle Me and see; for a spirit hath not flesh and bones, as ye see Me have."

And when He had thus spoken, He showed them His hands and His feet and His side.

Then were the disciples glad when they saw the Lord.

And while they yet believed not for joy and wondered, He said unto them, "Have ye here any meat?"

And they gave Him a piece of broiled fish and of a honeycomb. And He took it and did eat before them.

Then said Jesus to them again, "Peace be unto you; as My Father sent Me, even so send I you."

The Office of the Keys. And when He had said this, He breathed on them and saith unto them, *"Receive ye the Holy Ghost. Whosoever sins ye remit, they are remitted unto them; and whosoever sins ye retain, they are retained."*

Thomas. But Thomas, one of the Twelve, called Didymus, was not with them when Jesus came. The other disciples therefore said unto him, "We have seen the Lord."

But he said unto them, "Except I shall see in His hands the print of the nails and put my finger into the print of the nails and thrust my hands into His side, I will not believe."

And after eight days again His disciples were within and Thomas with them.

Then came Jesus, the doors being shut, and stood in the midst and said, "Peace be unto you."

Then said He to Thomas, "Reach hither thy finger and behold My hands, and reach hither thy hand and thrust it into My side; and be not faithless, but believing."

"My Lord and my God"

And Thomas answered and said unto Him, "*My Lord and my God.*"

Jesus saith unto him, "Thomas, because thou hast seen Me, thou hast believed. *Blessed are they that have not seen and yet have believed.*"

The Office of the Keys.

Luke 10, 16. He that heareth you heareth Me; and he that despiseth you despiseth Me; and he that despiseth Me despiseth Him that sent Me.

> Shine on the darkened and the cold,
> Recall the wanderers to Thy fold,
> Unite all those who walk apart,
> Confirm the weak and doubting heart. (512, 5.)

56. Christ's Appearance in Galilee
John 21, 1—19

At the Sea of Tiberias. After these things Jesus showed Himself again to the disciples at the Sea of Tiberias; and on this wise showed He Himself.

There were together Simon Peter, and Thomas, and Nathanael of Cana, in Galilee, and the sons of Zebedee, and two other of His disciples.

Simon Peter saith unto them, "I go a-fishing."

They say unto him, "We also go with thee."

They went forth and entered into a ship immediately; and that night they caught nothing.

But when the morning was now come, Jesus stood on the shore; but the disciples knew not that it was Jesus.

Then Jesus saith unto them, "Children, have ye any meat?"

They answered Him, "No."

And He said unto them, "Cast the net on the right side of the ship, and ye shall find."

They cast therefore, and now they were not able to draw it for the multitude of fishes.

Therefore that disciple whom Jesus loved saith unto Peter, "It is the Lord."

Now, when Simon Peter heard that it was the Lord, he girt his fisher's coat unto him and did cast himself into the sea. And the other disciples came in a little ship, (for they were not far from land, but as it were two hundred cubits,) dragging the net with fishes.

As soon, then, as they were come to land, they saw a fire of coals there and fish laid thereon and bread.

Jesus saith unto them, "Bring of the fish which ye have now caught."

Simon Peter went up and drew the net to land full of

great fishes, a hundred and fifty and three; and for all there were so many, yet was not the net broken.

Jesus saith unto them, "Come and dine."

And none of the disciples durst ask Him, "Who art Thou?" knowing that it was the Lord.

"Lovest thou Me?"

Jesus then cometh and taketh bread and giveth them and fish likewise.

Peter Reinstated in His Apostleship. So when they had dined, Jesus saith to Simon Peter, "Simon, son of Jonas, lovest thou Me more than these?"

He saith unto Him, "Yea, Lord; Thou knowest that I love Thee."

He saith unto him, "Feed My lambs."

He saith to him again the second time, "Simon, son of Jonas, lovest thou Me?"

He saith unto Him, "Yea, Lord; Thou knowest that I love Thee."

He saith unto him, "Feed My sheep."

He saith unto him the third time, "Simon, son of Jonas, lovest thou Me?"

Peter was grieved because He said unto him the third time, "Lovest thou Me?" And he said unto Him, "Lord, Thou knowest all things; Thou knowest that I love Thee."

Jesus saith unto him, "Feed My sheep. Verily, verily, I say unto thee, When thou wast young, thou girdedst thyself and walkedst whither thou wouldest; but when thou shalt be old, thou shalt stretch forth thy hands, and another shall gird thee and carry thee whither thou wouldest not."

This spake He, signifying by what death he should glorify God.[1]) And when He had spoken this, He saith unto him, "Follow Me."

First Article: Benevolent, merciful, gracious.
1 John 4, 8. God is Love.

> Oh, may Thy pastors faithful be,
> Not laboring for themselves, but Thee!
> Give grace to feed with wholesome food
> The sheep and lambs bought by Thy blood,
> To tend Thy flock, and thus to prove
> How dearly they the Shepherd love. (493, 2.)

---

1) Peter is said to have been crucified during the persecution in the reign of cruel Emperor Nero.

THE GREAT COMMISSION

57. The Ascension

Matt. 28, 16—20. Mark 16, 15—20. Luke 24, 49—53. Acts 1, 2—12

The Great Commission. Then the eleven disciples went away into Galilee, into a mountain where Jesus had appointed them. And when they saw Him, they worshiped Him.

And Jesus came and spake unto them, saying, *"All power is given unto Me in heaven and in earth. Go ye therefore*

"Go ye therefore and teach all nations"

and teach all nations, baptizing them in the name of the Father and of the Son and of the Holy Ghost; teaching them to observe all things whatsoever I have commanded you.

"And, lo, I am with you alway, even unto the end of the world. He that believeth and is baptized shall be saved, but he that believeth not shall be damned."

The Promise of the Spirit. And Jesus showed Himself alive after His Passion by many infallible proofs, being seen of His disciples forty days and speaking of the things pertaining to the kingdom of God.

And being assembled together with them, He commanded them that they should not depart from Jerusalem, but wait for the promise of the Father, "which," saith He, "ye have heard of Me. For John truly baptized with water; but ye shall be baptized with the Holy Ghost not many days hence.

"He was carried up into heaven"

Ye shall receive power after that the Holy Ghost is come upon you; and ye shall be witnesses unto Me both in Jerusalem, and in all Judea, and in Samaria, and unto the uttermost part of the earth."

The Ascension. And He led them out as far as to Bethany; and lifted up His hands and blessed them.

And it came to pass while He blessed them, He was parted from them and carried up into heaven while they beheld; and a cloud received Him out of their sight.

And while they looked steadfastly toward heaven as He went up, behold, two men stood by them in white apparel, which also said, "Ye men of Galilee, why stand ye gazing up into heaven? This same Jesus which is taken up from you into heaven shall so come in like manner as ye have seen Him go into heaven."

And they worshiped Him and returned to Jerusalem from the mount called Olivet with great joy. And they were continually in the Temple, praising and blessing God.

Second Article: "He ascended into heaven."
John 12, 26. Where I am, there shall also My servant be.

> The Head that once was crowned
> with thorns
> Is crowned with glory now;
> A royal diadem adorns
> The mighty Victor's brow. (219, 1.)

SUMMARY STUDY OF THE FOURTH PERIOD

1. Recall in a few sentences the leading events from the resurrection of Christ to His ascension.
2. Name as many proofs as you can that Christ rose from the dead.
3. Why was it so important for the disciples of Christ to be made certain of His resurrection from the dead, and why is this so important also for us?
4. Quote a number of statements from Luther's Small Catechism which refer to this period.
5. Name the comforts that Christ's resurrection from the dead affords to all believers.
6. What is the true meaning and glory of Christ's ascension into heaven?
7. Discuss various spiritual benefits that Christians should derive from the foregoing accounts.

"BECAUSE I LIVE, YE SHALL LIVE ALSO." John 14, 19.
"WHERE I AM, THERE SHALL ALSO MY SERVANT BE."
John 12, 26.

FIFTH PERIOD

THE FOUNDING AND THE GROWTH OF THE CHRISTIAN CHURCH

Isaiah had prophesied, chap. 53, 10: "When Thou shalt make His soul an offering for sin, He shall see His seed, He shall prolong His days, and the pleasure of the Lord shall prosper in His hand." Here the founding and the growth of the Christian Church are foretold. Having departed visibly from the earth, the glorified Savior poured out the Holy Spirit upon His disciples, who guided them into all truth and made them the God-inspired witnesses to the work of redemption which Jesus had finished. After beginning their witness in Jerusalem, they went into Judea, Samaria, and the uttermost parts of the earth, teaching and preaching the glad tidings of the grace of God in Christ Jesus. Those who believed and were baptized were saved. They were the "seed" of which Isaiah prophesied. The saving of souls by the preaching of the Gospel to the end of days is to be that "pleasure of the Lord" which is to prosper by the hand of the glorified Savior.

Of this the remaining stories in our Bible History treat. Here we witness the first-fruits of Christ's redemption, but we also learn of the scorn and bitterness with which the enemies of Christ opposed the preaching of the Gospel. Here we have the beginning of a work that has continued to the present day and will continue until Christ returns for Judgment.

58. Pentecost
Acts 2

The Outpouring of the Holy Ghost. And when the day of Pentecost was fully come, they were all with one accord in one place.

And suddenly there came a sound from heaven as of a rushing, mighty wind. And it filled all the house where they were sitting.

And there appeared unto them cloven tongues like as of fire, and it sat upon each of them.

And they were all filled with the Holy Ghost and began to speak with other tongues, as the Spirit gave them utterance.

The Multitudes. And there were dwelling at Jerusalem, Jews, devout men, out of every nation under heaven.

Now, when this was noised abroad, the multitude came together and were confounded because that every man heard them speak in his own language.

And they were all amazed and marveled, saying one to

"And they were all filled with the Holy Ghost"

another, "Behold, are not all these which speak Galileans? And how hear we every man in our own tongue wherein we were born?

"We do hear them speak in our tongues the wonderful works of God."

And they were all amazed and were in doubt, saying one to another, "What meaneth this?"

Others, mocking, said, "These men are full of new wine."

Peter's Sermon. But Peter, standing up with the Eleven, lifted up his voice and said unto them, "Ye men of Judea and all ye that dwell at Jerusalem, be this known unto you, and hearken to my words; for these are not drunken, as ye suppose, seeing it is but the third hour of the day.

"But this is that which was spoken by the prophet Joel: 'And it shall come to pass in the last days,' saith God, 'I will pour out of My Spirit upon all flesh; and your sons and your daughters shall prophesy, and your young men shall see visions, and your old men shall dream dreams. And on My servants and on My handmaidens I will pour out in those days of My Spirit; and they shall prophesy. And it shall come to pass that whosoever shall call on the name of the Lord shall be saved.'

"Ye men of Israel, hear these words: Jesus of Nazareth, a Man approved of God among you by wonders and miracles and signs, which God did by Him in the midst of you, as ye yourselves also know: Him, being delivered by the determinate counsel and foreknowledge of God, ye have taken and by wicked hands have crucified and slain; whom God hath raised up, whereof we all are witnesses.

"Therefore let all the house of Israel know assuredly that God hath made that same Jesus whom ye have crucified both Lord and Christ."

The First Christian Congregation. Now, when they heard this, they were pricked in their hearts and said, "Men and brethren, what shall we do?"

Then Peter said unto them, "Repent and be baptized, every one of you, in the name of Jesus Christ for the remission of sins, and ye shall receive the gift of the Holy Ghost. For the promise is unto you and your children and to all that are afar off, even as many as the Lord, our God, shall call."

Then they that gladly received his word were baptized;

and the same day there were added unto them about three thousand souls.

And they continued steadfastly in the apostles' doctrine, and fellowship, and in breaking of bread, and in prayers.

And fear came upon every soul; and many wonders and signs were done by the apostles.

Third Article.

1 Cor. 3, 16. Know ye not that ye are the temple of God and that the Spirit of God dwelleth in you?

> O Holy Spirit, enter in
> And in our hearts Thy work begin,
> Thy temple deign to make us. (235, 1 a.)

59. The Healing of the Lame Man
Acts 3 and 4

In Jesus' Name. Now, Peter and John went up together into the Temple at the hour of prayer, being the ninth hour.

And a certain man, lame from his birth, was carried, whom they laid daily at the gate of the Temple which is called Beautiful, to ask alms of them that entered into the Temple; who, seeing Peter and John about to go into the Temple, asked an alms.

And Peter, fastening his eyes upon him, with John, said, "Look on us." And he gave heed unto them, expecting to receive something of them.

Then Peter said, "Silver and gold have I none; but such as I have give I thee: In the name of Jesus Christ of Nazareth rise up and walk."

And he took him by the right hand and lifted him up; and immediately his feet and ankle-bones received strength.

And he, leaping up, stood and walked and entered with them into the Temple, walking and leaping and praising God. And all the people saw him walking and praising God.

Peter's Testimony. And as the lame man which was healed held Peter and John, all the people ran together unto them in the porch that is called Solomon's, greatly wondering.

And when Peter saw it, he answered unto the people, "Ye men of Israel, why marvel ye at this, or why look ye so earnestly on us, as though by our own power or holiness we had made this man to walk?

"In the name of Jesus Christ of Nazareth —"

"The God of Abraham and of Isaac and of Jacob, the God of our fathers, hath glorified His Son Jesus; whom ye delivered up, and denied Him in the presence of Pilate when he was determined to let Him go. But ye denied the Holy One and the Just and desired a murderer to be granted unto you; and killed the Prince of Life, whom God hath raised from the dead; whereof we are witnesses.

"And His name, through faith in His name, hath given

this man whom ye see and know this perfect soundness in the presence of you all.

"And now, brethren, I know that through ignorance ye did it, as did also your rulers.

"Repent ye therefore and be converted that your sins may be blotted out."

And many of them which heard the Word believed; and the number of the men was about five thousand.

Second Commandment. — Second Article: "His only Son, our Lord."

Mark 16, 17. 18. And these signs shall follow them that believe: In My name shall they cast out devils; they shall speak with new tongues; they shall take up serpents; and if they drink any deadly thing, it shall not hurt them; they shall lay hands on the sick, and they shall recover.

> O faithful God, thanks be to Thee
> Who dost forgive iniquity.
> Thou grantest help in sin's distress,
> And soul and body dost Thou bless. (321, 1.)

60. Ananias and Sapphira
Acts 4, 32—35; 5, 1—11

The Early Christians. And the multitude of them that believed were of one heart and of one soul; neither said any of them that aught of the things which he possessed was his own; but they had all things common.

And with great power gave the apostles witness of the resurrection of the Lord Jesus.

And as many as were possessors of lands or houses sold them and brought the prices of the things that were sold and laid them down at the apostles' feet; and distribution was made unto every man according as he had need.

The Death of Ananias. But a certain man, named Ananias, with Sapphira, his wife, sold a possession and kept back part of the price, his wife also being privy to it, and brought a certain part and laid it at the apostles' feet.

But Peter said, "Ananias, why hath Satan filled thine heart to lie to the Holy Ghost and to keep back part of the price of the land? While it remained, was it not thine own? And after it was sold, was it not in thine own power? Why hast thou conceived this thing in thine heart? Thou hast not lied unto men, but unto God."

"And Ananias gave up the ghost"

And Ananias, hearing these words, fell down and gave up the ghost.

And great fear came on all them that heard these things.

And the young men arose, wound him up, and carried him out, and buried him.

The Death of Sapphira. And it was about the space of three hours after, when his wife, not knowing what was done, came in.

And Peter answered unto her, "Tell me whether ye sold the land for so much."

And she said, "Yea, for so much."

Then Peter said unto her, "How is it that ye have agreed together to tempt the Spirit of the Lord? Behold, the feet of them which have buried thy husband are at the door and shall carry thee out."

Then fell she down straightway at his feet and yielded up the ghost.

And the young men came in and found her dead and, carrying her forth, buried her by her husband.

And great fear came upon all the Church and upon as many as heard these things.

Second Commandment: "Lie or deceive by His name."

Matt. 7, 21. Not every one that saith unto Me, Lord, Lord, shall enter into the kingdom of heaven, but he that doeth the will of My Father which is in heaven.

>Thou sacred Love, grace on us bestow,
>Set our hearts with heavenly fire aglow,
>That with hearts united we love each other,
>Of one mind, in peace with every brother.
>Lord, have mercy! (231, 3.)

61. Stephen
Acts 6, 7, and 8, 1

The Seven Elders. And in those days, when the number of the disciples was multiplied, there arose a murmuring of the Grecians against the Hebrews because their widows were neglected in the daily ministration.

Then the Twelve called the multitude of the disciples unto them and said, "It is not reason that we should leave the Word of God and serve tables. Wherefore, brethren, look ye out among you seven men of honest report, full of the Holy Ghost and wisdom, whom we may appoint over this business. But we will give ourselves continually to prayer and to the ministry of the Word."

And the saying pleased the whole multitude; and they chose Stephen, a man full of faith and of the Holy Ghost, and Philip, and Prochorus, and Nicanor, and Timon, and Parmenas, and Nicolas, a proselyte of Antioch.

Stephen Accused. And the Word of God increased; and the number of the disciples multiplied in Jerusalem greatly; and a great company of the priests were obedient to the faith.

And Stephen, a man full of faith and power, did great wonders and miracles among the people.

Then there arose certain men and disputed with Stephen.

And they were not able to resist the wisdom and the spirit by which he spake.

Then they suborned men, which said, "We have heard him speak blasphemous words against Moses and against God."

And they stirred up the people and the elders and the scribes, and came upon him, and caught him, and brought him to the Council.

And all that sat in the Council, looking steadfastly on him, saw his face as it had been the face of an angel.

Then said the high priest, "Are these things so?"

The Defense. But Stephen answered for himself and spake of the things which the God of Abraham, Isaac, and Jacob had done to their fathers and how their fathers had always resisted the will of God; and at last he said: "Ye stiff-necked, ye do always resist the Holy Ghost; as your fathers did, so do ye. Which of the prophets have not your fathers persecuted? And they have slain them which showed before of the coming of the Just One; of whom ye have been now the betrayers and murderers; who have received the Law and have not kept it."

When they heard these things, they were cut to the heart, and they gnashed on him with their teeth.

The First Martyr. But he, being full of the Holy Ghost, looked up steadfastly into heaven and saw the glory of God and Jesus standing on the right hand of God and said, "Behold, I see the heavens opened and the Son of Man standing on the right hand of God."

Then they cried out with a loud voice, and stopped their

"And they stoned Stephen"

ears, and ran upon him with one accord, and cast him out of the city, and stoned him.

And the witnesses laid down their clothes at a young man's feet whose name was Saul.

And they stoned Stephen, calling upon God and saying, "Lord Jesus, receive my spirit."

And he kneeled down and cried with a loud voice, "Lord, lay not this sin to their charge."

And when he had said this, he fell asleep.

And devout men carried Stephen to his burial and made great lamentation over him.

But Saul consented unto his death.

Eighth Commandment. — *Of Prayer in General:* "For whom shall we pray?"

Rom. 8, 18. I reckon that the sufferings of this present time are not worthy to be compared with the glory which shall be revealed in us.

>Thine honor, save, O Christ, our Lord!
>Hear Zion's cries and help afford;
>Destroy the wiles of mighty foes
>Who now Thy Word and truth oppose. (265, 1.)

---

62. The Eunuch of Ethiopia
Acts 8, 1—6. 26—39

The Persecution. And at that time there was a great persecution against the church which was at Jerusalem; and they were all scattered abroad throughout the regions of Judea and Samaria except the apostles.

As for Saul, he made havoc of the church, entering into every house, and, haling men and women, committed them to prison.

Therefore they that were scattered abroad went everywhere, preaching the Word.

Then Philip [1] went down to the city of Samaria and preached Christ unto them.

And the people with one accord gave heed unto those things which Philip spake, hearing and seeing the miracles which he did.

---

1) Philip the Evangelist (not the Apostle) was one of the seven men elected to distribute the alms of the congregation. (Lesson 61.)

The Eunuch. And the angel of the Lord spake unto Philip, saying, "Arise and go toward the south, unto the way that goeth down from Jerusalem unto Gaza, which is desert."

And he arose and went.

And, behold, a man of Ethiopia, a eunuch [2]) of great authority under Candace, queen of the Ethiopians, who had

"Understandest thou what thou readest?"

the charge of all her treasure and had come to Jerusalem for to worship, was returning and, sitting in his chariot, read Esaias, the prophet.

Then the Spirit said unto Philip, "Go near and join thyself to this chariot."

And Philip ran thither to him and heard him read the prophet Esaias and said, "Understandest thou what thou readest?"

---

2) A high official.

And he said, "How can I except some man should guide me?"

And he desired Philip that he would come up and sit with him.

The place of the Scripture which he read was this, *"He was led as a sheep to the slaughter; and like a lamb dumb before His shearer, so opened He not His mouth."*

And the eunuch answered Philip and said, "I pray thee, of whom speaketh the prophet this?"

Then Philip opened his mouth and began at the same scripture and preached unto him Jesus.

His Baptism. And as they went on their way, they came unto a certain water.

And the eunuch said, "See, here is water; what doth hinder me to be baptized?"

And Philip said, "If thou believest with all thine heart, thou mayest."

And he answered and said, *"I believe that Jesus Christ is the Son of God."*

And he commanded the chariot to stand still; and they went down into the water, and he baptized him.

And when they were come up out of the water, the Spirit of the Lord caught away Philip that the eunuch saw him no more.

And he went on his way rejoicing.

Baptism.

Rom. 10, 17. So, then, faith cometh by hearing and hearing by the Word of God.

Baptized into Thy name most holy,
  O Father, Son, and Holy Ghost,
I claim a place, though weak and lowly,
  Among Thy seed, Thy chosen host.
Buried with Christ and dead to sin,
Thy Spirit now shall live within. (298, 1.)

63. The Conversion of Saul
Acts 9, 1—31

Saul, the Persecutor. And Saul,[1)] yet breathing out threatenings and slaughter against the disciples of the Lord, went unto the high priest and desired of him letters to Damascus,[2)] that, if he found any of this way,[3)] whether they

"Saul, Saul, why persecutest thou Me?"

were men or women, he might bring them bound unto Jerusalem.

Jesus Appears to Saul. And as he journeyed, he came near Damascus. And suddenly there shined round about him a light from heaven.

---

1) Saul, whose name was changed to Paul, was born at Tarsus, the chief city of Cilicia, in Asia Minor.
2) Damascus is the most ancient and famous city of Syria, 133 miles northeast of Jerusalem.
3) Believers in Jesus.

Advanced Bible History.

And he fell to the earth and heard a voice saying unto him, "Saul, Saul, why persecutest thou Me?"

And he said, "Who art Thou, Lord?"

And the Lord said, "I am Jesus, whom thou persecutest; it is hard for thee to kick against the pricks." [4]

And he, trembling and astonished, said, "Lord, what wilt Thou have me to do?"

And the Lord said unto him, "Arise and go into the city, and it shall be told thee what thou must do."

And the men which journeyed with him stood speechless, hearing a voice, but seeing no man.

And Saul arose from the earth; and when his eyes were opened, he saw no man.

But they led him by the hand and brought him into Damascus.

And he was three days without sight and neither did eat nor drink.

Saul's Baptism. And there was a certain disciple at Damascus named Ananias; and to him said the Lord in a vision, "Ananias, arise and go into the street which is called Straight and inquire in the house of Judas for one called Saul of Tarsus; for, behold, he prayeth."

Then Ananias answered, "Lord, I have heard how much evil he hath done to Thy saints at Jerusalem; and here he hath authority from the chief priests to bind all that call on Thy name."

But the Lord said unto him, "Go thy way; for he is a chosen vessel unto Me to bear My name before the Gentiles and kings and the children of Israel. For I will show him how great things he must suffer for My name's sake."

---

[4] Pricks were long, sharp-pointed sticks, used to drive cattle by pricking them. The meaning here is that, if Saul would continue his persecution, he would but aggravate his unhappy condition.

And Ananias went his way and entered into the house and, putting his hands on him, said, "Brother Saul, the Lord, even Jesus, hath sent me that thou mightest receive thy sight and be filled with the Holy Ghost."

And immediately there fell from his eyes as it had been scales; and he received sight forthwith and arose and was baptized.

And when he had received meat, he was strengthened.

Paul's First Preaching. Then was Saul certain days with the disciples which were at Damascus. And straightway he preached Christ in the synagogs that He is the Son of God. But all that heard him were amazed.

And the Jews took counsel to kill him. But their laying wait was known of Saul. And they watched the gates day and night to kill him. Then the disciples took him by night and let him down in a basket by the wall.

And when Saul was come to Jerusalem, he assayed to join himself to the disciples; but they were all afraid of him and believed not that he was a disciple.

But Barnabas took him and brought him to the apostles and declared unto them how he had seen the Lord in the way and that He had spoken to him and how he had preached boldly at Damascus in the name of Jesus.

And he was with them coming in and going out at Jerusalem.

And he spake boldly in the name of the Lord Jesus and disputed against the Grecians; but they went about to slay him; which when the brethren knew, they brought him down to Caesarea and sent him forth to Tarsus.

Then had the churches rest throughout all Judea and Galilee and Samaria and were edified and, walking in the fear of the Lord and in the comfort of the Holy Ghost, were multiplied.

Third Article: Conversion.

Matt. 10, 32. Whosoever therefore shall confess Me before men, him will I confess also before My Father which is in heaven.

>Thy grace alone, O God,
> To me can pardon speak;
>Thy power alone, O Son of God,
> Can this sore bondage break. (389, 5.)

64. Cornelius
Acts 10

The Prayers and Alms of Cornelius. There was a certain man in Caesarea called Cornelius, a Roman centurion, a devout man, and one that feared God with all his house, which gave much alms to the people and prayed to God always.

He saw in a vision evidently, about the ninth hour of the day, an angel of God coming in to him and saying unto him, "Cornelius."

And he was afraid and said, "What is it, Lord?"

And He said unto him, "Thy prayers and thine alms are come up for a memorial before God. And now send men to Joppa and call for Simon Peter; he lodgeth with one Simon, a tanner, whose house is by the seaside; he shall tell thee what thou oughtest to do."

And Cornelius called two of his household servants and a devout soldier and sent them to Joppa.

Peter's Vision. On the morrow, as they went on their journey and drew nigh unto the city, Peter went up upon the housetop to pray, about the sixth hour.

And he became very hungry and would have eaten; but while they made ready, he fell into a trance and saw heaven opened and a certain vessel descending unto him, as it had been a great sheet knit at the four corners and let down to earth, wherein were all manner of four-footed beasts of the earth, and wild beasts, and creeping things, and fowls of the air.

And there came a voice to him, "Rise, Peter, kill, and eat."

But Peter said, "Not so, Lord; for I have never eaten anything that is common or unclean."

And the voice spake unto him again the second time, "What God hath cleansed, that call not thou common."

This was done thrice; and the vessel was received up again into heaven.

Now, while Peter doubted in himself what this vision which he had seen should mean, behold, the men which were sent from Cornelius stood before the gate and called and asked whether Peter were lodged there.

While Peter thought on the vision, the Spirit said unto him, "Behold, three men seek thee. Arise therefore and get thee down and go with them, doubting nothing; for I have sent them."

Then Peter went down to the men, and on the morrow he went away with them.

Peter Preaches to Cornelius. And Cornelius waited for them and had called together his kinsmen and near friends.

And as Peter was coming in, Cornelius met him, and fell down at his feet, and worshiped him, and said, "We are all here present before God to hear all things that are commanded thee of God."

Then Peter opened his mouth and said, "Of a truth I perceive that God is no respecter of persons; but in every nation he that feareth Him and worketh righteousness is accepted with Him. Ye know the word which God sent unto the children of Israel, preaching peace by Jesus Christ, (He is Lord of all,) whom they slew.

"Him God raised up the third day; and He commanded

us to preach unto the people and to testify that it is He which was ordained of God to be the Judge of quick and dead. To Him give all the prophets witness that through His name whosoever believeth in Him shall receive remission of sins."

Cornelius Receives the Holy Ghost and is Baptized. While Peter yet spake these words, the Holy Ghost fell on all them which heard the Word.

"God is no respecter of persons"

And the Jews which believed were astonished, as many as came with Peter, because that on the Gentiles also was poured out the gift of the Holy Ghost. For they heard them speak with tongues and magnify God.

Then answered Peter, "Can any man forbid water that these should not be baptized which have received the Holy Ghost as well as we?" And he commanded them to be baptized in the name of the Lord.

Third Article: Holy Ghost.

John 10, 16. And other sheep I have which are not of this fold; them also I must bring, and they shall hear My voice; and there shall be one fold and one Shepherd.

> Savior, sprinkle many nations;
> Fruitful let Thy sorrows be;
> By Thy pains and consolations
> Draw the Gentiles unto Thee. (510, 1 a.)

---

65. Peter's Deliverance
Acts 12, 1—19

Herod Persecutes the Church. Now, about that time, Herod the king [1] stretched forth his hands to vex certain of the church.

And he killed James, the brother of John, with the sword.

And because he saw it pleased the Jews, he proceeded further to take Peter also. (Then were the Days of Unleavened Bread.)

And when he had apprehended him, he put him in prison and delivered him to four quaternions of soldiers to keep him, intending after Easter to bring him forth to the people.

The Angel Delivers Peter. Peter therefore was kept in prison; but prayer was made without ceasing of the church unto God for him.

And when Herod would have brought him forth, the same night Peter was sleeping between two soldiers, bound with two chains; and the keepers before the door kept the prison.

And, behold, the angel of the Lord came upon him, and

---

[1] Herod Agrippa, grandson of Herod the Great, the murderer of the little children, nephew of Herod Antipas, the murderer of John the Baptist. He ruled 41—44 A. D.

a light shined in the prison; and he smote Peter on the side and raised him up, saying, "Arise up quickly."

And his chains fell off from his hands.

And the angel said unto him, "Gird thyself and bind on thy sandals." And so he did.

And he said unto him, "Cast thy garment about thee and follow me." And he went out and followed him and wist

"And they went out"

not that it was true which was done by the angel, but thought he saw a vision.

When they were past the first and the second ward, they came unto the iron gate that leadeth unto the city, which opened to them of his own accord.

And they went out and passed on through one street; and forthwith the angel departed from him.

Peter Joins the Christians. And when Peter was come to himself, he said, "Now I know of a surety that the Lord hath sent His angel and hath delivered me out of the hand of Herod and from all the expectation of the people of the Jews."

And when he had considered the thing, he came to the house of Mary, the mother of John, whose surname was Mark, where many were gathered together praying.

And as Peter knocked at the door of the gate, a damsel came to hearken, named Rhoda.

And when she knew Peter's voice, she opened not the gate for gladness, but ran in and told how Peter stood before the gate.

And they said unto her, "Thou art mad."

But she constantly affirmed that it was even so.

Then said they, "It is his angel."

But Peter continued knocking; and when they had opened the door and saw him, they were astonished. But he, beckoning unto them with the hand to hold their peace, declared unto them how the Lord had brought him out of the prison.

And he said, "Go, show these things unto James and to the brethren."

And he departed and went into another place.

The Keepers Put to Death. Now, as soon as it was day, there was no small stir among the soldiers what was become of Peter. And Herod commanded that the keepers be put to death.

First Article: Good Angels. "He guards and protects me from all evil."

Heb. 1, 14. Are they not all ministering spirits, sent forth to minister for them who shall be heirs of salvation?

With thy Savior at thy side,	All thy trust do thou repose
Foes need not alarm thee;	In the mighty Master,
In His promises confide,	Who in wisdom truly knows
And no ill can harm thee.	How to stem disaster. (540, 3.)

66. Paul's First Missionary Journey *
Acts 13 and 14

Paul in Cyprus. Now, there were in the church at Antioch, where the disciples of Jesus were first called Christians, certain prophets and teachers.

As they ministered to the Lord and fasted, the Holy Ghost said, "Separate me Barnabas and Saul for the work whereunto I have called them."

And when they had fasted and prayed and laid their hands on them, they sent them away. And they sailed to Cyprus.

Paul and the Sorcerer. And when they had gone through the isle unto Paphos, they found a certain sorcerer,[1] a false prophet, a Jew, whose name was Bar-jesus, which was with the deputy [2] of the country, Sergius Paulus, a prudent man; who called for Barnabas and Saul and desired to hear the Word of God. But the sorcerer withstood them, seeking to turn away the deputy from the faith.

Then Saul, (who also is called Paul,) filled with the Holy Ghost, set his eyes on him and said, "O full of all subtilty and all mischief, thou child of the devil, wilt thou not cease to pervert the right ways of the Lord? And now, behold, the hand of the Lord is upon thee, and thou shalt be blind, not seeing the sun for a season."

And immediately there fell on him a mist and a darkness; and he went about seeking some to lead him by the hand.

Then the deputy, when he saw what was done, believed, being astonished at the doctrine of the Lord.

In Pisidia. Now, when Paul and his company loosed

---

* Paul made three great missionary tours. Each of these began at Antioch, in Syria. The first tour occupied a period of about two years.

1) A magician and soothsayer.   2) Governor.

from Paphos, they came to Perga, in Pamphylia, and thence to Antioch, in Pisidia.

And they went into the synagog on the Sabbath-day and preached the glad tidings of forgiveness of sins through Jesus Christ.

And when the Jews were gone out of the synagog, the Gentiles besought that these words might be preached to them the next Sabbath.

And many of the Jews and religious proselytes [3] followed Paul and Barnabas, who, speaking to them, persuaded them to continue in the grace of God.

And the next Sabbath-day came almost the whole city together to hear the Word of God.

But when the Jews saw the multitudes, they were filled with envy and spake against those things which were spoken by Paul, contradicting and blaspheming.

Paul and Barnabas Turn to the Gentiles. Then Paul and Barnabas waxed bold and said, "It was necessary that the Word of God should first have been spoken to you; but seeing ye put it from you and judge yourselves unworthy of everlasting life, lo, we turn to the Gentiles."

And when the Gentiles heard this, they were glad.

And the Word of the Lord was published throughout all the region.

But the Jews raised persecution against Paul and Barnabas and expelled them out of their coasts.

But they shook off the dust of their feet against them and came unto Iconium.

At Lystra. In Iconium Paul and Barnabas abode a long time, speaking boldly in the Lord.

---

[3] Gentiles who had accepted the Jewish faith and were circumcised.

But the multitude of the city was divided; and part held with the Jews and part with the apostles.

And when there was an assault made both of the Gentiles and also of the Jews to stone them, they fled unto Lystra, and there they preached the Gospel.

And there sat a certain man at Lystra, a cripple from his birth, who never had walked. The same heard Paul

"We are also men"

speak; who, steadfastly beholding him and perceiving that he had faith to be healed, said with a loud voice, "Stand upright on thy feet." And he leaped and walked.

Paul and Barnabas Deified. And when the people saw what Paul had done, they lifted up their voices, saying, "The gods are come down to us in the likeness of men."

And they called Barnabas, Jupiter, and Paul, Mercurius, because he was the chief speaker.

Then the priest of Jupiter, which was before their city,

brought oxen and garlands unto the gates and would have done sacrifice with the people; which, when the apostles heard of, they rent their clothes and ran in among the people, crying out and saying, "Sirs, why do ye these things? We also are men of like passions with you and preach unto you that ye should turn from these vanities unto the living God, which made heaven, and earth, and the sea, and all things that are therein; who hath not left Himself without witness, in that He did good and gave us rain from heaven and fruitful seasons, filling our hearts with food and gladness."

And with these sayings scarce restrained they the people that they had not done sacrifice unto them.

Driven from the City. And there came thither certain Jews from Antioch and Iconium, who persuaded the people and, having stoned Paul, drew him out of the city, supposing he had been dead.

Howbeit, as the disciples stood round about him, he rose up and came into the city.

And the next day he departed with Barnabas to Derbe. And when they had preached the Gospel to that city and had taught many, they returned again to Lystra and to Iconium and Antioch, confirming the souls of the disciples and exhorting them to continue in the faith and that we must through much tribulation enter into the kingdom of God.

And they ordained elders in every church and passed throughout Pisidia and Pamphylia and then sailed to Antioch, from whence they had started.

Second Petition.

Luke 10, 16. He that heareth you heareth Me; and he that despiseth you despiseth Me; and he that despiseth Me despiseth Him that sent Me.

> Send Thou, O Lord, to every place
> Swift messengers before Thy face,
> The heralds of Thy wondrous grace,
>   Where Thou Thyself wilt come. (506, 1.)

67. Paul's Second Missionary Journey
Acts 15—18

Paul Called to Europe. And Paul chose Silas and went through Syria and Cilicia, confirming the churches.

And when they came to Troas, a vision appeared to Paul in the night; there stood a man of Macedonia and prayed him, saying, "Come over into Macedonia and help us."

And they sailed to Philippi, which is the chief city of that part of Macedonia, and preached the Gospel there.

And a certain woman, named Lydia, a seller of purple, heard them; whose heart the Lord opened that she attended unto the things which were spoken of Paul.

And she was baptized and her household.

Paul and Silas in Prison. But the multitude arose up against the apostles.

And the magistrates laid many stripes upon them and cast them into prison, charging the jailer to keep them safely; who, having received such a charge, thrust them into the inner prison and made their feet fast in the stocks.

And at midnight Paul and Silas prayed and sang praises unto God; and the prisoners heard them.

And suddenly there was a great earthquake, so that the foundations of the prison were shaken; and immediately all the doors were opened, and every one's bands were loosed.

The Jailer at Philippi. And the keeper of the prison awaking out of his sleep and seeing the prison-doors open, he drew out his sword and would have killed himself, supposing that the prisoners had been fled.

But Paul cried with a loud voice, saying, "Do thyself no harm; for we are all here."

Then he called for a light, and sprang in, and came trembling, and fell down before Paul and Silas, and brought them out, and said, "Sirs, what must I do to be saved?"

And they said, *"Believe on the Lord Jesus Christ, and thou shalt be saved and thy house."*

And he took them the same hour of the night and washed their stripes; and was baptized, he and all his, straightway.

Paul and Silas Released. And when it was day, the magistrates [1] sent, saying, "Let those men go."

"Sirs, what must I do to be saved?"

But Paul said, "They have beaten us openly, uncondemned, being Romans, and have cast us into prison; and now do they thrust us out privily? Nay, verily; but let them come themselves and fetch us out."

And the magistrates feared when they heard that they were Romans, and came and besought them, and brought them out, and desired them to depart out of the city.

At Athens. And Paul went to Athens.

And his spirit was stirred in him when he saw the city

---

1) Government officials.

wholly given to idolatry. Therefore disputed he in the synagog with the Jews and with the devout persons and in the market daily with them that met with him.

And they took him and brought him unto Areopagus,[2] saying, "May we know what this new doctrine, whereof thou speakest, is?"

Then Paul stood in the midst of Mars Hill and said, "Ye men of Athens, as I passed by and beheld your devotions, I found an altar with this inscription, 'TO THE UNKNOWN GOD.' Whom therefore ye ignorantly worship, Him declare I unto you.

"God, that made the world and all things therein, seeing that He is Lord of heaven and earth, dwelleth not in temples made with hands, but He is not far from every one of us; for in Him we live and move and have our being, as certain also of your own poets have said, 'For we are also His offspring.'

"Forasmuch, then, as we are the offspring of God, we ought not to think that the Godhead is like unto gold or silver or stone, graven by art and man's device.

"And the times of this ignorance God winked at, but now commandeth all men everywhere to repent, because He hath appointed a day in the which He will judge the world in righteousness by that Man whom He hath ordained and whom He hath raised from the dead."

And when they heard of the resurrection of the dead, some mocked.

Certain men, however, clave unto him and believed.

After these things Paul departed from Athens and came to Corinth and continued there a year and six months.

Thereafter he went down to Antioch.

---

2) Or Mars Hill, a hill of Athens. Here court was held, and here Paul was to tell the public of his "new doctrine."

Second Petition.

Matt. 28, 19. 20. Go ye therefore and teach all nations, baptizing them in the name of the Father and of the Son and of the Holy Ghost; teaching them to observe all things whatsoever I have commanded you. And, lo, I am with you alway, even unto the end of the world.

> O Christ, our true and only Light,
> Enlighten those who sit in night;
> Let those afar now hear Thy voice
> And in Thy fold with us rejoice. (512, 1.)

---

68. Paul's Third Missionary Journey
Acts 18—21

At Ephesus. And after Paul had spent some time at Antioch, he departed and went over all the country of Galatia and Phrygia in order, strengthening all the disciples, and then came to Ephesus.

And the name of the Lord Jesus was magnified.

And many that believed came and confessed and showed their deeds.

Many of them also which used curious arts brought their books together and burned them before all men; and they counted the price of them and found it fifty thousand pieces of silver.

So mightily grew the Word of God and prevailed.

The Silversmiths. And there arose no small stir. For a certain man, named Demetrius, a silversmith, which made silver shrines for Diana, brought no small gain unto the craftsmen, whom he called together and said, "Sirs, ye know that by this craft we have our wealth. Moreover, ye see and hear that not alone at Ephesus, but almost throughout all Asia this Paul hath persuaded and turned away much people, saying that they be no gods which are made with hands, so that not only this our craft is in danger to be set at naught,

Advanced Bible History.

but also that the temple of the great goddess Diana should be despised."

And when they heard these sayings, they were full of wrath and cried out, saying, "Great is Diana of the Ephesians!"

And the whole city was filled with confusion and rushed with one accord into the theater.

And when Paul would have entered in unto the people, the disciples suffered him not.[1]

Some therefore cried one thing and some another; for the assembly was confused; and the more part knew not wherefore they were come together.

And all with one voice, about the space of two hours, cried out, "Great is Diana of the Ephesians!"

The People Appeased. And when the town clerk had appeased the people, he said, "Ye men of Ephesus, ye ought to be quiet and to do nothing rashly. If Demetrius and the craftsmen have a matter against any man, the law is open. We are in danger to be called to account for this day's uproar." And when he had thus spoken, he dismissed the assembly.

And Paul called unto him the disciples and embraced them and departed into Macedonia.

And when he had gone over those parts, he came to Greece and there abode three months.

The Return. And Paul took ship and returned to Asia to Troas.

And Paul preached until midnight, ready to depart on the morrow.

And there sat in a window a certain young man named Eutychus, being fallen into a deep sleep; and as Paul was long preaching, he sunk down with sleep and fell down from the third loft and was taken up dead.

---

[1] Did not permit him to go.

And Paul went down and fell on him and, embracing him, said, "Trouble not yourselves; for his life is in him."

And they brought the young man alive and were not a little comforted.

Paul and Silas Come to Miletus. Paul determined to sail by Ephesus, to be at Jerusalem the day of Pentecost. And from Miletus he sent to Ephesus and called the elders of the church.

And they all wept sore and fell on Paul's neck and kissed him, sorrowing most of all for the words which he spake that they should see his face no more.

And they accompanied him unto the ship.

And they left Cyprus on the left hand and sailed into Syria and landed at Tyre.

Second Petition. — Second Commandment: Using Witchcraft.

Ps. 115, 3. 4. But our God is in the heavens; He hath done whatsoever He hath pleased. Their idols are silver and gold, the work of men's hands.

   Ye who confess Christ's holy name,
    To God give praise and glory!
   Ye who the Father's power proclaim,
    To God give praise and glory!
   All idols under foot be trod,
   The Lord is God! The Lord is God!
    To God all praise and glory! (19, 5.)

---

69. Paul the Prisoner
Acts 21—26

Arrested at Jerusalem. After those days they went up to Jerusalem.

And Paul declared to the brethren what things God had wrought among the Gentiles by his ministry.

And when they heard it, they glorified the Lord.

But when the Jews saw him in the Temple, they stirred

up the people and laid hands on him, crying out, "Men of Israel, help! This is the man that teacheth all men everywhere against the Law and this place."

And they took Paul and drew him out of the Temple; and forthwith the doors were shut.

And as they went about to kill him, tidings came unto the chief captain, who immediately took soldiers and centurions and ran down unto them; and when they saw the chief captain and the soldiers, they left beating of Paul.

Then the chief captain commanded him to be bound with two chains; and he demanded who he was and what he had done.

And Paul was led into the castle.

The Conspiracy against Paul. And when it was day, certain of the Jews banded together and bound themselves under a curse, saying that they would neither eat nor drink till they had killed Paul.

And they were more than forty which had made this conspiracy.

And when the chief captain heard of it, he called unto him two centurions, saying, "Make ready two hundred soldiers to go to Caesarea, and threescore and ten horsemen and two hundred spearmen, and bring Paul safe unto Felix, the governor." [1]

Then the soldiers, as it was commanded them, took Paul and brought him by night to Felix.

Before Festus. But after two years Festus came into Felix' room; [2] and Felix left Paul bound.

Then the high priest and the chief of the Jews laid many and grievous complaints against Paul, which they could not prove.

---

1) Of Judea.
2) In Felix's place; Festus became his successor in office.

But Festus, willing to do the Jews a pleasure, said to Paul, "Wilt thou go up to Jerusalem and there be judged of these things before me?"

Then said Paul, "I stand at Caesar's judgment-seat, where I ought to be judged; to the Jews have I done no wrong, as thou very well knowest. For if I be an offender or have

Paul before Agrippa

committed anything worthy of death, I refuse not to die; but if there be none of these things whereof these accuse me, no man may deliver me unto them. I appeal unto Caesar."

Then Festus answered, "Hast thou appealed unto Caesar? Unto Caesar shalt thou go."

Before Agrippa. But when King Agrippa,[3] with his sister Bernice, came to salute Festus, Paul was brought before them.

---

3) Herod Agrippa II.

Then Agrippa said unto Paul, "Thou art permitted to speak for thyself."

Then Paul stretched forth his hand and answered for himself.

Agrippa said unto Paul, "Almost thou persuadest me to be a Christian."

Second Commandment: False Swearing.

Matt. 5, 34. But I say unto you, Swear not at all.

Rom. 1, 16. I am not ashamed of the Gospel of Christ; for it is the power of God unto salvation to every one that believeth.

> Delay not, delay not, O sinner, to come,
> For mercy still lingers and calls thee today;
> Her voice is not heard in the vale of the tomb;
> Her message, unheeded, will soon pass away. (278, 2.)

70. Paul is Taken to Rome
Acts 27 and 28

Sailing for Italy. And when it was determined that we [1] should sail into Italy, they delivered Paul and certain other prisoners unto one named Julius, a centurion of Augustus' band.

And entering into a ship, they sailed under Cyprus to Crete.

And Julius courteously treated Paul.

And when sailing was now dangerous, Paul admonished them and said unto them, "Sirs, I perceive that this voyage will be with hurt and much damage, not only of the lading and ship, but also of our lives."

Nevertheless, the centurion believed the master and the

---

1) Luke, the writer of Acts, here refers to Paul, Aristarchus, and himself.

owner of the ship more than those things which were spoken by Paul.

And they departed thence.

The Storm. But not long after, there arose a tempestuous wind.

And when the ship was caught and could not bear up into the wind, we let her drive.

And we being exceedingly tossed with a tempest, the next day they lightened the ship; and the third day we cast out with our own hands the tackling of the ship.

And when neither sun nor stars in many days appeared and no small tempest lay on us, all hope that we should be saved was then taken away.

But after long abstinence, Paul stood forth in the midst of them and said, "Sirs, ye should have hearkened unto me and not have loosed from Crete and to have gained this harm and loss. And now I exhort you to be of good cheer; for there shall be no loss of any man's life among you but of the ship. For there stood by me this night the angel of God, whose I am and whom I serve, saying, 'Fear not, Paul; thou must be brought before Caesar; and, lo, God hath given thee all them that sail with thee.' Wherefore, sirs, be of good cheer; for I believe God that it shall be even as it was told me. Howbeit, we must be cast upon a certain island."

And he took bread and gave thanks to God in presence of them all; and when he had broken it, he began to eat.

Then were they all of good cheer, and they also took some meat.

And we were in all in the ship two hundred threescore and sixteen souls.

Shipwrecked. And falling into a place where two seas met, they ran the ship aground; and the forepart stuck fast and remained unmovable, but the hinder part was broken with the violence of the waves.

And the soldiers' counsel was to kill the prisoners lest any of them should swim out and escape.

But the centurion, willing to save Paul, kept them from their purpose and commanded that they which could swim should cast themselves first into the sea and get to land and the rest, some on boards and some on broken pieces of the ship.

And so it came to pass that they escaped all safe to land.

On the Island of Melita. And when they were escaped, then they knew that the island was called Melita.

And the barbarous people showed us no little kindness; for they kindled a fire and received us, every one, because of the present rain and because of the cold.

And when Paul had gathered a bundle of sticks and laid them on the fire, there came a viper out of the heat and fastened on his hand.

And when the barbarians saw the venomous beast hang on his hand, they said among themselves, "No doubt this man is a murderer, whom, though he hath escaped the sea, yet vengeance suffereth not to live."

And he shook off the beast into the fire and felt no harm.

Howbeit, they looked when he should have swollen or fallen down dead suddenly; but after they had looked a great while and saw no harm come to him, they changed their minds and said that he was a god.

Paul Heals Many. In the same quarters were possessions of Publius, the chief man of the island; who received us and lodged us three days courteously.

And the father of Publius lay sick; to whom Paul entered in, and prayed, and laid his hands on him, and healed him.

So when this was done, others also which had diseases in the island came and were healed; who also honored us with many honors; and when we departed, they laded us with such things as were necessary.

In Rome. And we departed in a ship, and landing at Syracuse, we came to Puteoli, where we found brethren.

Paul in Prison

And when the brethren in Rome heard of us, they came to meet us, whom when Paul saw, he thanked God and took courage.

And when we came to Rome, the centurion delivered the prisoners to the captain of the guard; but Paul was suffered to dwell by himself with a soldier that kept him.

And Paul dwelt two whole years in his own hired house and received all that came in unto him, preaching the kingdom of God and teaching those things which concern the Lord Jesus Christ with all confidence, no man forbidding him.

First Article: "Guards and protects me from all evil." — *Seventh Petition.*

Eph. 2, 20. Ye are built upon the foundation of the apostles and prophets, Jesus Christ Himself being the chief Corner-stone.

2 Tim. 4, 18. The Lord shall deliver me from every evil work and will preserve me unto His heavenly kingdom; to whom be glory forever and ever! Amen.

>From evil, Lord, deliver us;
The times and days are perilous.
Redeem us from eternal death;
And when we yield our dying breath,
Console us, grant us calm release,
And take our souls to Thee in peace. (458, 8.)

SUMMARY STUDY OF THE FIFTH PERIOD

1. Give various examples of the way in which the power and the spirit of Jesus continued in the disciples after His ascension.

2. Show by examples, a) how the Gospel of Christ was accepted by man, b) how the hatred against Christ continued.

3. Draw comparisons between the work of the early Church and the Church of to-day.

4. Show from three stories that the Christian Church was to comprise Gentiles as well as Jews.

5. Recount briefly the chief events in the life of Paul.

6. The growth of the early Church was rapid. How do you account for it?

7. What was the chief theme of all the sermons of the apostles?

8. Let pupils discuss the spiritual benefits derived from the accounts of this period for their own faith and life.

"BY HIS KNOWLEDGE SHALL MY RIGHTEOUS SERVANT JUSTIFY MANY." Is. 53, 11.

BOOKS OF THE BIBLE

Names and Sequence of All the Books of the Old and New Testaments, with the Number of Their Chapters

THE BOOKS OF THE OLD TESTAMENT

The Five Books of Moses
	Chapters
Genesis	50
Exodus	40
Leviticus	27
Numbers	36
Deuteronomy	34

Historical Books
Joshua	24
Judges	21
Ruth	4
1 Samuel	31
2 Samuel	24
1 Kings	22
2 Kings	25
1 Chronicles	29
2 Chronicles	36
Ezra	10
Nehemiah	13
Esther	10

Poetical Books
	Chapters
Job	42
Psalms	150
Proverbs	31
Ecclesiastes	12
Song of Solomon	8

The Prophets
Isaiah	66
Jeremiah	52
Lamentations	5
Ezekiel	48
Daniel	12
Hosea	14
Joel	3
Amos	9
Obadiah	1
Jonah	4
Micah	7
Nahum	3
Habakkuk	3
Zephaniah	3
Haggai	2
Zechariah	14
Malachi	4

THE BOOKS OF THE NEW TESTAMENT

	Chapters
Matthew	28
Mark	16
Luke	24
John	21
The Acts	28
Romans	16
1 Corinthians	16
2 Corinthians	13
Galatians	6
Ephesians	6
Philippians	4
Colossians	4
1 Thessalonians	5
2 Thessalonians	3

	Chapters
1 Timothy	6
2 Timothy	4
Titus	3
Philemon	1
Hebrews	13
James	5
1 Peter	5
2 Peter	3
1 John	5
2 John	1
3 John	1
Jude	1
Revelation	22

Pronouncing Vocabulary of Proper Names

Ab'a-na
A-bed'ne-gō
A-bī'jah
A-bī'ram
Ā'chan (k)
Ā'gag
A-has-ū-ē'rus
A-hī'jah
A-hĭm'e-lech (k)
Ā'ī
Aj'a-lon
Al-phaē'us
Am'a-lek
Am'ram
An-a-nī'as
An'ti-och (k)
Ār'a-rat
Ār-e-op'a-gus
Ār-i-ma-the'a
As'e-nath
Ash'ke-lon
As-syr'ia
Ăth'ens
Au-gus'tus

Bā'a-lim
Bab-y-lō'nish
Bā'laam
Bā'lak
Bär-ăb'bas
Bär-jē'sus
Bär'na-bas
Bär-thŏl'o-mew
Bath-shē'ba
Bē-er-shē'ba

Bē'li-al
Bel-shaz'zar
Beth'a-ny
Beth-ăb'a-ra
Bē-thĕs'da
Beth'pha-ge (j)
Bĕth'shan
Be-thū'el
Bil'dad

Caē'sar
Caĕs-a-rē'a
  Phi-lip'pī
Cal'va-ry
Can-dā'cē (see)
Ca-pēr'na-um
Cē'phas (s)
Chal-dē'ans (k)
Chal'dees (k)
Chē'rith (k)
Ci-li'ci-a (shi-a)
Clē'o-phas
Cor'inth
Cor-nē'li-us
Cy'prus (s)
Cy-rē'nē (s)
Cy-rē'ni-us (s)
Cy'rus (s)

Dā'gon
Da-mas'cus
Dăn'ites
Da-rī'us
Dā'than
De-lī'lah

De-mē'tri-us
Der'bē
Did'y-mus
Dī-an'a
Dō'eg

Eb-en-ē'zer
Ē'dom
Ē'dom-ite
Ē'lī
Ē-li'ab
Ē'li, Ē'li, lā'ma
  sā-băch-thā'nī
E-li-ē'zer
Ē'līm
E-lĭm'e-lech (k)
Ĕl'i-phaz
El'kā-nah
Em'ma-us or
  Em-mā'us
Ĕn-gē'dī
Ĕph'pha-tha
E-phē'sians (zhanz)
Eph'e-sus
Ē'phra-im
E-sā'ias
Esh'col
Eū'nuch (k)
Eū'ty-chus (k)

Gal-i-lē'an
Gā'za
Gē-hā'zi
Gen-nes'a-ret
Ger'ge-sēnes (seens)

[445]

Geth-sĕm′a-nē
Gib′e-ah
Gib′e-on
Gil-bō′ah
Gil′gal
Gŏl′go-tha
Gō-lī′ath
Go-mor′rah
Gō′shen
Grē′cians (shans)

Hag′gā-ī
Hā′man
Hā′ran
Hē′bron
Hĕ-rō′di-as
Hez-e-kī′ah
Hit′tītes
Hoph′nī
Hō′reb
Ho-shē′a

Ī-cō′ni-um
Ish-bō′sheth
Ish′ma-el-ites
Is′sa-char (k)

Jā′besh-gil′e-ad
Ja-ī′rus
Jā′pheth
Je-hō′a-haz
Je-hoi′a-chin (k)
Je-hoi′a-kim
Jer-o-bō′am
Jesh′ū-a
Jē′thro
Jez′e-bel

Joch′e-bed (k)
Josh′ū-a
Ju′pi-ter (ōō)

Kā′desh
Kid′ron
Kir′jath-jē′a-rim
Kish
Kī′shon
Kō′rah

Lā′mech (k)
Lē′ah
Leb-baē′us
Lўs′tra

Mac-e-dō′ni-a (s)
Mach-pē′lah (k)
Mag′da-lēne or
  Mag-da-le′ne
Mā-ha-nā′im
Mal′chus (k)
Mam′rē
Ma-năs′seh
Ma-nō′ah
Mā′rah
Mas′sah
Mēdes
Mĕl′i-ta
Mē′ne, mē′ne, tē′kel,
  u-phär′sin
Me-phib′o-sheth
Mer-cū′ri-us
Mer′i-bah
Mē′shach (k)
Mes-o-po-tā′mia
Me-thu′se-lah

Mī′chal (k)
Mid′i-an
Mid′i-an-ites
Mī-lē′tus
Mir′i-am
Miz′pah
Mōr′de-cāi
Mō-rī′ah

Nā′a-man
Nā′both
Nā′hor
Nā′in
Naph′ta-lī
Na-than′a-el
Naz′a-rite
Nic-ō-dē′mus
Nic′o-las
Nin′e-vĕh

Ō′bed
Ol′i-vet

Pam-phўl′i-a
Pā′phos
Pär′me-nas
Pe-nī′el
Per′ga
Phā′raōh (roh)
Phār′i-sees
Phär′pär
Phi-lip′pī
Phĭ-lĭs′tĭnes
Phin′e-has
Phrўg′i-a (frĭj)
Pī′late
Pis′gah

PRONOUNCING VOCABULARY OF PROPER NAMES

Pī-sĭd′ĭ-a
Pī′thom
Pon′ti-us (or shus)
Pot′i-phär
Pot-i-phē′rah
Proch′o-rus (k)
Pub′li-us
Pŭ-tē′o-lī

Rā-am′ses
Rab-bō′nī
Rab′sha-kĕh
Rā′chel
Rā′hab
Rā′mah
Rā′moth–gil′e-ad
Rē′hob
Rē-ho-bō′am
Reph′i-dim
Rhō′da

Sa-bē′ans
Sad′du-cees
Sa-lō′me

Sap-phī′ra
(Saf-fī′ra)
Sā′rā-ī (or -rā)
Sen-nach′e-rib (k)
Ser′gi-us Pau′lus (ji)
Shā′drach (k)
Shā′lem
Shal-ma-nē′ser
Shē′chem (k)
Shim′e-ī
Shī′nar
Shur (ōō)
Shu′shan (ōō)
Sī′chem (k)
Sī′na-ī (or nī)
Stē′phen (ven)
Sȳ′char
Syr′a-cūse

Tăl′i-tha, cū′mī
Tar′sus
Tet′rärch
Tī-bē′ri-as

Ti-bē′ri-us
Tim′nath
Tī′mon
Tir′zah
Tish′bīte
Tȳre

Ū-rī′ah

Vash′tī

Zac-chaē′us
Zach-a-rī′as
Zā′dok
Zär′e-phăth
Zeb′e-dee
Zeb′ū-lŭn
Zech-a-rī′ah
Zed-e-kī′ah
Ze-rub′ba-bel
Zī′don
Zī-dō′ni-ans
Zĭp-pō′rah
Zō′phar

NOTE. — Except in the name Rachel, the digraph ch in proper names of the Bible has the sound of k.

No. 1.

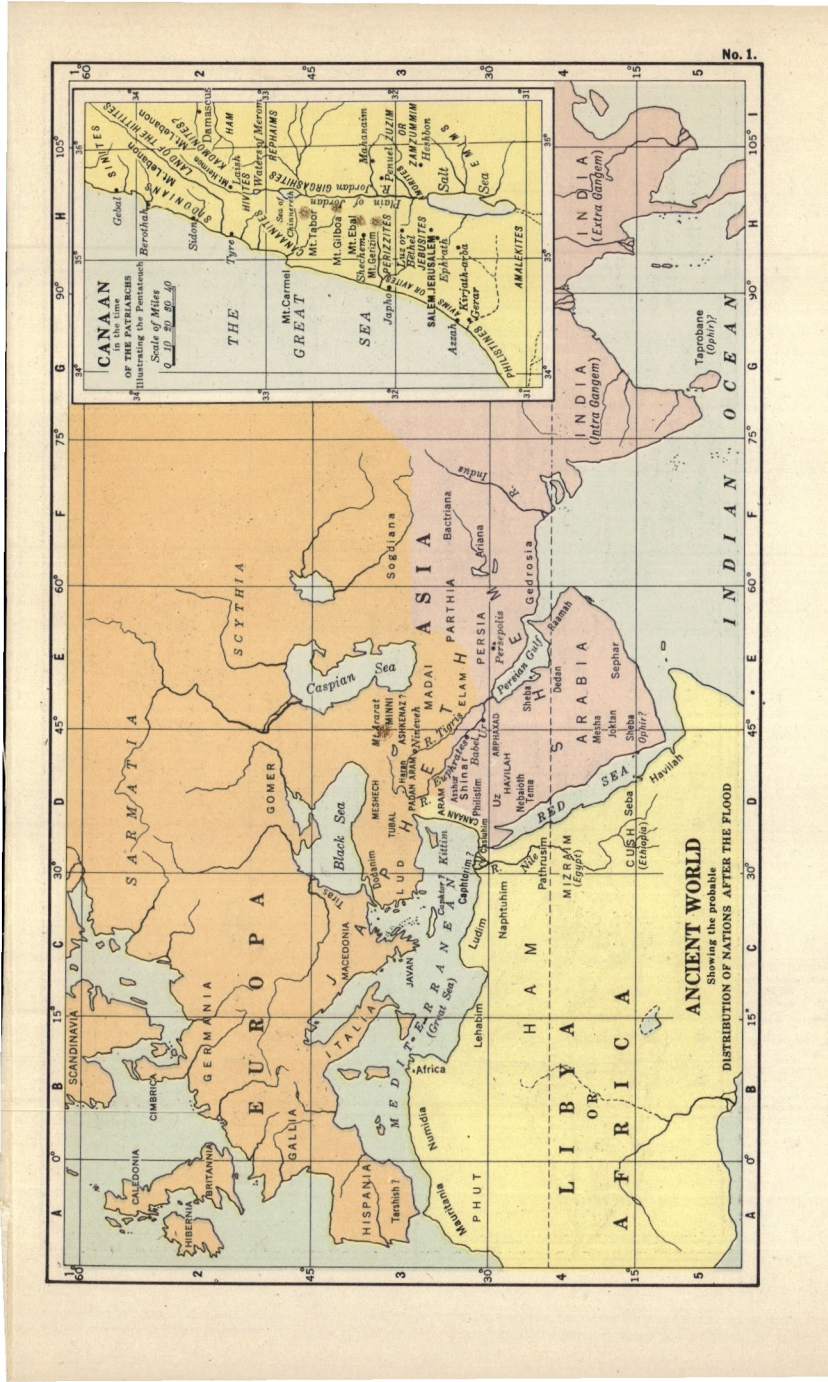

ANCIENT WORLD
Showing the probable
DISTRIBUTION OF NATIONS AFTER THE FLOOD

CANAAN
in the time
OF THE PATRIARCHS
Illustrating the Pentateuch
Scale of Miles

EGYPT
& THE SINAI PENINSULA
WITH THE JOURNEYINGS OF THE ISRAELITES

Scale of Miles
0 10 20 30 40 50 60

Probable route ----

CANAAN
as divided among
THE TWELVE TRIBES
Scale of Miles
0 10 20 30
Cities of Refuge are underlined
A 30′ B 35° C 30′ D 36° E 30′
Longitude East of Greenwich
Zidon
Zarephath
PHENICIA
Mount Lebanon
R. Jordan
Mount Hermon
N. Taura
N. Abanah (Pharpar)
N. el Barada
DAMASCUS
Nahr el Awaj
R. Leontes
Ijon
TYRE
Abel-beth-maachah
Dan or Laish
GESHUR
Kanah
Horem
Ladder of Tyrus
Hammon
Kedesh Naphtali
Ramah
Plain of Nasor
Waters of Merom
Abdon
Hebron
Hazor
Achzib
NAPHTALI
BASHAN
Aere
ASHER
GOLAN
ARGOB
ACCHO
Hannathon
Hukkok
Beth Dagon
Cabul
Sea of Chinnereth
Golan
Rimmon
Ashteroth Karnaim
ZEBULON
Aphek
MANASSEH
R. Kishon
Hammath
Mount Carmel
Harosheth
Daberath
Mt. Tabor
R. Hieromax
HAURAN
Chesulloth
Adami
HAVOTH JAIR
Jokneam
The Great Plain of Esdraelon
Endor
Hill of Moreh
Shunem
Edrei
Ramath Mizpeh
Megiddo
Valley of Jezreel
LAND OF TOB
Tob
Arbela
Jezreel
ISSACHAR
Taanach
Beth Shean
Mt. Gilboa
Bozrah
Engannim
Dothan
Abel Meholah
Jabesh Gilead
Plain of Sharon
Tirzah
GAD
Thebez
MANASSEH
SAMARIA
Mt. Ebal
Gerasa
Ramoth Gilead
Shechem
Mt. Gerizim
Sychar
Succoth
River Jordan
Gilgal
Gibeah Phinehas
R. Jabbok
Rakkon
R. Kanah
Mahanaim
Me Jurkon
Timnath Serah
Mount Ephraim
Shiloh
Adam
JOPPA or Japho
Bene Berak
EPHRAIM
Penuel
Jehud
Gilgal
Jogbehah
DAN
Ophrah
BETHEL
Rock Rimmon
Rabbath Ammon
Lod
Ai-Hai-Aiath
BENJAMIN
Beth Nimrah
Jabneel
Ekron
Beth-Horon
Lower
Upper
AMMON
Gezer
Gibeon
Michmash
JERICHO
Geba
Anathoth
Gilgal
Ajalon
Zoar
Heshbon
Elealeh
Zorah
JERUSALEM
Mt. of Olives
Shittim V.
Valley of Sorek
Timnath
Beth-Jesimoth
Ashdod
Beth Shemesh
Kirjath Jearim
Brook of Kidron
Mt. Pisgah
Mt. Nebo
BETHLEHEM
Beth Peor
Medeba
Ashkelon
Vale of Elah
REUBEN
Adullam
Tekoa
Gedor
Ataroth
Eglon
Mareshah
Plain of Mamre
Kiriathaim
JUDAH
HEBRON
Beth Gamul
GAZA
Lachish
Adoraim
Ziph
En Gedi
Bezer
Dibon
Dumah
Carmel
Aroer
Gerar
Debir
Maon
R. Arnon
Sharuhen
Wilderness of Judah
THE SALT SEA
En Rimmon
Eshtemoa
Jattir
Ar of Moab
Rabbath Moab
BEERSHEBA
Arad
Adadah
MOAB
City of Salt
Kir of Moab
Aroer
NEGEB
Bered?
Ziklag?
Reboboth
Ascent of Akrabbim
The Brook Zered
SIMEON
Tophel
Zephath
Hezron
Arabah
Wilderness of Zin
Bozrah
EDOM
THE DOMINIONS OF
DAVID & SOLOMON
Scale of Miles
0 20 40 60 80 100
Tiphsah (Thapsacus)
Hamath
ARAM OR SYRIA
Arvad
HAMATH
Kedesh of the Hittites
Tadmor (Palmyra)
Gebal
Great Desert
GREAT SEA
Berothah
Sidon
DAMASCUS
Tyre
Mt. Hermon
Dan
Mt. Carmel
Sea of Chinnereth
Kenath
Salcah
ISRAEL
Joppa
Rabbath Ammon
JERUSALEM
Heshbon
Gaza
JUDAH
Rabbath Moab
Tophel
Desert of Paran
Elath

ASSYRIA
& OTHER COUNTRIES ADJOINING CANAAN
ILLUSTRATING THE CAPTIVITIES OF THE JEWS

No. 5.

PALESTINE
Showing Elevations in Feet
Over 6000
4000 to 6000
2000 to 4000
1000 to 2000
Sea Level to 1000
Below Sea Level
Scale of Miles
0 5 10 15 20 25
Sidon
PHENICIA
Mount Lebanon
R. Jordan
Mount Hermon
DAMASCUS
R. Leontes
TYRE
Dan
Waters of Merom
BASHAN
GALILEE
Sea of Galilee
R. Kishon
Mt. Carmel
NAZARETH
R. Yarmuk
DECAPOLIS
CÆSAREA
Dothan
SAMARIA
SAMARIA
Sychar
R. Jordan
Apollonia
R. Jabbok
Joppa
Shiloh
Penuel
Mahanaim
AMMON
BETHEL
JERICHO
Azotus
JERUSALEM
Bethany
BETHLEHEM
Askelon
JUDÆA
DEAD SEA
HEBRON
Gaza
R. Arnon
MOAB
BEERSHEBA
EDOM OR IDUMEA

No. 6

PALESTINE
NORTHERN DIVISION

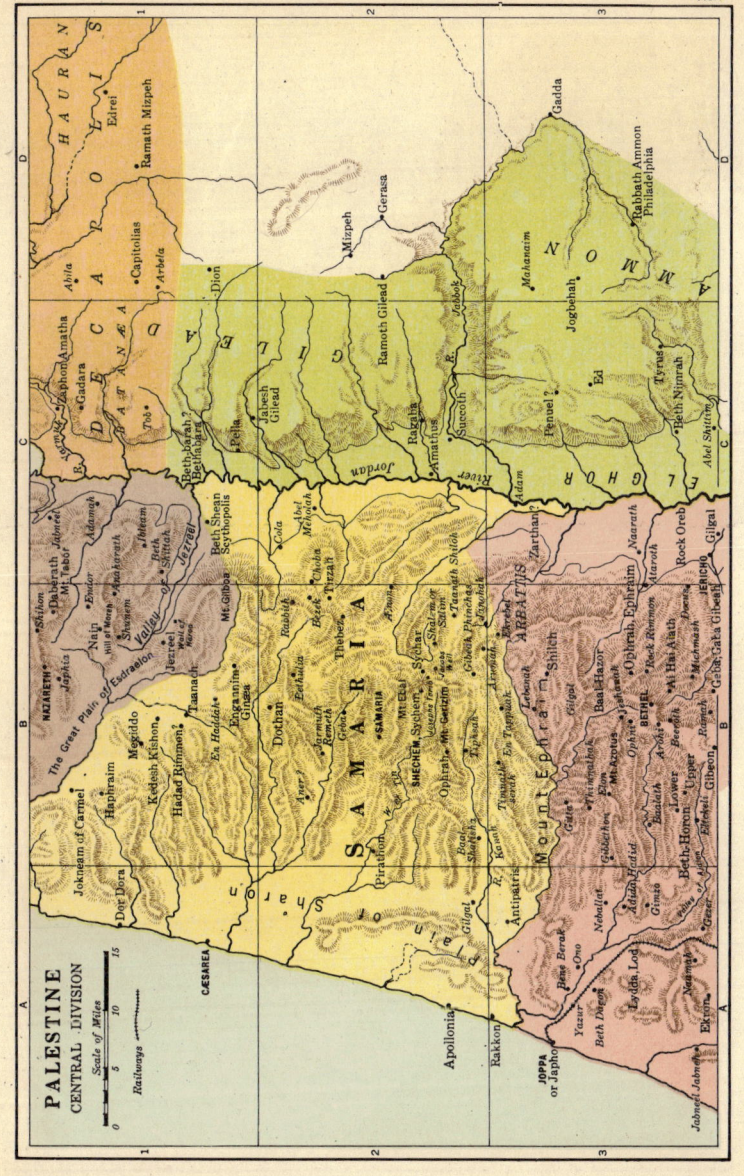

PALESTINE
CENTRAL DIVISION

PALESTINE
SOUTHERN DIVISION
Scale of Miles
0 5 10 15
Railways

PALESTINE
Illustrating
THE NEW TESTAMENT

No. 10

ANCIENT JERUSALEM
Scale of ¼ Mile

MODERN JERUSALEM
Scale of ¼ Mile

ENVIRONS OF JERUSALEM

Scale of Miles
0 1 2 3 4
The Figures show the Elevations

SCENE OF PAUL'S JOURNEYS
& OF THE EARLY CHURCHES